To:

MASON

FAMILY D.

GREAT FRIENDS

Almost

"A Time to be Remembered"

A Memoir
by

Donald Thomsen

authorHOUSE®

AuthorHouse™
1663 Liberty Drive
Bloomington, IN 47403
www.authorhouse.com
Phone: 1-800-839-8640

First published by AuthorHouse 11/18/2010

ISBN: 978-1-4520-8805-1 (e)
ISBN: 978-1-4520-6373-7 (sc)

Printed in the United States of America

This book is printed on acid-free paper.

Because of the dynamic nature of the Internet, any Web addresses or links contained in this book may have changed since publication and may no longer be valid. The views expressed in this work are solely those of the author and do not necessarily reflect the views of the publisher, and the publisher hereby disclaims any responsibility for them.

"Act as if what you do makes a difference . . . It does."

— William James

Table of Contents

Prologue

*Never be bullied into silence. Never allow
yourself to be made a victim. Accept no one's
definition of your life; define yourself.*
— Harvey Fierstein

This book is dedicated to my children who have
encouraged me for years to write down my life
experiences, especially my daughter Syndee, who at
one time sent me a "fill in the blanks" journal to make
it as easy as possible. And to my beautiful wife, who
had to put up with so much and encouraged me from
beginning to end.

As I started jotting down the outline of my memoirs
and noting interesting events in my childhood, I was
hoping that I would be able to recall those events that
happened so long ago before senility set in. Much to
my surprise once I got into it, it flowed back as if it had
happened yesterday. Few things have I enjoyed as much
as the three months it took me to write this book.

In the back of my mind, I've had this dark, contrived
recollection of my childhood as being isolated, poverty
stricken, and deprived of modern conveniences which
retarded my growth and development as a child and

teenager. Upon reflection, that previous conception couldn't be farther from the truth. My childhood and adolescence was . . . *priceless*!

Every day of my early life was a new adventure. My imagination and curiosity spurred me on to constant new discoveries. On very few occasions did I venture more than fifty miles form my little farm community. My worldly life experiences had to come to pass by proxy, my inspiration and stimuli being the radio and comic books.

Due to the remote location and scarcity of children my age, I had few—but genuine friends. My family gave me the freedom and encouragement to act out my fantasies, to make mistakes and learn there were consequences for those mistakes. I was able to reap rewards and accolades when I would *almost* succeed at various ventures—as long as I played by the rules. I knew my boundaries and the penalties that surely would follow if I strayed beyond those confines. I didn't have to search for my limitations, as a lot of children do nowadays. The rules of the game were clearly defined before the activities began. I experienced things, people traditions, and a moral integrity that no amount of influence of money or possessions could have purchased. In fact, wealth would have *polluted* my growth.

I was raised in a society where self sufficiency was paramount. If a problem presented itself, **you** handled it.

If the problem was beyond your capability and resources to cope with, you had a support group ready to step in and assist, many times without being asked. The local churches took care of their flocks, and the entire community pitched in when disasters (man-made or natural) occurred. It has always taken a village to raise a child.

Life-changing transactions and decisions were made and sealed with a handshake. We didn't have any Joneses' to keep up with. Those in our town who had considerable wealth never flaunted it . . . there was no class envy, the town drunk was still treated with respect.

There was no need for attorneys. I don't think anyone even knew one. A real doctor was visited only in cases of the most extreme injuries or maladies, and folks still regularly lived into their nineties.

These people worked hard and freely shared the fruits of their labor. You couldn't visit anyone's house without them inviting you to their gardens to pick a mess of whatever was ripe. If the garden was out of season, they would invite you to the cellar to take a few jars of preserves home with you (just bring back the jar). These folks always planted and raised an abundance of crops and livestock, not for the purpose of *having* to share but for the purpose of being *able* to share.

My wife (I luckily found a wonderful soul mate

who has put up with me for fifty years) and I have raised four children, all married. We have six grandchildren spread out all over the country.

Having the luxury of time and experience on this earth, I have come to the conclusion that *all* people are basically good, possessing a sense of right and wrong and a charitable spirit. Problems arise when societies start dictating our values, when others start defining the meaning of success and failure, when certain classes of people are deemed more or less worthy of emulation, when those whose occupations produce the least are the most revered, when position and possessions start to take precedence over God, family, values and country.

If you are reading this thumbnail overture on humanity, you have likely decided to read my book. My intention is to introduce or re-introduce my readers to a time in our history that a few would like to forget, but that most (if the truth be known) kind of miss. I tried to make my story light hearted easy to read and yet informative. My attempt is to take you by the hand. Join me and experience (through my eyes) firsthand my exciting, hilarious childhood, through adolescence, graduation and into the Navy at an early seventeen years of age.

I decided to use only the first names of the key characters in my story to protect the innocent and attempt not to alienate *all* my friends and relatives. I have nothing but the utmost love and respect for the people I was raised with and have written about, you know who I mean. If by poking fun at you and telling our deep dark secrets, I have offended you in any way . . . tough . . . suck it up . . . and get on with life.

CHAPTER ONE

A Night of Terror

*I have been through some terrible things in
my life, some of which really happened.*
— Mark Twain

The era: the late 1930s, and then into the '40s, and
'50s. The tail end of the Great Depression. There
were rumors of war lingering on the horizon.

The place: a small rented sharecropper's farm located
three miles outside a tiny, poverty-stricken community
in rural Nebraska.

It was late in the evening. My father had already
gone to bed. My mother was finishing up her nightly
chores and would soon retire. My brother, my closest kin
(eight-and-a-half years my senior), and I just finished
listening to the scary program *Inner Sanctum*, on our
battery-powered radio.

My mother, father, brother, and I had regular nightly

1

radio programs we listened to after supper, when we finished clean-up and homework.

Collectively, the family liked to listen to early evening favorites like *Amos and Andy* and *Fibber McGee n' Molly*. Those were the only programs my mom and dad afforded themselves because they both went to bed early at the end of their busy day.

After our parents finished their radio entertainment, my brother and I listened to the really scary programs. The ones we liked were: *The Shadow, Inner Sanctum* and *Mystery Theater*. However, I wouldn't listen to these programs without Lloyd being nearby—they just scared the heck out of me.

I now realize that the human mind coupled with an overactive imagination could create a much more vivid, horrifying, perceived reality than any *Chainsaw Massacre* or *Jason* movie ever could.

The weather conditions became troubling. A storm was brewing, with a cold, brisk wind blowing out of the north. The overcast sky produced distant lightning flashes and threatening claps of thunder. These menacing conditions caused the night to be unusually dark. It was very spooky.

Luckily I didn't have to sleep alone. I slept with my brother. The big problem: After the spooky programs I always had to go to the bathroom in the dark, alone, and scared to death!

My mother used to tell me, "If you're too scared to go by yourself, stop listening to those frightening programs at night!" But I just couldn't stop listening. It was like an addiction.

I tried my hardest to go to the bathroom before the programs came on, but it never worked. Out of habit, I always went just before bedtime, because you sure as heck didn't want to get up out of a warm bed and go outside in the cold and dark night, especially if the weather was bad—like this night.

I, a child of seven, was warily groping my way down the lengthy path to the outhouse. We had no electricity. My choices of illumination were either a kerosene lantern or a weak, piece-of-crap flashlight. With the wind blowing so hard the lantern wasn't going to stay lit, leaving me with the flashlight. Back then, batteries were not what they are today, so the light was dim. You could only see a little way in front of you—enough, hopefully, that you wouldn't trip over anything. While making my way to the privy, I remembered, when younger, how thankful I felt when Mom would make my brother, Lloyd, accompany me to the outhouse on those dark, dark, cold, stormy nights—like this night.

We had an unusual *two-hole* outhouse; the traditional models usually had only one hole. I can recall my Mom asking Dad, "Why in the world would anyone build a two-hole outhouse? I wouldn't want to share that intimate experience with anyone else, would you?" Personally, I preferred the larger dimensions of the upscale two-holer. I didn't feel quite so claustrophobic.

When making those lonely trips to the outhouse by myself, I always took an old baseball bat with me for protection.

I had mixed emotions about the quality of illumination of the flashlight. On one hand, I wanted to brightly light up everything so I could clearly see what *may* be lurking out there, anything dangerous and life-threatening. On the other hand, I wasn't sure I really wanted to see what my mind eye told me was *definitely* out there.

I will never forget the horrifying event that occurred that fateful dark evening. While stealthily making my way to the privy with flashlight and my trusty baseball bat, I had my senses tuned to any threatening sound or movement that would warn me of immediate danger. So far, so good . . . I made it to the outhouse without incident, had my pants down and was warily doing my business while shining the flashlight around to keep watch as best as I could while concentrating on the job at hand.

All of a sudden these terrible, bloodcurdling screeching sounds started, a loud banging and flapping noise erupted—it was spine-tingling! The most terrifying part: At first I thought some strange creature was trying to break into the structure to devour me, but—even more frightening, I realized the hideous sounds were coming from *inside* the outhouse—where I was! If you have ever been inside an outhouse you would know there isn't much room in there, even for a modern, upscale two-holer like ours. If there is *something* that can make that much bone-chilling noise and those loud thumping and flapping sounds . . . in there with me . . . and only one way out—*I'm dead!*

I jumped up, dropped the flashlight and in the pitch blackness started swinging the bat back and forth with all my might—in case whatever was going to try to kill me could be between me and the door. I fiercely battered the inside walls of the outhouse with the bat for a time, until I realized, Hey—*I'm still alive . . . I can actually get out the door and make a break for the house.* The distance I had to sprint was about twenty-five to thirty yards. I wish someone could have timed me because I'm sure it would have been a world record, even in the dark, while holding up my pants with one hand.

I ran into the house and breathlessly told my mother and my brother about my ordeal. They both tried to assure me I had imagined the whole thing, but neither was willing to go out there to see if what I had just related was in fact true, particularly since the piece-of-crap flashlight was still in the outhouse.

My dad had been in bed for some time because he

had to get up before sunrise to start his daily chores. Therefore, he didn't like to be awakened under any circumstances, but I figured since our whole family was in peril, I would risk retribution—I woke him up. I told him what had happened and suggested he get his gun and investigate. I convinced him of the impending danger that was about to befall all of us. He got up, got dressed, lit the kerosene lantern and started for the outhouse, but without any protection!

I encouraged him to take his gun, or at least take my bat, since it had saved my life. I figured he would need something to kill that monster, but he assured me he could take care of any menacing situation without a weapon.

Wow, that's my dad, what a guy!

I waited in the house, huddled close to my mom and brother, all the while thinking, *the three of us will have to go help him at any minute. It's the least we can do if the creature has him.*

Surprisingly my dad came back unscathed and told us what had happened. He looked directly at me and said, "Someone left the door of the outhouse open and one of our roosters decided to go inside, out of the weather, to keep warm and fell in the hole. When Donnie went in the outhouse he scared him. All the noise he heard was the bird's panicked attempt to escape."

I replied, "What'd-ya' mean? . . . I scared *him?*

What about me?—he tried to kill me. I could have had a heart-attack!"

My dad informed me that since I was the one who probably left the door open, it was up to me to get the rooster out in the morning, and went back to bed. How humiliating. I was the one who was attacked, and now I had to figure a way to rescue the attacker.

In the morning I took a look at the situation in the light of day. The rooster was definitely down there.

We raised a lot of chickens and if you want chickens that lay eggs that give you more chickens—you gotta have roosters. This rooster was the head honcho, the one that taught the younger roosters how to do their job; (mostly by example . . . might add). Can you imagine, having a job like that of a *head rooster*? All you can eat, and you could have any chick on the farm—any time. Think about that scenario for a while. With those benefits, I didn't feel quite so sorry for him sitting in that hole; a little humility once in a while didn't hurt anyone, or in this case, *anything*, even a super-virile rooster.

What I had here was a poser. I couldn't just reach down and grab him because it was a fairly new "poop pit," so it was still a relatively deep hole. I wouldn't want to touch him anyway, as he was a smelly slob right now. He added a whole new dimension to the phrase, *someone's in deep do-do*. I could drop a noose down and try to rope him (I was getting good at roping, while fantasizing in my role as "*Tom Mix*"), but the way my luck was running I would probably snag him around the neck and hang him on the way up.

I considered getting my dad's gun and shooting the darn thing. I wouldn't have to worry about his dead body smelling the place up, because the outhouse smelled that way most of the time anyway, but how would I explain to my dad what had happened to his prize rooster? . . . He was the "cock-of-the-walk!"

I got to thinking, *how do we normally catch the other chickens when we are going to have one for supper?*

When we wanted to select a chicken to have over for dinner, one member of our family (usually me) would go into the henhouse at dusk, when the chickens went to roost. They were really docile at that time and you could do about anything with them you wanted.

In our chicken house, the roosts were built in tiers, along one wall, all facing the same direction. You opened the door and there they were, all sitting in their stadium seats. At the sound of the door opening, they all, slowly turned their heads at the same time and looked at you. Something would make a sound at the other end of the building and they would all slowly turn their heads and look that direction. It was like they were all watching a boring tennis match. Little did they know that one of them was going to get ejected from the grandstands for heckling, or in their case,—*cackling*.

Under each tier was a trough lined with straw to catch the eggs. It was so easy; you could just walk under the tiered roosts, gather the eggs or pick off a chicken for eating. You would then take the condemned bird and put it in a crate, which was an honorary *invitation to dinner*.

The next day, we took the condemned fowl out of the crate and humanely administer the lethal injection (it really was just an axe we used to chop wood for the fire).

By the way, have you ever heard the phrase, "Running around like a chicken with its head cut off?" That's a gigantic understatement. If those fools would show that much enthusiasm *before* they lost their head, they wouldn't be so easy to catch.

It was an awesome responsibility. When you selected a victim to invite to supper, you were the judge and jury.

Back to the *doo-doo* bird problem at hand.

I found a long stiff wire, went to the tool shed where we had an anvil and a hammer. I made a long loop, an open-ended slot (like a drawn-out letter U) with the slot width being the size of a chicken's leg. Chicken legs are very sturdy, all bone with tough scales on them.

I knew the foot was bigger than the leg. If I could

reach down and slip that slotted loop around a leg I could pull the rooster up without it slipping off. The plan was, after I got him up just slip the loop off and he could run away. I didn't have to touch him, which suited me just fine considering the condition he was in!

It worked like a charm. In fact, my family used my invention from then on because with my device you could catch a chicken any time of the day, not just at dusk, without the condemned bird having to think about his death sentence overnight. I shoulda' got the Nobel Prize for that one.

The only inconvenience the rooster had endured, besides a few hours of fasting, was he wasn't quite as popular with the ladies . . . until after the next rain.

It took me awhile to live that embarrassing event down. It was especially troubling since it wasn't definitely proven that I was the one who left the door open. Unfortunately, in our family there was no appellate process.

Going to the outhouse in the dark was never easy for me and *like dying;* I would put it off as long as possible. It was a miracle I didn't come down with some rare digestive bowel disorder.

Mom and Dad, in their "Sunday-go-to-meet'in" duds.
(notice dad's dress sox's with new overalls)

CHAPTER TWO

The Family

*In these times you have to be an optimist
to open your eyes when you awake in the
morning.*

— Carl Sandburg

My story starts with my birth: April 19, 1938. I was born at home with a mid-wife's assistance. My parents were well past middle age, although I never figured how you determine the middle of something when you don't know how long it's going to be.

They were humble farmers. My father, James, a child of an immigrant family from Denmark, was born in 1888. He was a successful farmer at the time of his marriage, in 1913, to my mother Pearl, also a farmer's daughter, but of modest means. A short time after inheriting a prosperous family farm from his father my dad mortgaged the assets of his inherited enterprise and used the proceeds to purchase an additional farming complex which was vested entirely in the rearing of swine (pigs to you city folks). He felt it was a wise decision to leverage his assets and expand his small empire. At the time it was a sound business decision which was fully sanctioned by the local banker, especially since just experiencing the "booming" economy of the *Roaring Twenties*.

However, the Great Depression of the *Thirties* changed all that. His timing was impeccable. In very short time-period a wide spread epidemic of Swine cholera depleted the entire livestock assets of his newly acquired venture. That calamity placed an unexpected burden on the operation of his original farm which was struggling due to the devastating national financial collapse. Trying to operate two farms that were no longer producing a profit, and saddled with a crushing mortgage on both entities, he unfortunately lost both ventures to foreclosure, as did most small farmers in the Midwestern states. My mother never forgave my dad for his (in her mind) stupid business decisions.

Those few affluent farmers with large land holdings, and ample cash reserves, actually fared quite well. They began buying up the devalued small farms that were being foreclosed upon by local banks. Some farmers prospered further by subletting their newly acquired farm units back to the less fortunate previous landowners on a sharecropper basis.

Even after the financial humbling of our family, I was always impressed by my father's unselfish nature. He was very charitable in sharing his meager possessions and time. He helped anyone (within his ability) with anything they needed, but he was strangely reluctant to ask for help from anyone else, unless there was absolutely no other option.

My dad had no time for religion. His God was the land. He would say, "If you do your part in preparing and nurturing the soil, the land will reward you in abundance." He would also follow up with, "If you are foolish and neglectful, the land will also punish you accordingly."

His stated philosophy: "You aren't entitled to economic rewards unless you *physically* put in an honest day's work with your hands."

He only had an eighth-grade education, but could read and understand complicated documents, i.e. insurance policies, deeds of trust, etc. Many times, neighbors would bring these types of documents to our home for him to decipher. My mother pleaded with him to go into that line of work and give up farming, but to no avail. Farming was his life's blood.

James took pride in his family, and his ability to adapt to most anything fate threw at him. However, one of his prideful shortcomings was his disdain and intolerance of nonsense and disrespect. He demanded total respect and obedience from his children and was, at times, quick to anger and swift in reprimanding those who fell short of his expectations. My father's ire was at times explosive—but short-lived.

He was a fair man and his punishments were usually (especially in my case,) well-deserved. I knew he loved and cared for me, even though open displays of affection were few, if any. It just wasn't his way.

Strangely, even though my father was a strong fulsome man, he had the tendency to shed tears at the most unusual occasions. It was sometimes embarrassing and I had always perceived it as a weakness. My mother hated this unusual emotional behavior and would always bring it to his attention by saying, "James, act like a man."

My mother, Pearl, was born in 1895. Like my dad she also had an eighth-grade education. She was raised in a sod house in the plains of western Nebraska. Her description of its modest architecture pointed out that the structure had only the barest of necessities. There weren't a lot of trees on the plains, consequently lumber was very expensive. By design the earthen abodes required only a minimal amount of lumber, namely a door and one or more windows.

One thing that was in abundance was sod. The

sod squares, cut from the soil, had long grass roots in them and thus were tough yet flexible. Not only were the walls constructed of sod, but most roofs as well, which sometimes led to wet bedding and clothes after a heavy rain.

Most sod houses had dirt floors that were packed to a concrete consistency, they needed to be swept daily to keep the dust to a minimum. These structures proved to be energy-efficient: They were cool in the hot summer and warm in winter. Some folks whitewashed the interiors to lighten them up. Some also covered the exterior with various siding materials for protection from the, at times, severe weather, which was hard on such structures.

Because of the remote locations and primitive construction of these sod homesteads, the inhabitants had to contend with a lot of critters infiltrating their living areas. My mother had a sizable scar on her upper lip. I asked, "How did you happen to get the scar?"

She said, "I got that from a large rat that had crawled into my crib when I was a baby, and bit me on the lip."

She said, "There were stories of children being killed from lethal rat attacks in the sod houses." Mother related other incidents, one being, "Often, at night, the local wolves would stand on their hind legs and look into the windows of our home." She remembered their sneering faces eerily glowing through the flimsy single-paned windows . . . now that's really scary!

Mom's parents were humble farmers and raisers of livestock. She would tell me stories of her childhood, how she would ride her horse to bring in the milking stock from the grazing range.

I asked her if she enjoyed riding a horse.

She said, "I spent every waking moment I was allowed riding my horse—I loved it. I was the happiest on horseback."

She told me she used a saddle equipped with stirrup chaps (leather envelopes that covered her feet.) On one occasion, her horse shied and my mother thought he had stepped in a prairie dog hole. When she looked down to check her mount she noticed that a large rattlesnake had, in fact, struck the leather cover and had imbedded its fangs and was hanging from her stirrup.

"What did you do?" I asked.

She said, "I didn't panic. I used my riding crop to beat the snake off my stirrup. It was difficult getting rid of the snake and still keep my horse under control."

I thought, *my mother had to be a pretty savvy horsewoman to accomplish that feat.*

I was the last of six children. My father was fifty years old and my mother was forty-three when I came into the world. I was probably an unexpected surprise. The only indication I had of how they felt about this blessed event was the manner of *aggressive* birth control they practiced from that point on. To my knowledge, my parents *never* slept in the same bedroom, not just bed, again. Who says the abstinence method doesn't work? It certainly did for them, because I was the last child born into the family.

My brother, Lloyd, had the status of being the "baby of the family" until I showed up. He also had all the perks that went with the title. The status, fame and fortune of being "the baby" were then, by birthright, passed down to me. Little did I know the awesome responsibility that came with the title. That *baby* moniker really sticks with you. I think the last time I remember my mother introducing me as the *baby* was to a nurse on her death bed. I was forty-seven.

I don't remember too much about my early childhood; I think I started to become coherent right before I started school. I do, however, recall clearly the approach of my kindergarten year in school. My brother, in his infinite wisdom and with his usual caring attitude, tried to prepare me for school. He told me what I could expect when school started. He said, "Your schoolwork will be really hard and you will have study every night into the wee hours, just to keep up."

He told me the teachers were really mean and yelled at you constantly. The most frightening thing, he warned, was that the principal paddled at least one kid each day and you never knew which day was going to be your turn. Obviously, I was really looking forward to that ordeal.

Then came the first day of school. The teacher introduced herself and seemed to be really nice, but I knew the inside scoop. She wasn't fooling me for one minute. I didn't know what the principal looked like, but I didn't figure he would pick me on the very first day so that paddling part didn't worry me too much.

The room I was in was shared by the kindergarten, first, and second grades. There were less than a dozen pupils total in those three grades combined, so it didn't take long to get to know each other. I was told there were less than 100 pupils in the whole school which went through the twelfth grade.

After the kindergarten class introductions, we were issued a Dick and Jane workbook, a coloring book with crayons and we were indoctrinated in the intricate usage of the sandbox. I knew after the first day that everything my brother warned me of was true. With my heavy curriculum and all the rules affixed to using the complex sandbox . . . this was going to be a tough year.

I especially enjoyed recess and lunch. The school was big enough to have a cafeteria kitchen and a hot lunch program. I was privileged that one of my older sisters, Lucille, was one of two people who prepared the meals. How much pride could one kid be allowed to have? My sister a lunch lady and a *townie*! A townie was anyone living within the city limits, and this title carried a lot of status to those who lived in the countryside. Since I lived three miles outside the boundaries, I was considered *almost* a townie.

I had two other relatives that lived in town, Uncle Fred and Aunt Mary (my dad's sister). In itself this relationship wasn't unusual, but in a way it was kinda weird, because the more I got out into the world and met more people, I found out, that *everybody*, had an Uncle Fred and Aunt Mary. It was like everyone was issued one set to every family, sorta' like uniforms in the military.

Their house was right next to the school. Sometimes I would go there after school and wait for someone to pick me up and take me home. Then came all the "after school" duties and chores prior to supper. After clean-up, homework and an occasional bath we could settle down to our much anticipated radio programs.

Third, fourth, and fifth grades in one room with one teacher. (I'm in the back row, first on the left)

CHAPTER THREE

Life on the Farm

*Any idiot can face a crisis – its day to day
living that wears you out.*
— Anton Chekhov

The living conditions on our farm were very primitive: no electricity, no running water. All water used domestically, and for the livestock, was pumped by hand from a well. The only heat in the house was a pot-bellied coal-fired stove in the kitchen/dining area.

My mother cooked with a wood-fired stove, which gave off very little warmth in the winter time and waaay too much in the summer. None of the rest of the house or the bedrooms was heated and of course there was no insulation, whatever that was.

The wash house also had a wood-fired cook stove. This stove was used to heat water for bathing, the laundry, and also was used to do all the canning and food processing at harvest time.

The bathing process was as follows: Mom or Dad made a fire in the washhouse wood stove; I pumped by hand an adequate amount of water to fill a boiler (a deep vat) which was heated on the stove; I pumped another two to three reserve buckets of cold water. Then, using a bucket, I filled a galvanized wash tub (*almost*, big enough to set in) with the desired mixture of the hot and cold water. The tub was set by the stove, the distance from the stove depended on the weather outside. Once I had the preferred water temperature and correct volume, I took a bath, using Mom's homemade lye soap. Every member of our family insisted on taking a bath alone I *never* saw any other family member naked.

There was a drain in the middle of the washhouse floor where you poured the soapy, dirty bath water. Come to think of it, I don't know where that water went because we had no plumbing or sewer line.

Wrapped in a towel trying not to freeze my butt off, I refilled the tub with clean water and rinsed off.

With all the time and trouble this procedure involved, one can better understand the infamous *Saturday night* bathing schedules the rural farm folks sensibly applied.

Since we had no refrigeration, all leftovers and harvested foodstuffs had to be canned within a reasonable time frame so they wouldn't spoil. The seasons were the determining factor as to when this chore had to be completed.

The canned goods and perishables were stored in the cellar, a brick-lined cave underground with a flat wooden door. The cellar temperature fluctuated, but it was always cooler in the summer and stayed above freezing in the winter.

The cellar also did double duty as a refuge shelter when we were visited by the tornados that frequented our area. The terrain was so flat that it allowed inclement weather to sneak up on you relatively fast. We always knew when a tornado was approaching: It would get very dark and still, not a breath of air.

If we were fortunate to be home, at the time of the impending storm, everyone had assigned tasks prior to going into the cellar. Any stock that happened to be inside the barn had to be let out. The high-velocity whirlwinds seemed to do the most damage to the tallest structures so this procedure, at least, gave the animals a fighting chance of survival.

My job was to open all the windows in the house; because the wind funnel would create a vacuum around the outside of the house, causing any closed windows to explode outward.

We would take adequate food and drink, and a kerosene lamp with plenty of fuel into the cellar with us. This extended supply of essentials were critical, because if by chance the storm destroyed one of the local structures and deposited the debris or maybe a large tree on top of the door of the cellar, it might be several days before anyone would find us.

We could always eat some of the canned food and drink from the water storage we had. A shallow pit back in the corner was used to deposit our bodily waste if an extended stay became necessary.

It was exciting to hurry and go through all the preparations against the potential damage of those storms, but I always felt sorry for all the animals on the farm. They were really on their own. We were prepared for the worst, but fortunately the storm fronts usually passed quickly.

I heard stories of some strange happenings during, and in the aftermath of tornados. One story always stood out as one of the weirdest. A farmer had just finished milking his cows and was walking away from the barn with two full (to the brim) buckets of fresh milk. The storm came up and he set the buckets down and ran to the safety of his cellar.

When the storm had passed, his barn and much of his livestock had been destroyed. But there were those two buckets of milk, still filled to the brim, left completely untouched, not even dirty.

There were also stories of shafts of wheat straw

driven through trees and telephone poles, and other odd destruction. I never, personally, witnessed anything that strange in my lifetime. We were lucky none of those tornados ever touched down on our farm, although some were mighty close.

* * *

Our small farm complex and dwellings were rented from a relatively wealthy local farmer, along with additional acreage. The total acreage was sufficient to raise food for human and animal consumption, and enough extra to raise crops and livestock to sell on the open market.

The rent for these small farms was a negotiated share of the marketable crops they raised and harvested. That is how the practice got the name "sharecropping."

My father would borrow enough money from the local Farmers and Merchants Bank to buy seed to plant a crop and winter feed for the few animals he raised for us to eat, including the surplus livestock he raised to market for income, and other basic living essentials.

The main drawback to this 'credit farming' was the risk of the investment in time and money not paying off as intended. A lot of variables were at play: the weather condition, the individual farmer's planning ability, and the most important ingredient—a lot of luck.

Obviously there was no income while the crops and the animals he was to sell matured. Consequently, dad was forced to work elsewhere until the crops could be harvested and the excess animals sold. Unfortunately, there was no work to be had locally. With no other choice available, my father went to work on the WPA. The Works Progress Administration (renamed in 1939 to the Work Projects Administration) was the largest New Deal agency, created by Franklin Delano Roosevelt's presidential order.

This program, employing millions of people affected almost every locality in the United States, especially rural and Western mountain populations. The program also redistributed food, clothing and housing to those in need. Periodically, in dad's absence, a government truck would come by our little farm and bring canned food and essentials to sustain a reasonable caliber of existence. My mother was thoroughly humiliated by this service, but had to accept the hand she was dealt.

My dad went to Flagstaff, Arizona, and worked as a carpenter's helper. Worker pay at the WPA was based on three factors: the region of the country, the degree of urbanization, and the individual's skill. It varied from $19/month to $94/month. Since my dad's skill level was on the lower end of the scale, his income must have been also.

He worked at this government job for six months at a time and would come home in time for the harvest and planting of the new crops. While he was gone, my mother, brother, and sister worked the farm. I was just a toddler then. This was a great burden on Mom and she hated every minute of it.

All the local sharecroppers would use *communal* labor and farm implements to harvest their crops. They formed co-ops and pooled their resources to get the job done. One farmer would obtain a necessary piece of equipment, like a mower, another farmer would purchase a bailer, another a corn sheller, another a combine, and so on.

When Dad was home and harvest time came he and all the other sharecroppers neighbors would gather at a designated farm and collectively work from daylight to dark until the harvest was completed, they then move onto the next farm, until everyone was serviced.

Whole families would go from farm to farm. The women would cook the meals, make provisions, and set up resting places for the men. Some families provided tents, or made up their outbuildings to accommodate sleeping overnight. Everyone not actively involved in the harvest, helped take care of the children.

After the evening meal they would gather around a fire, and interact in various ways. Some would quilt, others told stories, the children played games, and all enjoyed each other's company. They would then rest and start over the next day.

Because of the limited funds of our family, and

most of our neighbors and relatives, the children had to innovate and use their imagination to entertain themselves.

The youngsters indulged in activities that needed no specialized accessories or props. Most of the games involved hiding, running, and role-playing, i.e. cops and robbers, cowboys and Indians and a variety of comic book scenarios. When there weren't enough participants, there were a few board games that as many as two people could play and children could master. Games like regular checkers and Chinese checkers, played with marbles. The most popular games were "kick the can" (the urban cousin of hide and seek), and" anti-anti-over," (a game of throwing a ball back and forth over the roof of a house.)

The town of Valparaiso was comprised of one main, graveled street (a two-lane road) with all the businesses located on one side. We had the usual small town businesses. The most active were the blacksmith shop; a farm implement/hardware store; a gas station/repair garage; a barber shop (where everybody congregated and swapped gossip); an ice house; two grocery stores and two beer joints with restaurants, pool tables and shuffleboard. A couple of the unusual establishments were a one room jailhouse (why? we had no cops); a town hall/meeting room/ auditorium/skating rink/ theater/anything else that came to mind; and a two-story rooming house (for the life of me I can't ever remember anyone staying there).

On the other side of the street was the railroad tracks (the mainstay of the town); a grain elevator and feed store; railroad depot with telegraph/ticket sales/freight dock; the volunteer fire department, and the VFW hall and meeting room. That's it for Main Street!

There was a large (at least I thought so at the time), two-story brick building that served as the consolidated county school. The first floor was the grade school, with kindergarten, first, and second grades in one room with one teacher. Third, fourth, and fifth grades were in another room with a teacher, and sixth, seventh and eighth grades in the remaining room with yet another teacher. There was a home economics room, woodworking shop, and a small cafeteria with kitchen, all connected by a hallway with restrooms at each end.

On the second floor was the high school with classrooms, chemistry lab, gymnasium/auditorium, and principal's office, also connected by a long hallway with restrooms at each end. The high school had grades nine through twelve. For a long time I thought the reason they called it "high school" was because it was located on the top floor.

The mainstay of the local commerce was agriculture, and the railroad was the life-line that tied it all together. Other than the few civic businesses that employed very few residents, one's vocation was limited to either farming or working for the railroad. I knew at an early age that I didn't want to participate in either of those occupations. I wanted to be a businessman!

You notice I didn't mention any doctor's or dentist offices; that's because there weren't any. The nearest doctor was twenty-five miles away and he was a chiropractor, but in those days chiropractors treated you for everything and I mean *everything*!

There was a "circuit" dentist that traveled from town to town. He would come by every six to eight months; his time frame dictated how you scheduled your tooth-aches.

An unfortunate painful encounter I had with the roving dentist comes to mind. When I was in elementary school I developed a cavity, one of the few I have ever had. My mother made an appointment for one of the rare occasions when the dentist was available. The dentist was set up in one of the vacant offices over the bank. I went in and sat in his big black, portable folding chair. He examined me and discovered the cavity. He said he would have to drill out the defective portion of the tooth and fill it with a silver alloy. I said OK—like I had a choice.

He had this drill contraption that ran by pumping a foot treadle, like my mom's Singer sewing machine. He didn't use anything to deaden the pain and as he was drilling he hit the nerve, which he *solemnly* promised me he wouldn't do. I know I left a clear set of fingerprints firmly imbedded in the arms of his portable black chair, probably still there to this day.

After a few years of working for the WPA, Dad quit because he couldn't stand being away from me and the family for that long a time.

Knowing he would have to supplement his lost income, he and my Uncle Fred decided to partner up and do carpentry work together. Uncle Fred used his contacts and got them both a job at a new airport being built in Lincoln, approximately thirty miles away. I am not sure how my dad made the transition from carpenter's helper to a full-fledged *real* carpenter, but he seemed to pull it off.

Dad was very accident-prone; he was always bashing a finger or cutting himself with a saw. He constantly had a bandage on him somewhere. Thank God they didn't have power tools back then.

My father's typical day was to arise before sun-up, and do his morning chores, which included milking two cows and putting the milk in containers and then in the cellar so it would stay cool in the summer and not freeze in the winter. He then got ready for Uncle Fred to come by and pick him up. Together they would drive the thirty miles to be at work by 8:00 am. If it rained and the dirt road we lived on was too muddy, he had to walk two miles to the graveled portion of the road.

He and Uncle Fred would do carpentry work for eight hours, and then drive the same thirty miles back home. Dad then did his evening chores, which also entailed milking the same two cows again and processing the day's milk with a hand-crank separator, separating the whole milk, the cream and the whey. We had a stainless steel can for cream (provided by the ice-cream factory in Lincoln,) which we kept in the cellar until it was full. The lid was sealed, a name tag attached and hauled over to a designated spot next to the railroad tracks. The local train would come by the next day and pick it up and leave another clean can, with a receipt inside. The voucher was honored anywhere in town for trade, this was how the local railroad line got the term, "the milk run."

I felt proud that the folks who lived in *the big city* of Lincoln would buy ice cream that was partly made from cream—from *our* cows.

Part of the cream our cows produced would be made into butter in a hand-crank churn. The butter would be lightly salted and pressed into wooden butter moulds. The whole milk was used for drinking and cooking, but the best use (in my opinion) was homemade ice cream.

You are probably wondering how we made ice cream

without refrigeration; well, it wasn't easy. We had to buy a half block of ice from the ice-house in town, and some rock salt. When we got the ice and the salt we had to quickly go straight home, where the 'hand-cranked' ice cream maker was waiting. Mom would have the ice cream mixture already in the canister with the wooden paddle (called the dasher) and she would be standing by, waiting. All of us took turns cranking the mechanism, adding more rock salt and ice as it melted. When the crank became too hard to turn, as if by magic . . . you had ice cream, really good ice cream.

Mom would pull the dasher out of the canister, and then the *mock* battle would begin over who got to lick the wooden paddle while she dished up the ice cream. In my opinion, there was an upside to not having refrigeration: All the ice cream had to be eaten quickly. Sometimes, however, if you ate it too quickly you got a "brain freeze," which was really painful. What wasn't initially eaten was supposed to go into the slop bucket for the pigs. We all made sure none of our pigs *ever* tasted ice cream!

Dad always said, "Those were the good old days." I thought he was delusional!

Mom's typical day was to get up at daybreak and fix breakfast, and get my brother and me ready and off for school. Most of the time she would take us to school in the car, but if the roads were too muddy or

impassable we would walk the three miles (all up hill—
both ways).

Once a week she would do laundry. This entailed pumping enough water to fill a boiler (the same one we used for bathing) and heating it on our backup wood stove in the wash house. She then filled a galvanized wash tub and scrubbed the clothes on a wooden washboard. The clothes were rinsed and hung on the clotheslines.

On the really cold winter days, the clothes would freeze solid on the clothesline. Mom would take Dad's bib overalls and shirts in the house where it was warm and lay them all over the kitchen and living room close to the stove to thaw out and dry. Until the clothes thawed, the place looked like a morgue after a catastrophic disaster, with rigid bodies lying all over the place. If any clothes needed ironing she had a flat iron, which was heated on the stove.

Over time, Dad accumulated a little extra money and bought Mom a gasoline-powered washing machine made by Maytag. It consisted of a tub and set of wringer rollers on the top, with a Briggs & Stratton "kick start" engine. The new modern laundry procedure was: Fill the tub with hot water and soap (she made her own soap from lye and ashes). She would then "kick start" the engine. The machine had two levers; one turned on the agitator in the tub, the other operated the wringers.

When the washing cycle was finished she repeated with the rinse cycle to get the soap out, and the wet clothes were put through the wringer rollers.

If Mom did laundry when I was home, I liked to help. My job was to run the clothes through the wringers. I folded the clothing item to the width of the wringer rollers, and then I would push the garment into the two counter-rotating rollers. You had to be careful to quickly pull your hands back when the winger caught the clothing and started to pull it through. I sadly recall one time—I was feeding the wet clothes through the wringers and all of a sudden both arms were caught clear up to my shoulders and the engine was straining and trying its best to squeeze my whole body completely through the rollers. My mother heard me screaming and quickly came and stopped the motor. Fortunately, the wringer assembly had a quick-release lever which opened the rollers. Thankfully the manufacturer anticipated someone like me screwing up and not paying attention, so I didn't have to permanently wear the darn contraption.

We didn't have a lot of money to spend on new clothes, so Mom had to do a lot of repair work on the old stuff. She had an old Singer sewing machine. Sometimes she would have to make new shirt or a dress when the old ones were beyond repair. These new garments were made from the sack material the livestock feed came in. Mother picked out all the feedstock and it wasn't by the brand name, it was solely by the colors and prints on the bag that influenced her. I'm sure the animals that had to eat the feed she picked out were hoping the manufactures of the *best-tasting food* were also the *best fashion designers*.

I wore "hand me downs" until I started school, mostly bib overalls, long-sleeved shirts and high-topped shoes.

Mom would make preparations for our evening meal, which sometimes included killing and dressing a chicken. Keep in mind we had no electricity, which meant no refrigeration, so everything had to be consumed fresh or canned. Most all leftovers were given to the dog or the pigs, in the form of slop. We never bought dog or cat food. I don't know if it was even offered to the farming community. Dogs ate what you ate or they didn't eat. The cats were on their own— they had to kill varmints for their vittles.

My brother and I had chores to do before we went to school and also when we came home in the evening. We were kept busy, but nothing on the level of our parents.

If the road was passable, mother or dad drove us to town when we went. We had a 1938 Ford sedan with a V-8 engine. It was a modest, good car—very dependable.

* * *

Because of our remote location, access to any credible medical assistance was out of the question, except in extreme emergencies. My parents had a remedy for every ailment known to man, most passed down from generation to generation. Once when I was carrying a glass jar of popcorn downstairs and I fell, the jar broke and cut the palm of my hand really bad. Instead of taking me to the doctor to get stitches, my mother put mercurochrome in the cut and hard-boiled some eggs (no . . . we hadn't decided to pause for breakfast at this crucial time). She carefully peeled the skin away from the inside of the shell, closed the wound as best as she could and stuck that egg skin over the cut just like a tire patch. She then put a big bandage on my hand and I got out of chores for four to five days. Believe it or not, it worked. Till this day you can barely see the scar.

On another occasion I got a sticker (briar, for you city folks) in my finger and developed blood poisoning; it was my middle finger and it was so swollen it looked like I had a second thumb growing where it shouldn't. The finger turned dark and a red streak was moving up my arm. As my mother seemed to be the medic in the family, she took my dad's shaving razor (straight razor—no safety razors in our house) and made a small incision where the sticker was, then made a poultice from bread and whole milk. She put a big glob on the sore, wrapped the hand in waxed paper and bandaged it tightly. I had to wear a clean cloth glove. She repeated this procedure daily until eventually the swelling went down and the color returned to my finger and I survived and still had all my digits.

There were other remedies of elixirs and herbs for diarrhea, constipation, fever, and chills. I seem to remember a lot of the medicine was the same for all the problems; black strap molasses or cod-liver oil seemed to cure most ailments.

Vicks VapoRub was the new cure-all if you had a cough, cold or fever. Mom would "grease you up" with Vicks *everywhere* and would even rub it on, *and in,* your nose. If the cold persisted, she would heat Vicks in a pan of water and we had to breathe the medicated vapor while holding our heads under a towel draped over the steaming pan.

Then there was the dreaded 'mustard plaster,' a mixture of mustard and flour formed into a paste and covered with waxed paper; it was used for chronic congestion. The downside was, if it was left on too long it would cause a chemical burn, even blisters. It had to be removed very carefully because, on occasion, a good portion of your skin could come off with it. The weirdest remedy of all was applied when I would get the croup, a deep heaving cough. My dad always administered this cure. He would give me a teaspoon of *kerosene* (fuel oil) mixed with sugar. He always instructed me not to cough around any open flame. I think he was kidding . . . *wasn't he??*

If the military and the CIA were aware of these home remedies I'm sure they included these techniques in their enhanced interrogation procedures against the enemy.

In addition to these cures we had the "BIG (medical) BOOK," A huge leather-bound tome with gory pictures and everything you needed to know (and a whole lot of things at least I didn't want to know) about *any* medical problem and its cures.

If you couldn't find your problem and several remedies in the "BIG BOOK" you probably didn't have a problem, just a fixation, as my mother would say. She was right I would browse through the book and I'll be darned if I didn't have just about everything in there, with the exception of the pregnancy thing.

I would peruse the book and feel just terrible afterwards— but I couldn't leave it alone. It was another one of those addictions . . . I tried looking that up too. They didn't offer a cure for addictions, probably so they could sell more "BIG BOOKS"!

The "BIG BOOK" was bigger than the Sears Roebuck catalog, which next to the Burpee's seed catalog and the Farmer's Almanac was the most revered publication accepted by the rural farmer and his family, probably by *all mankind*, if the truth be known.

Speaking of the Sears Roebuck catalogs, the *wish book from heaven*, it was used by every member of every family. Once you were finished with it, a new one always appeared, as if by magic. The old catalogs still had many uses: a booster chair for the children; keeping the doors open in the summertime; and *the* most important use of all—it served as toilet paper for the outhouses. You had to tear out each page, then wrinkle it up and smooth it out again or else it wouldn't work, because the paper was too slick. Store-bought toilet paper was a luxury, ill-afforded in most households.

Another alternative for store-bought toilet paper that worked well was "popcorn." Just hold on . . . let me explain. Most farmers raised popcorn; it was the *social crop* of the era. When someone visited and you wanted something to do, collectively, around the fire—everybody just shelled popcorn and told stories. Remember, no TV.

As a bonus, in addition to having great popcorn to eat, it produced very soft (velvety) cobs, unlike field corn (the type fed to livestock) which was *rough as a cob*. Some varieties of popcorn produced a white cob and others a red cob. A lot of outhouses would stock a small bin, with both colors. The theory was you wiped with a red cob, and then you used a white cob to see if you needed another red one. See, all along you thought us county folks were backward and simple . . . Pretty cool, huh?

My dad wanted my brother and me to be farmers like him, but we had different ideas, which were encouraged by our mother. Mom *hated* farming life, if you could call it a life. She never thought they were "the good old days" like dad did.

My dad wanted my brother and me to learn to milk the cows. Mother, not wanting us to get caught up in that demanding chore, took us aside one day and warned us not to learn. She said, "Just act stupid," and we figured we could handle that easy enough.

Mother warned, "Once you two learn to milk, you will be doing all the milking—*all the time*. One thing about milk cows, once you started milking them you had to do it twice a day, every day . . . *forever!* If you missed a milking session, the cow would come looking for you, and it could get really ugly. My brother and I held up our end on most of the chores assigned to us, but we drew the line on milking. In hindsight that was pretty selfish of us, but when times get tough, you gotta do what a guy's gotta do.

My mom used say, "Living on a farm is a dog-eat-dog life."

I had a dog named Spunk, but I never saw him eat another dog. I don't think they do that—do they??

When I was eight years old, my mother decided she was tired of not having any money to spend and tired of the isolation on the farm. She decided to get herself a job as a clerk, working at the dry-goods store in town. I'm not sure why they called it dry goods because they sold a lot of wet stuff too. It was a combination grocery, delicatessen, clothing, shoes, animal feed, candy, baby chickens, and an all-around supply store.

The name of the dry-goods enterprise, painted on the front window was *Schmidt and Son, "Valparaiso's Greatest Store,"* Valparaiso, Nebraska; Phone number 5. (No kidding . . . just dial the number five).

My dad didn't react well to the idea of my mom working outside the home. He said, "A man should be the one working and supporting the family; the woman should be the homemaker."

My mother was small of stature but very headstrong. Once she made up her mind you might just as well back off. She was informing us what she planned to do—I don't think she was asking for permission. Dad's objections may have been a little selfish. I think he was just worried he might not get his supper right at five o'clock every night.

The deal my mother made with our family was: she would still do most of her wifely duties but with considerable more help and support from my brother and me. She would make advanced preparations for the evening meal before she went to work, so we would still have supper close to the regular time, and my brother and I had the cleanup. These conditions softened the embarrassment my father was having by his wife working in public. There were times when mom didn't want to cook. On those rare occasions she would fix a meal at the deli portion of Mr. Schmidt's store and bring it home for us all to eat. Maybe that's where the fast-food idea got started . . . you think??

As a point of information the town's name, Valparaiso, supposedly was an old Indian name meaning the *"Valley of Paradise,"* which was strange because it wasn't a valley at all, flat as a pancake, and according to my mom, *"It sure as hell wasn't paradise."*

My dad's description and explanation was much better: the *Valley of the Polacks.* The biggest drawback of living with a majority of European immigrant farm families from Poland, Slovakia, and Czechoslovakia was, you couldn't tell any good Polack jokes because, to them, they weren't funny . . . just statements of fact! They had a funny application of the English language, they would use terminology like: "Drive the hill, over" or "Throw the cow over the fence, some hay." Weird, right?

I was ecstatic over Mom's decision to work because that meant I didn't have to go straight home after school. I would have about three hours every day to do about anything I wanted, as long as I kept my grades up. My mother figured I couldn't get into too much trouble since everybody in town knew me, plus we could ride home together.

Another benefit of this arrangement was, since I would be spending so much time in the big city, I would technically be considered a "townie," a promotion from my present *almost a "townie"* status. My social standing was rapidly improving.

The town rolled up the streets every weeknight at about 6:00 o'clock with the exception of Wednesday and Saturday nights. Wednesday night the stores stayed open until 9:00 p.m. and Saturday until 11:00 p.m. Sunday, everything was closed with the exception of the two beer joints. They opened at noon, when the Catholic Church services were over, and closed at 6:00 p.m.

On Wednesdays, my mother got off at 2:00 in the afternoon for three hours then had to be back at 5:00 and work until 9:00. So after school we would all go home for supper and then go back to town. Every Wednesday night was free show night. Weather permitting, the movie would be shown outside next to the grain elevator. If it was raining or too cold, they would set up chairs in the town hall. I had been going to the movies even before I started school.

I don't know who picked out the movies or what the criteria were in the decision-making process, but sometimes they had some real losers. No matter what was playing, the newsreels and the two cartoons they played before each movie were always good. Everybody liked the newsreels because the war was still going on, and while we heard about what was happening on the radio, newsreels were the only way you could *see* what was actually happening overseas. I remember everyone always felt so patriotic they would stand up and cheer while watching the newsreel.

If the movie was not going to be good, or one we had already seen a couple of times, my few friends and I would leave after the cartoons and go the barber shop and watch the barber give haircuts and shaves and listen to all the gossip.

At one time I thought I would like to be a barber. I liked the contact you had with people while they let you cut their hair. I especially enjoyed watching the customers lay back in the chair while the barber put hot towels over their faces. And those razors . . . the customers had to have a lot of trust in you—you could do some real damage to someone you didn't like. The barber seemed to know about everything that was going on and what was happening to everyone in town.

During my newfound after-school free time, I visited just about every business in town that would let me hang out with them. I was quickly building my resume to become a businessman. Speaking of knowing what's going on with everything and everyone in town, it didn't take me long to find out who really knew what was what.

I made several visits to the post office and got to know the husband-and-wife team who operated the facility. I assumed, because there was a war going on, the information that flowed through the post office would be under a high-security lock-down. Even so, on occasion I was allowed to go behind the scenes and see how it operated. I must not have been perceived as a high-security risk.

Right away I spotted a glaring potential security breach. It just so happened, the most efficient and cheapest way to communicate with the outside world was by the post card. It only cost one cent to mail a post card, anywhere. You would be surprised how much detailed information you could put in a relatively small space, which anyone could read. I was really surprised we won the war with a discrepancy of that magnitude. I am not saying that the couple who ran the post office actually read any of the postcards, but the possibility of innocently noticing pertinent, personal information from time to time certainly existed.

Another business that had access to critical intelligence was the telephone company. I spent quite a bit of time with the lady who manned (or should I say wo-manned) the day shift. She operated this weird-looking switchboard that consisted of what looked like a sheet of pegboard with a bunch of wires attached to it. It was very *high-tech*, but I figured it out right away.

This is how it worked: Someone on one end of the wires would want to make a call. The telephones of that time didn't have a dial, just a hand crank. Each telephone had a mouthpiece that you talked into and a listening device on a cord that you held up to your ear. When you vigorously turned the crank several times it generated enough power to light a bulb located on the pegboard console, above the jack connecting to the phone making the call.

The operator, who was the lady I hung out with a lot, sat in front of the switchboard with headphones on. She also wore a device that looked like she had been gored by a buffalo and the horn broke off and was imbedded in her chest. This was the part she talked into. When the light came on she would flip a switch and ask, "Number please." The caller would either tell her the name of the party or give her the number, i.e. *Schmidt & Son* store or give the actual number—in the case of *Schmidt & Son* . . . Number five. (I bet you still don't believe me, do you?)

She would then pull the wire from the location that was blinking and plug it into the number five jack, flip a toggle switch and the phone at Schmidt & Son store would ring . . . amazing! When one of the lights (the caller's or callee's) went out, that was a signal that they were finished talking, the wire would then be pulled out of the number five jack and it automatically slid back into the switchboard—isn't technology wonderful?

The operator lady couldn't hear the two-party conversation while the wire was plugged in *unless* she flipped the toggle switch while the conversation was on-going. Then she could actually hear both sides of the dialogue.

While visiting her, I noticed she often flipped the switch and would listen to the conversations. I asked, "Why do you listen to some people talk?"

She replied innocently, "Sometimes the lights don't go out when they're supposed to, so I have to *sneak* in a little listen—just to make sure they haven't already finished." Now I seriously doubt she ever *intentionally* listened in on other people's conversations, but in our interactions, over time, she seemed to know as much about everything and everyone as the barber and the postal clerks.

On Wednesday nights I spent a lot of time in one of the beer joints. You didn't have to be twenty-one to frequent the establishments. Anyone could go in because they served food and had pool tables and shuffleboard but you had to be twenty-one to drink beer.

Television was just starting to come on the scene. The first ones were of course black and white and had small oval or round screens. Each beer joint in town had a TV. In order for everyone to see the thing, they placed a large magnifying glass in front of the set and it *almost* made it possible to recognize what program was playing.

I loved watching wrestling. I was amazed those guys were in such good shape and really tough; they had to be because while they were in the ring they just beat the hell out of each other for almost an hour. If you weren't tough you couldn't take a beating like that and not bleed—I was really impressed. The best wrestlers were the midgets; boy, those little guys were fast.

I couldn't make heads or tails out of the other TV programs because there was so much noise in the beer joint you couldn't hear what the people on the programs were saying. Therefore, I just stuck to wrestling; I didn't need the sound, because I knew most of the celebrity athletes by sight.

CHAPTER FOUR

A First Stab at Capitalism

Imagination rules the world.
— Napoleon Bonaparte

I was about to experience the "Chance of a Lifetime!" An opportunity had presented itself that could fulfill my lifelong dream (of course I was only eight) of untold *wealth*!!

How I spent the three hours after school until Mom got off work was pretty much up to me. The only rule she insisted on was I had to periodically let her know where I was and what I was up to. She constantly told me, "You have an *overactive* imagination—that sometimes got you into some strange situations." Well, guess what, I had to be creative*!* I mostly played by myself (not by choice . . . no kids my age were close) and didn't have a lot of toys.

My older brother's one compulsive hobby was a

fantastic collection of action comic books. (I need to ask him someday how he afforded that many. They were ten cents apiece at the time.) I could enjoy his comic books as much as I wanted, *after* he had finished the initial reading.

My life experiences, outside of my limited, familiar environment were, by proxy, through the actions and adventures of my comic book and radio super heroes like Red Ryder, Tom Mix, The Lone Ranger, Dick Tracy, Buck Rogers, Gene Autry, The Shadow, Captain Marvel, Superman, Batman & Robin, Plastic-Man (never could quite figure that guy out) and many others.

The comic books were my *window* to the outside world. The best parts of the comics were the ads in the back of each publication. Each one offered different but incredible products that anyone, in their right mind, would die to own. To possess these valuable items, all you had to do was send off a few breakfast cereal box tops or labels, and by return mail you could own the world. The downside was you had to eat all that crappy cereal, plus it was expensive. My mom didn't want to admit we couldn't afford to buy the cereal so she would tell me that the stuff tasted terrible and wasn't good for me.

I tried to explain to her about the advantages of eating the cereal. I needed to send in the box tops and get all the good things advertised in the comic books. Instead she informed me it was her responsibility to make sure I got a nutritional, well-balanced breakfast—and cereal wasn't it!

I was a little upset. Because of her outdated logic, I had to eat eggs cooked various ways, bacon, ham or sausage, biscuits with gravy, pancakes with syrup and fruit, when in season—every day—with no box tops to send in, like the other kids. It just wasn't right!

I discovered something amazing while hanging out at the store, where she worked. On occasion, I would help my mom stock shelves with new merchandise. I didn't get paid, but it was something to do and it helped her out.

I realized that some of the products delivered to the store were damaged during delivery, and occasionally similar damage would occur while being handled during the shelf-stocking procedure. The store owner, Mr. Schmidt, couldn't sell these items. He would keep the damaged merchandise in the back of the store until the delivery guy came with new deliveries. The delivery guy worked for a warehouse representing most all the popular cereal brands and he would credit Mr. Schmidt and pick up the damaged items. Being a natural-born entrepreneur . . . *I had an idea*. One day when he was making a delivery, I asked him, "What do you do with the damaged cereal boxes you pick up?"

He said, the companies he delivered for, couldn't sell the merchandise once the products had been damaged. When he got back to his warehouse, the contents of the damaged containers were dumped into a large bin. The unsalable product in turn was sold to a hog farmer.

What I really wanted to know was this: "What did you do with the boxes?" I asked.

Much to my glee, he said, "We throw the boxes away."

That was more than I could have hoped for, so I asked him, with my fingers crossed behind my back, "Would you mind if I cut the box tops off the boxes before you picked them up?" He answered, "Heck no, go right ahead."

I had just found *a gold mine, the keys to the city, the big Kahuna.*

It was hard to imagine the magnitude of this business venture I was about to embark on. I had accessed the ability to capitalize on *all* the comic book and radio ad goodies known to man. What I didn't want to keep, I could sell to my friends.

What a BONANZA! . . . I could hardly sleep thinking what I was going to do with all the money and stuff, and the best part was I didn't have to buy or eat any of that crappy cereal.

I started to put my plan in action. I got out the comic books and made a list of all the stuff I wanted.

Between the comic books and the radio ads, my list grew and grew.

I decided that with so much stuff to choose from I had to prioritize. I narrowed my list down to about six or eight items. I then compiled an inventory of the brands of cereal, and the amount and kinds of box tops and labels; I would need to get started.

My list was composed of the following:

1. A Lone Ranger "six-shooter" ring. Not just any ring. This one, according to the picture in the ad, had fire and smoke coming out of the barrel. It had a whistle on the side so you could call your horse—I didn't have a horse, but I had a dog. Most importantly, it had a secret compartment to hide hush-hush messages. I didn't have any, but I planned to devote some time into coming up with something, knowing they would have to be very important—if you had to hide them. This item required six Kix box tops (I figured this would be more—what a bargain!). Shipping was free.

2. A set of lead soldiers with a tank and a Jeep. I figured, with the war and all, I should do my part and play some patriotic games. This required seven Ralston Wheat Chex box tops. Again, shipping was free.

3. An authentic, (according to the ad) Dick Tracey "2-way" wrist radio. I should get two of these if I was going to talk to someone besides myself. Mr. Tracy's life had been saved on numerous occasions by using these

modern devices. Each one required six Cheerios box tops, with free shipping

4. A Buck Rogers decoding "Death Ray" gun. It also was authentic (according to the ad), just like the one Buck used in the comic books and on the radio. I figured I would write the messages I was going to hide in my Lone Ranger ring, in code. Even if someone found them by accident, they couldn't read them until they were decoded using the Buck Rogers decoder. The intrigue was going to be great fun. This item was a biggie; you needed ten Wheaties box tops and a dime for shipping—must be a heavy package. With all that "high-technology," the instruction manual was probably what made it so weighty.

5. A family of sea monkeys, a whole family. The ad's picture showed the little devils playing in the water. It said they were friendly. I could always use some more friends. Amazingly, this item took only two Shredded Wheat (un-frosted) box tops, another bargain . . . I mean . . . you got a *whole family!*

6. A Charles Atlas muscle-building book. This was the one where the big bully kicked sand in the face of the little guy, and stole his girlfriend (some girlfriend). But then the little guy got the Charles Atlas muscle-building book, got strong and beat the crap out of the bully and got his pretty girlfriend back.

I had to have the muscle-building book because

that happened to me a lot (well, not really, but it might someday), especially if I ever got to go to the beach (wherever that was). Heck, if it got you the girl, it had to be worth it. It took three Ovaltine labels plus seven pennies for shipping (must be a really big book—probably lifting it was part of the muscle-building program).

7. A pair of X-Ray vision glasses. The pictures on the ads showed a guy looking through walls and through people's clothes. I could see where they would come in handy, but I made a promise to myself that I wouldn't look though my mother's clothes. I was surprised how cheap these were—only a couple of bubble gum wrappers (Double Bubble). With all the technology that must have gone into making them, I guessed, they would have been a lot more expensive, free shipping too—*Wow*!

8. Last but not least, the Harry Blackstone Magic Kit. I always wanted to be a magician. My dad always said, "It was good to have a trade to fall back on." This was a big item, as the cost was ten Wheaties box tops and ten cents shipping. I considered the magic kit a good deal, because of all the money I could make putting on magic shows.

Now that I had my prioritized list, I would have to start checking the damaged inventory. I really wanted the Lone Ranger ring, so I was especially watching for the damaged Kix boxes.

Right away I discovered a logistical problem. Unfortunately, I couldn't dictate which boxes and jars were going to be damaged. The waiting was pure agony and, I have to admit, it was a real challenge not to hurry things along and *intentionally* damage some of the items I really needed. Fortunately, having listened to too many cop programs on the radio and realizing the bad guys always got caught, I decided to go straight and let happenstance take its course. Besides, I didn't want to get my mom in any trouble.

Finally, after what seemed like forever, I had all the box tops and labels I needed but not all the money for shipping, so I had to make some more tough choices.

Every Wednesday and Saturday, when my dad would give me a nickel for candy (you wouldn't believe how much candy you could get for a nickel back then), he would always say "don't spend it all in one place." This wasn't too tough since only three places sold candy and a lot of it was the same type. I didn't have much trouble spreading the wealth around.

My plan was to cut down on the candy for a couple of weeks and save up for the return postage on my items. I even hit Mom up for some extra money. She was usually an easy touch now that she was working. With her contributions I wouldn't have to cut down too far on the candy and still reach my goals. *Tough business decisions*!

I finally balanced the equation, and had enough money for the return mail expenses; I was ready to send off for the much anticipated treasures.

After getting all the instructions for mailing from the postmaster, Mr. Christiansen, I stuffed everything in envelopes, which the postal clerks gave me free of charge. I put on all the addresses like they told me to do and took them to the post office to start reaping the rewards of my venture.

I gave the letters to Mrs. Christensen and started to leave, but she stopped me and told me I needed fourteen cents more for the postage to send them. I was devastated. No one told me you had to pay to send things *both ways*.

I asked, "When did they start that?" I also asked, "Would it be cheaper to put them all in one envelope, since they are all going to the same city, Battle Creek, Michigan?"

She said, "You can't do that because they are all going to different companies, albeit in the same city."

There was one of my first important lesson in Business 101; you have to budget in for unexpected overhead and transportation costs. I also learned about discretionary spending. It was quite apparent that I had to "cut out some more pork (in my case, candy)." I also decided to cancel the X-Ray glasses. I figured looking though walls and people's clothes isn't such a big deal after all.

After two more weeks of budgeting and candy rationing, I revisited the post office and successfully mailed everything.

With great expectations, I checked the post office box every day. We had one of those boxes with the secret combination dial to get in it, but if I forgot the combination Mrs. Christensen would just hand it to me—so much for interstate commerce security.

I lost interest in keeping track of more damaged goods, for a while. I figured I have so much stuff coming; I won't have much time for any other activities anyway.

After about three weeks, I received my first item. I don't know how far away Battle Creek, Michigan, was or how they sent the mail, but it seemed they could have *walked* it to me faster.

My first arrival was, much to my delight, the Lone Ranger "six-shooter" ring. I could hardly wait to open it, but I decided I would wait until I got home, where I had the privacy and the uninterrupted time to read about all the great things this marvelous piece of equipment could do.

After arriving home and finishing all my chores, I went into my bedroom: it was time for the unveiling. With sweaty hands, I took it out of the box; so far it was, *as advertised*, a ring . . . with an adjustable band. It had a "six-shooter" mounted on the top, just like the ad said, but that was about as far as the "as advertised" description went.

Fire and smoke couldn't come out of the barrel because it was solid. The thing that made the fire and smoke was a tiny mechanism, like a Zippo lighter. It had a piece of flint, which, when you flicked it, would spark and if you *really squinted*, you could see a little wisp of smoke trailing up from the flint.

I ran outside near where my dog was and blew the whistle. I did this several times, but after a while I came to the reality that the high-pitched sound must only work on horses, because Spunk wouldn't come. He just looked at me like, "Why the hell are you making all that noise?"

I checked for the one last feature and sure enough it was there, a hollowed-out hole, underneath, where the "six-shooter" was mounted on the ring. The cavity was really tiny but I suppose you could hide a secret message in there . . . if you didn't have much to say. The gun on the top of the ring stuck up so high that I couldn't put my hand in my pocket to get anything out; I had to take the ring off first. That's OK, I thought, *I am sure the wonderful advantages will eventually far outweigh the inconveniences.* So I put it away and got ready for bed.

The next morning I decided I would wear my ring

all day, thinking it was probably like a pair of shoes you had to break in before they got comfortable.

I had to do some chores—first I had to pump water for the livestock.

I filled the first bucket and reached down to pick it up, bumped the ring on the well spout and broke the "six-shooter" off the ring mounting, the Zippo mechanism fell apart, the flint fell out and everything else fell into the bucket of water, which ruined the whistle.

I just stood there amazed, *awestruck*. The whole thing disintegrated in a matter of seconds, right before my eyes. I was devastated I wanted to cry but then I remembered, not all is lost, "I've got a lot of *better* stuff coming." So I was back to the post office vigil.

Within a couple of days the next item arrived—the Buck Rogers "authentic" *Death Ray* gun. I unwrapped it and at first glance, it too appeared to be *as advertised*. It looked just like the real thing.

I looked further in the box and found a battery and instructions on how to install it. I thought: *Battery powered, this thing is going to do amazing stuff, just like the one Buck used in the comic book*. It was getting exciting.

I installed the battery and held it out away from me, not knowing exactly what to expect, and pulled the trigger. Nothing happened. I surmised that because it was new, it probably had to get warmed up.

I held it out away from me again, shaded my eyes and pulled the trigger. This time I noticed a faint little glow coming from the front of the gun.

I ran inside where it was darker and pulled the trigger again and you could see the glow a little better, but it definitely wasn't even close to a *Death Ray*! It didn't even put out as much light as our old "piece of crap" flashlight. I thought, *Well, that was impressive.*

What about the decoder? It was supposed to be a decoder too—where was the decoder? In a panic, I tore though the box looking for an instruction book for the decoder, and finally found it.

I had to snap off one of the handle grips and sure enough inside was the decoder mechanism; it consisted of two different sized wheels set up like dials, the smaller one was mounted on top of the larger one. You could move them separately, and on the outside of the wheels there was a ring of numbers; as you turned each wheel independently of each other, little windows would open and you could see letters appear. Then you lined everything up with the two arrows on the edge of the handle and you could decipher the code, to which I thought: *This is the most confusing thing I've ever done in my entire life!*

It took me almost twenty minutes to decipher my first name—and *I knew what it was*! If you had to decode a really important, lengthy message, the war would be over before they figured out what you wanted to tell'em!

I was batting zero for two with my treasures. One consolation—*it can't get any worse.* My spirits weren't completely dampened. I still had a lot of great stuff coming, but right now the X-Ray glasses were looking better all the time.

The next to arrive were the lead solders with the tank and the Jeep. I unwrapped them with less excitement than before, trying to keep my expectations down, but I was pleasantly surprised to find they were exactly "as advertised." I got six soldiers in various stages of action, and each with various weapons. I got a tank that actually looked like a tank, and a Jeep that *pretty much* looked like a Jeep.

I played with them for about fifteen minutes; I had a "crack" fighting force but nobody to fight. I attempted to pit them against each other but that just didn't seem right. I didn't want to give anyone the impression I thought they were a bunch of traitors, so I put them on my shelf in my bedroom and never touched them again. At least I didn't get totally screwed, as with the other items. Back to the post office watch.

I got two items on the next delivery, the sea monkeys and the Dick Tracy wrist radios. I couldn't decide which one to open first but finally I discerned that the sea monkeys probably would be anxious to get out of the box, but since they would probably take the most time to acclimate, I had to put them in water, watch them grow, and then I had to train them, I figured I would save them for last. Besides, I could then give them my undivided attention while I was befriending them.

I quickly opened the wrist radios and again *as advertised* they looked just like Dick Tracy's actual wrist radio. I had good feeling about these; each one had a movable dial that adjusted the frequency. I looked for batteries but, strangely enough, there were none. The radios sounded hollow, so I figured they must operate by some kind of advanced "air" power.

I talked my mother into taking one and we carefully adjusted them to the same frequency and separated, at quite a distance, and talked to each other, but heard *nothing* . . . I had this sinking feeling again surely, Dick Tracy, fighter for truth and justice, wouldn't disappoint me.

Maybe they were just out of range so Mom and I talked into the radios as we walked toward each other and, as if a miracle was happening, all of a sudden they started to work. They must have been "sound powered" (like the telephones on a Navy ship) because the closer we came to each other and the louder we talked—the better we could hear each other.

I was so excited, and was really glad I had gotten

two of them. They worked so well and they could be used anywhere—as long as you weren't too far apart.

I wondered why my mother kept looking at me kinda funny, and was shaking her head.

Finally she said, "Donnie, I don't want to play anymore," and went into the house. I guess she was too overwhelmed by this advanced technology.

This seemed to be my lucky day, so on to the sea monkeys. I opened the box, expecting to see some kind of a life chamber, an air lock or tiny fish bowl . . . something. The ad said they were alive. You were just supposed to put them in water, they would become active. They would then become a happy, fun loving, talented family.

I didn't find anything like that at all; what I found were some dried-up pieces of dirt in an envelope, which I dumped out outside in the trash barrel, but I never found the sea monkey family—they must have escaped en route. At first I was sad that they were gone but then I figured it was OK—as long as they were together as a family.

Both the *Charles Atlas* muscle-building book and the magic kit eventually came and they were both worth all the trouble I had getting them. The muscle-building book people wanted me to buy a whole set of muscle-building weights, but we couldn't afford them, so I used pieces of machinery and bricks instead. I followed the instructions and the pictures. I really think I got stronger over time. I had no doubt that I would be ready for the beach and the bully if the occasion ever arrived.

The kit included a pamphlet showing how to do a whole bunch of strong man feats: like tearing a telephone book and a deck of cards in half, how to drive a nail through a board with your bare hands, how to bend nails bare-handed and so forth. There was a trick to most of the feats, but it still took a fair amount of strength.

I worked on those demonstrations for years until I could do all of them fairly well to one degree or another. Tearing the telephone book wasn't really fair because our telephone book was only two pages . . . double-spaced!

I really enjoyed the magic kit and got pretty good at most of the tricks, especially the card tricks. I have expanded the scope of the tricks over the years and really do them quite well. I have always done card tricks at family parties, and the kids really like them.

All said and done, this entrepreneurial venture took about two months to complete, but was it worth it? You bet! I told my parents and brother what I had done and my brother laughed at me for being so gullible, but he used my Charles Atlas book almost as much as I did.

My dad said, "There are no shortcuts in life. You

have to work hard with your hands to make anything of yourself." (I'm certain there was some real wisdom there, but I wasn't sure how it applied to my situation. I think he thought I was trying to make a fast buck without working. But I thought what I had done *was work*.)

My mother squatted down and looked me in the eye. She was only about five feet two inches tall so she didn't have far to go, and said, "Donnie, did you really think by just sending in a few box tops you were going to get a *real* ray gun, *real* radios, *real* live monkeys and X-Ray glasses?"

I said, "But Mom, the ads had pictures and everything. They said it all was *authentic* . . . how could they do that when they knew it wasn't true?"

She told me that what I had done and the ideas I had were good, and it didn't cost me anything but my time, so I didn't really fail, and if I learned that everything that sounds good, *isn't always,* then it was worth all the effort I had put into it!

I was proud of myself because I got all that stuff without having to buy anything or eat any of their crappy cereal, plus I got a lot of worldly experience . . . so who really won? All it cost me was postage and a little time. I did get some good things that I still use to this day; I cut down on my candy intake; and I learned a lot. I was *almost* a successful business kid—at least for a short period of time.

CHAPTER FIVE

Exposure to "High Technology"

Do you realize if it weren't for Edison we'd be watching TV by candlelight?
— Al Boliska

Had the townsfolk only known what evil was being brought into their midst.

I spent a lot of time in the store where my mother worked. I got to know the owner, Mr. Schmidt, really well. He bought fresh eggs from the local farmers and resold them to his customers. He also sold baby chicks to those who wanted to just raise a few chickens for eating. He would buy these (resale) baby chicks from a local hatchery.

Just about every farmer raising a lot of chickens had several roosters. Raising chickens to have eggs to eat and sell was all well and good, but if you planned to eat some of the chickens you raised you had to replace them once in a while. Why buy them when you have a bunch of chick factories "on the hoof." For this reason you need roosters to fertilize the eggs that need to be hatched.

Funny thing about chickens (other than being so stupid that they eat their own crap), all the females are potential layers but only a few are sitters, ones that have the patience to become a mother.

One of my chores was to collect the eggs. I never knew when it would happen or which chicken it would happen to, but on occasion one of the hens would be reluctant to give up her eggs. She would peck at you, and try to keep you from taking her potential offspring. At first, you never knew if she was "broody" (experiencing maternal instincts) or she was just being a biddy, wanting to hoard her eggs.

After a few of days of this behavior it was obvious that she was ready to make a total commitment to motherhood. At that time, I would load her up with more eggs (as many as she could cover without breaking them) while assuming the head rooster named "Killer" and his henchmen had done their jobs, and she was sitting on fertile eggs.

All you had to do then was to make sure she got feed and water for twenty-one days and she would take it from there. All chickens are pretty proud of themselves when they lay an egg. They cackle and strut like they are saying, "Hey, come here and look at this beauty. Let's see you top this one." But when they have been sitting in one spot for twenty-one days and those eggs start hatching: "*Hey, it's party time,*" she lets everyone know. All her friends come over to oooh and aaaah over the chicks and congratulate her on a job well done.

Then of course there's "Killer" and the boys. They come around and strut, crow and try to take credit for everything. Then like a typical *chauvinistic* fowl, "Killer" goes off in search of some other "cute chick" and delegated his paternal obligations to the ladies.

I called the head rooster "Killer" because of the episode involving him going inside the outhouse one evening to get warm. He's the one that fell in the hole. The general consensus, although never proved beyond a shadow of doubt, was that I was the one who left the door open. Whether it was true or not didn't matter . . . *the rooster believed it was me.*

He must have really resented the episode, even after all the trouble I went to getting him out of "deep doo-doo." He figured that I was the cause of all the embarrassment and isolation he had to endure until after the next big rain, and he wanted to get even.

I didn't know chickens held grudges. It was either that or Dad was putting steroids in his feed. Ever since the incident he had an attitude. He would periodically chase me when I went to the henhouse to gather eggs. He was an old rooster and he had really long spurs on the backs of his legs. He would run and jump at me and try to dig his spurs into my legs. That's the first time I ever had a bird pull a knife on me! I'm thinking, *some day I'll get that "cocky" bastard!*

I helped out a lot around the dry goods store. Mainly my motive was to help my mom but it was also a good way to kill time. Mr. Schmidt didn't pay me but I had a lot of perks, like every once in a while when he was weighing out candy for someone he would toss me a couple of pieces and that was more than enough to make me happy.

Mr. Schmidt, making a sound business decision, determining that it would be more profitable to hatch his own baby chicks, instead of buying them from the hatchery. He followed through on his judgment and bought one of the latest model incubators and a *high tech* egg candler.

He was buying eggs from many of the farmers, anyway, and although he resold most of the eggs for food, now he was also able to hatch the fertile ones and sell the baby chicks at a greater profit margin. In order to accomplish this task, he would have to determine which eggs he had bought were fertile and which were not.

The *high tech* candler he purchased basically consisted of a bright light behind what looked like an egg carton with the bottom cut out. You placed the eggs into the carton and the bright light would shine through the egg. If it was fertile, the yolk would be a different color and shape.

I enjoyed candling eggs. I filled and stacked the trays with, hopefully, fertile eggs. When all the trays were filled, they were placed in the incubator and it was turned on. The timer and temperature were preset. Once the eggs started on the incubation period, the temperature could not vary more than two to three degrees, between 100-103 degrees Fahrenheit, for twenty-one days. Then as if by magic, you had a whole bunch of noisy baby chicks.

I worried if I was doing it right because rarely did every egg in the trays hatch (I think this is where the saying, "Don't count your chickens before they hatch," came from). But since I was only candling every once in a while, and since it took twenty-one days to tell if you screwed up or not, I quit worrying. Besides, it would be hard for me to get fired since; technically, I didn't work there because I didn't get paid.

So there was another lesson logged away in my entrepreneur business 101 training experiences. If you want *real* job security, get a job where no one can prove you screwed up, or one where you don't get paid or—as a last resort—*go into politics*!

One of my other favorite things to do at the store was operate the shoe machine. The store sold many diverse items, one of them being shoes. I liked playing in that department. They had one of those metal flat things you put your foot on and slide all the tabs in toward your foot and it measures your foot size so the shoe clerk would know about what size for customers to try on. Now keep in mind this store was no PAYLESS SHOES. The sizes were few and the styles even fewer. Back then, everyone bought shoes sparingly, you got the most wear possible out of each pair.

When you bought shoes for children, you always made sure *you had room to grow*. Using that philosophy, your shoes actually fit you for just a short time before they wore out.

We didn't have a cobbler who repaired shoes. The closest thing we had was the blacksmith (wrong kind of shoes). I can remember wearing one pair of shoes for a long time and wearing holes in the soles. When that happened, my mom would cut cardboard (the heaviest she could find) insoles and slip them in the shoe. This worked pretty well as long as you didn't step on a sharp pebble, or in a water puddle. The cardboard liners didn't work when it rained or snowed. When the weather was bad I wore my "four buckle" overshoes all the time. I wore one pair of shoes so long my toes are still crooked—no kidding.

Anyway, it was so important to get the proper fit that Mr. Schmidt decided to buy one of those *newfangled* X-ray shoe machines. It was basically a wooden box pedestal with a cabinet on top. You stepped up on it and shoved both feet as far into the slot as you could. The box height was about belt-high to an adult. On top of the box there were three adjustable viewing ports which made it possible for three people, the salesman, the customer and in some cases the parent of a child customer, to look inside and actually see the outline of the shoes, but the really amazing benefit was, you could also see the outline of the feet and even the bones of the feet. In addition to the viewing ports was a handle. It operated a long pointer so the salesman could call attention to the areas he wanted the customer to focus one.

It was a fascinating device. Most of the upscale *national* shoe stores advertised it as an infallible miracle to get the "perfect fit." I think nowadays it would have been termed *an attractive nuisance.*

I was so fascinated by it I spent at least an hour a day playing with it. I loved looking at my feet, and anything else I could get in the slot. I enjoyed showing it to my friends and just about everyone else who came into the store.

A few months later in one of our science classes at school, someone had to do a report on X-ray machines and their dangers . . . *dangers?* The pupil giving the report was pointing out the devastating side effects of too much radiation. There were pictures of cancer patients with huge tumors and sores caused by excess radiation. The people who were affected the worst were the radiation technicians, the ones actually operating the X-ray machine.

The article showed the technicians operating the machines, while standing behind a lead shield, and wearing a lead-lined apron with extra lead below the waist, to protect his or her vital organs . . . especially the *reproductive organs!*

I felt cold chills going down my spine and the hair standing up on the nape of my neck. I raised my hand to ask permission—*I had to leave the room*!! This was devastating!

I'm thinking. . . *"OH MY GOD!"* I'm quickly trying to calculate: *How many hours have I spent with my body parts in that damn killing machine?* I knew I didn't have the protection of any lead shield or apron. The only protection I had was my bib overalls and holey shoes.

The *horror* of it all! I was almost in tears thinking how lonely I was going to be. I'd never be able to get married and have children since my only chance at fatherhood had just been snuffed out. I wondered just how much longer I would still be able to go the bathroom. And *what I would use?*

For a long time I was afraid to take off my shoes because I feared my feet would still remain in them! How would I make a living and get around with feet that were going to look like *two burnt matches?*

Talk about being traumatized. I was afraid to tell my mom about what I had found out. I remember her saying that she was ashamed to show my brother off to her friends when he was little. For some reason his hair grew down almost to his eyebrows. He was being shunned and his only problem was he didn't have a forehead. What would she think of me when I didn't have any feet, couldn't get work, or give her any grandkids?

My imagination was waaaaay out of control. I went to Mr. Schmidt to tell him that he had to do something about that death machine that was going to destroy the whole town, or maybe *all mankind*, for that matter. That monster made Buck Roger's *Death Ray* gun look like a water pistol.

Mr. Schmidt tried to convince me that the shoe machine was only putting out low-level radiation. It was actually a fluoroscope and it wouldn't hurt anyone. He impressed upon me that he sure wouldn't appreciate me telling everyone that his new "high-tech" shoe machine was going to alter the town's population. I told him that I wouldn't say anything, but I never got close to that *evil machine* again.

I found out later that the X-ray shoe machines were outlawed in the late 1950s.

I have often wondered . . . how differently I would have turned out if . . . I would have never encountered that *diabolical* high- tech invention?

CHAPTER SIX

The Wild Man from Borneo

*A man who carries a cat by the tail learns
something he can learn in no other way.*
— Mark Twain

Every year a carnival company would come to our small town. The show was relatively large for only traveling the small-town circuit. The carnival had an ample amount of quality rides, side shows and concession stands. The game booths, where you would pay money and try to win a prize, were the main attractions. They seemed to be the real moneymakers. I really enjoyed all the carnivals because school was always out for summer break and the attractions were an exciting diversion to a sometimes mundane summer. *Little did I know this year's carnival was going to erupt into a horrible nightmare!*

I was only nine years old at the time and not allowed

to stay at home alone on the farm while the rest of the family was at work.

The owners of the carnival always hired some of the local folks to help set up and tear down the tents and booths. This cut down on their overhead because they didn't have to carry a lot of laborers on their staff. I had a lot of time on my hands so I always made myself available to help set up and stock the carnival booths, for which they paid me in money and ride tickets.

The one area my mother warned me never to go around was the "hootchy cootchy" show, as she called it. I don't know why it bothered her so, because the ladies that worked the tent seemed *really* friendly with all the guys. I was always curious about what went on in there, and I must say I was tempted to take a peek, but I didn't. If staying away was all I had to do so Mom would give me a free rein the rest of the summer, it was a small price to pay.

I was fascinated with the "freak" shows and always tried to get on their setup crews. You met some of the nicest and most interesting people there.

Luckily this year, I was again able to get on the freak-show tent crew. As I was helping set up their attraction, I met and talked with the first black man I ever had contact with. He was a really friendly fella and we seemed to hit it off well, and we talked for some time.

I always picked up enough money working setup for

the carnival to do all the things I wanted to. Plus my dad and mom always gave me a little extra money for special occasions like this, so I was in "hog heaven" (for you city folks—that's a good place).

The first night the carnival opened, I went straight to the midway. I was really anxious to go see the freak show. Its tent had big signs outside showing a *bearded lady*, *a guy with big snakes*, a *two-headed cow*, *a man that was turning to stone, and the world's strongest man.* The feature exhibit was "*The Wild Man From Borneo.*" How could anyone pass on that lineup?

I paid my money and went into the tent by myself, like I did most things. They had little stages set up inside, so you could view the different "freaks of nature."

The bearded lady was *as advertised,* a fat lady with a beard, she didn't do anything special just sat there doing what she obviously did best . . . being fat. I moved on.

The stage with the big snakes was kinda' neat. The sign said these snakes were "man-eating" pythons and they were *big.* The guy on the stage invited volunteers from the audience to come up and help him handle the snakes and, of course, I volunteered. Me being the brave curious type. I figured, "If these things are "man-eating," they probably wouldn't even bother with someone my size." He told me that they had already eaten, so he was *pretty sure* they weren't still hungry (everyone laughed).

Once I got up on the stage, he started wrapping those two *huge* snakes around my shoulders, boy, I found out they weren't just big, they were also really *heavy*. I knew they were friendly because of the way they were squeezing me. As they got tighter and tighter I realized I could hardly move my arms!

The snake handler always had a hold of their heads and again assured me, and the crowd, that as long as he held onto their heads they couldn't swallow me—he didn't think. *I'm sweating, and everyone laughed again.* I was starting to lose confidence in this guy's ability to handle snakes, or to be funny, for that matter. What a time for my imagination to kick in. I'm thinking, *He said the snakes had already eaten,* and it suddenly hits me: *These are "man-eating" monsters . . . what. . . or who, did he feed them?* OK, I'm at the point now that I don't wanna' play any more. I yell out, "Get these things off me!" The snake handler sees my impending panic and starts removing the snakes as fast as he can.

When I am free and off the stage, he tells everyone to give me "a big hand" and they all start clapping and patting me on the back. All of a sudden I've gone from "snake bait" to super hero in the blink of an eye. The snake guy gave me some additional ride tickets for helping him, so all in all it was a good learning experience. I filed this pearl of wisdom away in my ever-growing business memory bank, *"Don't ever volunteer for anything again!"*

The two-headed cow was bogus. It wasn't alive, *it was stuffed,* and not a really good job either. It sorta' looked like they just sewed another head onto a regular dead calf. I was really disappointed.

The man who was turning to stone just looked like a guy with a bad rash, sorta' like my Uncle Art, who was caught out in the open in a gas attack in the First World War.

The "world's strongest man" was pretty good. He would flex his impressive muscles and would roll his stomach muscles around and around in a circle (it looked like something was alive in there and trying to get out—spooky!). He did a lot of strength feats. I 'm sure he was a graduate of the Charles Atlas course I was taking.

But where was the featured attraction? Where was "The wild man from Borneo?" That's the one I really wanted to see.

I noticed that in the back of the tent there was a plywood framed wall, with four sides. It had canvas tacked over it to form a cage about ten feet high. There was simulated barbed wire strung along the top of the walls, to either keep the public out or . . . *to keep something hideous in.* I couldn't tell which. They had built a sort of scaffolding all the way around the cage so you could walk up the stairs and stand on it and look down into the pit.

Standing on the walkway were two big guys stationed on the corners, holding clubs. Every once in a while they would beat on the walls with their clubs and shout in the pit, "Sit down". . . "Get away from that". . . "Put that down!"

I'm trying to imagine, *"What the heck is in there?"*

There was about half a dozen men and women standing on the walkway, looking in the pit. You could hear growling and a drum beating periodically. There must *really* be a wild man from a place called Borneo (wherever that is) in there!

Here's my thought process, *"Borneo must be a bad place if it made you wild. Sometimes my mom used to tell my brother and me to calm down, because we were getting too wild. Maybe this guy didn't have a mom to remind him to calm down and his behavior just got out of hand. Maybe he didn't have a mom at all. Maybe he—Oh Never Mind!*

There was a guy standing on a box in front of the cage-like enclosure, telling everyone to "step right up" to see the vicious, wild cannibal who was captured in the deepest part of the East Asian rain forests. *Step right up,* but it'll cost you an extra 10 cents to see him.

Wait a minute. They didn't tell you that on the outside—10 cents? *That's highway robbery.* I'm standing there contemplating, "What better use would I have for the dime it was going to cost me to see this thing?" and then I decided, I may never have another chance in this lifetime to see another "wild man from Borneo" or any other place else for that matter. *I gotta' go.*

I gave the guy a dime and got up on the walkway, stood on my tiptoes, and looked down into the pit. Of course I have my eyes closed so the initial shock won't be too great. I needed time to absorb this hideous creature *sloooowly.* I gradually opened my eyes and the sight I beheld was *horrifying.* There was a washtub full of bloody water set in the middle of the pit. Strewn around the floor of the pit were live and dead chickens, in various stages of dismemberment—feathers, body parts, guts and blood scattered all over.

There were also several small to medium-sized snakes crawling around in the pit. And there next to the washtub was a man (I think it was a man) sitting on a wooden stool with what looked like a leopard-skin dress on and a necklace made of animal claws around his neck. He had long scraggly matted hair hanging in his eyes. He was filthy!

His filthy condition reminded of the time I was slopping the pigs right after a big rain, and I slipped in the mud and fell backward. Both buckets of slop spilled on top of me. Every time I tried to get up I would slip back down and roll in the mud and pig crap; now that's *filthy*! This guy looked like that and worse.

He had an African drum next to him and he would periodically beat on it with a part of a chicken carcass.

Every once in a while he would let out a loud growl and jump up at a wall, like he was trying to escape. The guards on the walkway would beat on the walls and yell at him to sit back down. *This guy was in bad shape*!

I couldn't take my eyes off him, and he would just glare out from under his matted hair at everyone. I noticed one of the snakes was starting to crawl over his foot and he reached down, grabbed the snake and bit its head off. . I'm Talking . . . Bit . . . It . . . Off! He then proceeded to peel it like a banana and eat it! Everyone in the audience groaned and some of the ladies had to close their eyes.

He would play with some of the other snakes that were still alive. Then all of a sudden he would reach under his stool, grab a snake and throw it in the audience while laughing hysterically. Actually it wasn't a real snake, just a strip of rubber sliced from an old inner tube. But everyone thought he was throwing a real snake.

The guards would beat on the walls with the clubs, yell at him, and try to make him stop.

One of the rubber strips landed on a big Polack farmer's girlfriend's head and she had hysterics, screaming and trying to get this *perceived* snake off her head. Her boyfriend was so mad—he was trying going to go over the wall to get to the *"Wild Man from Borneo,"* barbed wire be damned. He was going to take this guy out; he didn't care where he was from! The guards grabbed the farmer and took him outside, kicking and screaming. I guess they figured the "*Wild Man from Borneo*" wouldn't stand a chance with an "*Irate Polack farmer from Saunders County, Nebraska.*"

I was feeling sorry for this poor creature. Everybody was yelling at him, beating on the walls and he had nowhere to hide. He had no place to bathe or go to the bathroom. He obviously was hungry if he had to resort to eating raw chickens and snakes. I was trying to imagine what he could be thinking as he stared at his tormentors through his mass of matted hair.

The longer I kept staring at the "Wild Man," the more he started to look familiar, and at last I figured it out—*it was Moses!* (The black man I had met the day before). My Gosh. What had they done to him? He must have gone crazy overnight!

I could appreciate and understand how he could have gotten that filthy that quickly (because of my pig sty experience), but *how had his hair grown that fast?*

The whole scenario reminded me of a mystery program I had listened to on the radio called *"Inner Sanctum."* This was a story about a good man named Dr. Jekyll. He was trying out a new drug and was accidently transformed into the evil Mr. Hyde, and killed everybody he came in contact with. Obviously, this "Wild Man" was dangerous like Mr. Hyde because he had to have those guards with clubs watch over him.

The carnival people must have given him this same type of secret potion (probably by mistake) that turned him into this hideous monster. Not knowing what else to do with him, they put him in this pit to keep him away from the rest of the people. The carnival owners, being the shrewd business people they were, probably figured they might just as well make some money off a bad situation.

My evening was ruined. I left the carnival and went to the barbershop, where a lot of the folks hung out in the evening. I was going to tell the people what I saw, but after careful consideration I knew they wouldn't believe me so I just watched haircuts and shaves until my mom got off from work and we went home.

I had trouble sleeping that night. I did a lot of thinking. I remembered, however, on the radio program the evil Mr. Hyde always turned back into the good Dr. Jekyll the next day, and he didn't ever remember what had happened the night before. I was hoping that would happen to Moses, because I really liked the guy.

The next day I went to town with my mom, and after she went to work I went back to the carnival site and started looking around. Sure enough I saw Moses—*he looked normal*. You wouldn't believe how relieved I was.

I stopped him and asked, "Do you remember me?"

He said, "I do."

Then I asked, "Do you remember anything about last night?"

He said, "Sure, what about last night?"

I knew the experience I was about to relate to him was going to come as a great shock, so I tried to recount what I had seen as gently and painlessly as possible without alarming him too much.

Of all things, he started to laugh. He laughed on and on until he could hardly get his breath.

I guess I wasn't as tactful as I had tried to be. He was *hysterical*. I really felt sorry for him; it must have been devastating to hear something that unbelievable. Finally when he caught his breath, he said, "Donnie, *that's my job!*"

"Say what?" I said. "What are you talkin' about— *your job*"?

Moses replied," It's what I do. I'm the show's GEEK!"

I wasn't sure what a GEEK was. I know my brother has called me a geek a few times but I never looked or acted like that.

He said, "It was all an act. I play like I'm this wild man. The people love being scared."

"What about eating the live snakes and chickens. Don't they feed you well at the carnival?" I asked.

Moses said, "It's just part of my act. The weirder I

make it look the more people come to see me. If you had watched more closely you would have seen that I really didn't eat the snakes or the chickens. I put the meat in my mouth and made it look like I was drooling, when what I was actually doing was spitting the stuff out. I wouldn't really eat that stuff. *It could make you sick.*"

But, I said, "I saw you bite the head off the snake and *you really did that*. I'll bet the snake didn't think it was part of the act!"

He said he was sorry it upset me so, but being a *geek* was really a good job, actually one of the best paid positions in the carnival, because it always brought in the most money.

I was glad for Moses that he didn't really turn into Mr. Hyde, but I felt kind of used and lied to. I had really felt sorry for him, and anguished over his hopeless condition. I lost a good night's sleep worrying if he would be all right the next day. I was beginning to understand that things were not always as they seemed, that people would sometimes deceive you, to get you to spend money you wouldn't normally spend. I knew that I would have to start looking beyond the obvious. I began to feel my innocent childhood starting to slip away.

CHAPTER SEVEN

My Second Stab at Capitalism

A child of five would understand this. Send someone to fetch a child of five.

— Groucho Marx

I was always looking for new ways to make money. What I planned to do this summer was not one of my more memorable endeavors. The only reason I am revealing this fiasco is so some other young entrepreneur won't make the same mistake.

One Saturday earlier during the school year, John the guy who owned the busiest beer joint, took me and a couple of my friends to a circus in Lincoln. John always liked me for some reason. I guess it was because I was always available for odd jobs and I worked cheap. I had decided to become an independent businessperson so I spent a lot of time visiting all the businesses in town, especially his, because his seemed to be one of the more successful ones.

Anyway, he took us to the circus. It wasn't Barnum, Bailey and Ringling Bros. by any means but it was big enough to impress me. They had a trapeze act, clowns, a strongman and a magician which were my favorites among all the acts and of course there were animals.

John bought us all cotton candy, sodas and a program. I noticed a sign on the tent that all the performances were sold out. That really stuck in my mind. Entertainment was something the public would spend money on, even during a depression.

After school was out for the summer, I wanted to do something to stay busy and also make some money. Remembering the trip to the circus led to my next business venture. I was ten years old at the time.

I got together with my friend Jack, who was two years older and two grades ahead of me in school. He lived about 1 ½ miles farther outside of town than I did. We were about the same size and we liked most of the same things. What I really liked about him was his imagination—his was about extreme as mine and, the best part, he was easy to motivate.

I took him aside and laid out a plan of action. I got out the program from the circus. I reminded him that all the performances were sold out. I also reminded him that the carnivals that came to our town were always busy and well-attended, entertainment was the business to be in.

I told Jack, "We need to put on an exciting show, sell tickets and make a lot of money over the summer." He looked kinda' skeptical but the more we discussed it the better he liked the idea.

We decided to take stock of the talents we had and what we could learn in a short period of time. I was getting pretty good with my magic kit. I told him I could teach him some of my Charles Atlas feats.

I knew Jack had a BB gun shooting gallery.

I was getting proficient with a lariat and I could rope most anything. (last year, I even roped one of the barnyard cats, but it got away and we had just recently found its body in the cornfield—not one of my more memorable events.) We explored all our options and decided we had enough talent to put on a great show. Jack would be the announcer and present the various acts, because I was a little shy. We just needed a grand finale act.

I was really impressed with the trapeze guys at the circus so that's what we'd do. I told Jack my idea and showed him a picture in the program. He looked at me kinda' strange-like and said "I'm not going to do that."

I said, "We don't have to be that high it the air. We could have a 'low level' High Trapeze Act." The hay mound in the barn was mostly empty at the beginning of summertime before we would start filling it up again with new hay for winter. There was always a lot of loose hay left over on the floor, so it would break our fall if we made a mistake.

We started making plans and divided up all the things we needed to do. We had to schedule all the training sessions for each act; we had to coordinate the timing so we would get good at everything at the same time. We figured it would take us about two weeks to get *really* good at everything we planned to perform.

We didn't have any rope for the trapeze swings, but my dad had a big ball of bailing twine and I figured we could braid three strands together like Mom did her hair sometimes, and that ought to be strong enough. I found some old pick handles to use for the bars. Jack was starting to get into the spirit, everything was coming together, and we were both getting excited.

We planned and accumulated all the items we thought we would need. It took us about four days and we were ready to start our rigorous training sessions.

Two important ideas came to me that we had forgotten: first, they always sold refreshments at the circus and the carnival. I figured my mom could make a lot of popcorn. We didn't have cotton candy like the big shows did, but Mom made great candy apples. I was sure she wouldn't mind making a few dozen of them in her spare time.

Jack was going to ask his mom if she could make

something yummy also. Man, we could make a fortune on just the treats alone.

The second important idea was, who could we get to print up all the tickets? We decided we would ask our mothers about the food this evening, and tomorrow I would ask around town about the tickets.

Later that night after supper and cleanup, I took my mom aside and told her of our plan and asked if she would mind making the food for all the people that would be coming to the show.

I was really excited, but my mom (doing that head-shaking thing again) took hold of my shoulders, sat me down, squatted down to look me in the eye, and said, "Donnie, calm down a minute and listen to me. I know you and Jack are excited about this show but *who are you going to sell all the tickets to. Who do you think will come all the way out here to see your show?*" Right off, the only person I could come up with was Jack, and he would probably want to get in for free . . . *how did I miss that important point?*

Thank God I talked to Mom first before I tried to get someone to print up tickets, and really thank God, I didn't tell my brother. I made my mother promise to *never* tell anyone about my plan.

It was about a week before Jack would talk to me again and when he did, he asked if I would *please* not include him in any more of my schemes. He must have had a similar reaction from his mom.

There was another idea to put into my business 101 memory bank. *Don't commit a lot of time and resources to a project until you have done an in-depth market study!*

CHAPTER EIGHT

Unexpected Promotion

*Education is learning what you didn't even
know you didn't know.*
— Daniel J. Boorstin

One of the biggest decisions in my young life was going to be determined by everyone . . . but me!

My fifth-grade school-year was a milestone for me. Other than the few glitches in my businessman planning, things were going great. However, we had a family "poser" to solve regarding my school activities. I was about to be promoted to the sixth grade. I was doing well in the fifth grade, near the top of my class, but due to some students moving and some students not having good enough grades to go on to the sixth grade, *I was going to be the only one in the sixth grade.*

Here was the "poser": the principal said I would probably be too bored if I had to go through the fifth grade again since I didn't have any problems with it, but if they put me ahead into the seventh grade, it would mean that I would be a sixteen-year-old graduating senior. He did not give us the option of my being the only one in the sixth grade. He said, "*That just wouldn't work*." He told my parents to think about it for a few days before making their decision.

My whole family and the school administrators were involved in the decision-making process with the exception of *me . . . imagine that*!

Personally, I was leaning toward just being the only one in the sixth grade. Think about it: I wouldn't have any problem staying at the top of my class. I would definitely be the teacher's pet. When we went on class field trips I pretty much had my choice of where I sat in the car, and I didn't have to raise my hand to get noticed. That's probably why I wasn't in on the decision- making process.

The general consensus of the family was that I should skip a grade and move into the seventh instead of retaking the fifth grade. What would be strange was that some of my upperclassmen, the ones whom I hung around with, would now be my classmates, which did seem pretty cool.

After all was said and done, I was OK with the decision and looking forward to my accelerated status in school. In my mind, I would be an *instant* celebrity! I could brag to the new kids that came into our classroom that I got to skip a grade. They *didn't have to know* it wasn't because of scholastic achievement, but due to student attrition.

I remember one incident when I was in the fifth grade. One of my friends, Wayne (a "townie"), was three grades ahead of me. Wayne was a great guy but school wasn't (let's say) his highest priority in life. Sometimes he would just frustrate the heck out of his teachers.

The classroom teachers were allowed to administer minor punishment for misbehavior in class. Most of them would take a ruler and smack you across your knuckles, which would raise welts that would sometimes swell up. Because of Wayne's *special* relationship with his teachers his hands always looked like a couple of sacks of doorknobs. If the infractions warranted stronger punishment, the offending student, would be sent to the principal's office for further evaluation.

One day we heard all this commotion in the hallway. With a loud bang, the door to our classroom burst open and here came Wayne's teacher pushing Wayne, *still sitting in his desk*, into our room. She skidded his desk to the rear of the room and turned around and stomped out and slammed the door. We all assumed she probably wasn't *entirely* happy with Wayne's academic endeavors that particular day.

Things happened fast in our school. My friend Wayne went from being three grades ahead of me to only one grade ahead of me in the span of one year . . . *that's life in the big city*!

CHAPTER NINE

Bareback Riding

Everywhere is within walking distance if you have the time.

— Steven Wright

My "Wild West" rodeo days took a turn for the worse!

The closest kid near my age lived about a mile from me. Her name was Sharon and she was one year behind me in school. She had a horse and every once in a while would ride over to visit me. She didn't go *anywhere* unless she was on that darn horse.

She was OK for a girl, but she was a little "chunky." Her biggest problem? She thought she was Annie Oakley or Dale Evans, always wearing denim pants with a cowgirl vest, boots and a Western hat.

When she came over she rarely got off the horse. She would just steer him over close to me so we could chat.

I always thought her horse was going to step on me, so to play it safe I would get up on our front porch when we talked. Sharon never really talked about anything interesting—mostly about horses and cowgirl things.

One time she asked me if I had ever ridden a horse. Now I never had much to do with horses, even though my dad had a team of big workhorses that he would set me on when he was leading them to and from the field, but they really weren't riding horses. They were really tall. I didn't like to be up that high, and they were so wide my legs wouldn't go around them like you see in the comic books. I being a typical *macho* male, when she asked me the question, I said, "Sure, ride em all the time. I even rode a cow once. Bet you haven't done that."

Of course her answer was, "Who would want to?"

I didn't elaborate right away, but it was true. We had two milk cows. One was a Jersey, named Bess. That breed of milk cow is brown with big floppy ears and the biggest eyes you've ever seen. She was just like a pet. You could scratch her ears and she would rub on you and sometimes try to lick you. I quickly found out you never let a cow lick you because its tongue is so rough it gives you a rash; secondly, most cows are always chewing something. Other than her feeding time, I never saw Bess put anything in her mouth, but all of a sudden she would be chewing something. After a while she would swallow it and, before long, as if by magic, she would be chewing it again.

It reminded me of my Uncle Fred when he chewed tobacco. I asked my dad once if the cow was chewing tobacco. He said, "No, it's her cud and she chews it to help her digestion." The chewing didn't bother me, but right before swallowing it she would always give out a big burp and it smelled terrible.

I tried it once. I tied a piece of string on a wad of bubble gum and swallowed it and tried to pull it back up and chew it again. I gagged and almost choked to death. I ended up having to swallow the string too. I don't know why it didn't work. My brother promised me it would be easy to do. He said he did it all the time. His throat must have been bigger than mine.

Back to riding the cow. When Bess was lying down, I enjoyed getting on top of her and play like I was riding a bucking bronco. I did it often, but one day she decided she didn't want to play any more and she got up before I could get off. There I was on her back and she started walking! Now, she wasn't as tall as the workhorses, but I was still too high to jump off her back when she was moving. I tried to get her to stop so I could slide off, but she wouldn't. I called her every bad name I could think of but nothing worked so I just rode . . . and rode . . . and rode. I don't know how far we went but it seemed like miles. I'm thinking, "*What if we both get lost?*" Finally, she must have figured she had taught me my lesson and stopped, lay down and started chewing that darn cud again. I got off, kicked her in the butt and started walking home, which seemed like forever.

I couldn't tell that story to Sharon. It just didn't sound *manly* enough, so I said, "You ought to try it sometime," and left it at that.

When Sharon would get ready to leave she would always pull back on the reins and smack her horse on the butt and he would rear up, just like in the movies. Then the horse would let out a big fart as Sharon waved her hat and rode off into the sunset.

I guess she thought that was pretty impressive. I did, however, come to appreciate her parting gesture because when she waved that hat I knew she was leaving, along with her "gassy" horse.

CHAPTER TEN

"May Day, May Day!"

All you need is love. But a little chocolate now and then doesn't hurt.

— Charles M. Schulz

I didn't have much to do with girls in my earlier years in elementary school. I was always small for my age. But I was cute, so it wasn't like I couldn't hang out with a girl if I had wanted to. I just didn't want to . . . until I changed my mind!

We had an unusual custom at our school. On the first day of May, the classroom of the Third, fourth, and fifth grades would celebrate the occasion by the boys delivering May baskets to all the girls' homes and the girls would do the same to the boys. There were eight girls and nine boys in our classroom.

The week before May Day we would make the baskets in school and then we would fill them with candy and goodies, stuff girls and guys would like prior to delivery. My mom did most of the filling because I had no idea what a girl would like.

We did the delivery swap on the first Saturday after May 1st because it was tough to get around to all the houses, on a weekday, before it got dark. The houses were spread out all around the town and surrounding suburbs. All the classmates were supposed to be home that day; the girls would deliver their baskets before noon and the boys in the afternoon.

The way it worked: Your parent stopped the car away from the house you were visiting, you snuck up to their door, put the basket down, knocked on the door and then ran back to the car before the girl could catch you, because if she caught you *she could kiss you*. The whole exercise seemed kinda' dumb to me and a waste of good candy, but everyone in our classroom got excited about it, especially the girls, so I tried to enjoy it.

The first year I participated I guess I won because I didn't get caught once. I was small but I was fast. I didn't catch one girl (on purpose of course) so I didn't have to kiss anyone, and I was really proud of myself. The game was fun but I thought it still was a waste of good candy.

On the following Monday in school, all the guys were talking and they would say things like: "Did you get to kiss so-and-so?" "I kissed so-and-so twice;" "Man, so-and-so really was a great kisser;" and stuff like that. The girls would be in little groups and when I would come close they would look at me and giggle. What was I missing here? I thought the whole point was not to get caught and not try too hard to catch anyone else.

Come to think of it, the girls *looked like* they were trying to get away, but they seemed like they were really slow. I remembered them being a lot faster when we played dodge ball on the playground.

The whole thing was a mystery to me, so I asked my brother what was up. He being the ever-caring and patient sibling, said to me (in his usual kind and caring voice), *"You dumb idiot, you didn't even get one kiss?" "You wasted all that candy and didn't even catch one girl? I thought you were faster than that. What a wimp. Some of those girls can't even run that fast—get away from me."*

I know, back in those days I wasn't the sharpest tack in the box, but slowly I was beginning to get the big picture as far as girls were concerned.

The next couple of years during the May basket event I swapped tactics, a total reverse of the first year. This time I ran a lot faster when I was chasing the girls (especially the pretty ones) and a lot slower when I was being chased, and I'll have to admit it was a lot more fun and rewarding for the amount of candy and goodies expended. My brother was proud of me.

CHAPTER ELEVEN

Fighting Spectacle

A peace is of the nature of a conquest; for then both parties nobly are subdued, and neither party a loser.

—William Shakespeare

One of my most unforgettable fights was strangely one I neither won nor lost!

While continuing my quest to become a businessman, I noticed, the people who ran the local businesses seemed to be a little better off than most. However, not *everyone* fared the same. For example: There were two similar beer joints in town. Both establishments were similar in services offered; they served beer, had pool tables, shuffleboard, TV, and served food.

My good friend, John, owned the busiest, although not the cleanest. Fortunately, there were no health inspectors that visited his establishment. If there had been, he would have had to find a different line of work. John's place had a large grill and kitchen where they prepared basic family-style meals. The grill and exhaust vent were so caked with grease and soot that it had to have been a fire and health hazard. Their specialty was *great* hamburgers—they were so greasy the juice would run down your arms.

They had a dog (a scrawny little Mexican Chihuahua) aptly named "Puddles." This dog had free rein of the kitchen and bar area. You can guess why they called it Puddles. John and his wife, Marge, one or the other, constantly held their dog while cooking or serving food and drink. John would even set the dog on the bar while drawing a beer from the tap or serving customers their food. And Puddles would do his thing.

Harry, was the owner of the other beer joint. For some reason, Harry's place was never as busy. His place was spotless; he served great food in a friendly, quiet, family atmosphere. His shuffleboard and pool tables were similar in quality. Harry's place was different. He was at the end of the street and it was a much quieter. He got most of the local "townie" business. But I don't think the locals drank as much or spent as much as the farming society.

John's place was always full, especially on the nights when the town businesses were open late (Wednesdays and Saturdays). His place was rowdier, and he always had some kind of special deal going on. For example, when all the pig farmers castrated the young pigs, they brought the testicles into John's place and he put on a "mountain oyster" feed. As long as you bought beer, you could have all the "mountain oysters" you could eat (don't get all uppity and curl your nose; if you haven't tried 'em, don't knock 'em). That was always a big weekend. It would even bring in the ladies. He would have pool and shuffleboard tournaments, and sometimes he would have a special price on beer during certain times of the day. I really think he must have been the guy that started "Happy Hour."

I realized any business could be relatively successful as long as it met the customer's needs. There was room for both places in this small town. I filed all of this business knowledge away in my Business 101 memory bank. *Marketing seemed to be the key once you identified your customer base and their needs.*

The farmers that came into town to let off steam preferred John's place because he kinda let them police themselves (to a point). Hardly a weekend passed when someone hadn't gotten drunk and started a fight. John's main rule was, if you had to fight you didn't do it in his place you had to take it outside. He had a good-sized billy club under his bar that seemed to work to enforce his rules.

There was an unwritten rule that if you were going to

fight, you had to do it under the town's one street light, which was located over the biggest intersection (we only had two) so the fight would be visible to everyone.

This rule applied even if the quarrel occurred earlier in the week. The fight had to be scheduled on Saturday night so everyone could watch. Wednesday night wasn't as good a time to schedule a fight because that was when they had the free shows, and by the time they were over most people wanted to go home, so you couldn't draw as big a crowd. Even so, on rare occasions, a fight would happen on Wednesday nights if the parties just couldn't wait.

One time in high school I got into a tussle with one of my farmer schoolmates. It was a rather heated argument without any punches thrown. I wanted to go ahead and fight and get it over with, but he decided to evoke the Saturday-night rule, and insisted we postpone it until the weekend, under the street light.

I was fairly easygoing. I could get mad and throw a few punches. If I won OK, if I lost, *almost* OK, but I usually got over it quickly and never held a grudge. How do you fight if you are not angry? I wasn't in it for the money!

‾He began to advertise the fight like a title match at Madison Square Garden. I didn't like the idea of possibly losing a fight in front of a group of people, which was always the risk. If you had a private fight (win or lose) you could spin it anyway you wanted—*who's to know?*

Most of the farm kids didn't know anyone in town except other farm kids, until they started high school. He and I had not known each other before we had the disagreement. He wasn't any bigger than I. Prior to our squabble, I saw him in a "mini" fight with another kid on the playground. He had acted sorta like a weenie, so I was sure I could take him.

It was four days until the scheduled fight and the event was starting to play havoc with my mind. Maybe I couldn't beat him after all; maybe he wasn't at his best in that scuffle I saw him participate in. The more I thought about it, the more this "weenie" was morphing into *Joe Louis*. This fiasco was also turning into a *grudge match* between the farmers and the "townies" (I was now considered a "townie" because I got to spend so much time in town). Since my closest friends were "townies," they were starting to put pressure on me to make sure I held up their reputation. I realized this event was getting blown all out of proportion!

I thought I would need an edge, so I did the only thing any self-respecting young man, under this much stress, would do . . . I wrote an anonymous note and slipped it into his homeroom desk. It said *"Don't fight this guy. He is a killer!"* I knew his friends were putting as much pressure on him to win as mine were putting on me, so neither one of us could gracefully back out. With two more days left until the fight, I slipped him another note, which said, *"This guy doesn't fight fair. I don't want you to get hurt—really bad!"*

I noticed him staring at me more often the following day when we passed each other in the hallways. I tried to swell up to my full five-foot-seven inches and walked with a swagger and a smirk. I could see he was having second thoughts like I was, so it was working. On Friday afternoon, I left the last note stating, *"If you talked to this guy, real nice, I think he would be willing to call off the fight. Don't be a fool—save yourself a lot of pain!"*

I did all I could do, if he showed up Saturday night I would have to go through with it and so would he.

Saturday night came and he was there. So was everybody else and they were anxious to see a fight . . . it got dark . . . we walked out under the street light (it was just like Gary Cooper in the movie *High Noon*). We stood, circled and stared at each other with our most menacing glares and then he said, "I'm not mad at you anymore," and I told him, "I was never mad at you, we just had an argument." We shook hands and walked away. Nobody lost face, nobody got hurt and the only people who were disappointed were the ones who came to see a fight.

We were pretty good friends after that. I always wondered if he ever mentioned the notes to anyone. He probably wondered who was looking out for his welfare. That was one of the longest weeks in memory. The business lesson I took from this was *"never underestimate your competition."*

Chapter Twelve

Day to Day Living During Wartime

I have never advocated war except as a means of peace.

— Ulysses S. Grant

Keep in mind the visitors that frequented the local business establishments were of all stripes. But most were of the same ethnic background. They were folks who made their living with their hands; they fought the elements, the Depression, and some of their sons were off fighting a war.

Most all spoke a language that was foreign to a lot of the locals. They were mostly God-fearing Catholics, with large families, law-abiding, and watched out for their neighbors. They worked hard, played hard, and most of the time played fair. There were no law officers in town, in fact, not even in the county. Everyone policed themselves. To my knowledge no one ever locked their doors or closed their windows, in the summertime anyway (too damn hot). We had an elected town council who made policy and decided what activities would take place and when.

We had a volunteer Fire Department to protect the town from catastrophic fire danger. It was fun to watch when the telephone operator would sound the fire alarm (a huge siren mounted on a pole in the center of town). You would see men streaming out of their businesses, some wearing their specialty business and working attire, running full speed to man the fire trucks. It made you proud of the dedication of these guys.

When we had activities like the annual carnival and athletic events the town fathers would appoint town constables to manage traffic and crowd control—if you can visualize a crowd in a town of 200 people. Can you imagine trying to run a township these days under these rules? What do you think would happen? *Does Dodge City come to mind?*

I can't remember any major thefts, murders, gang activities or rapes. (Unless you count a few farm animals a horny farm boy may have had his way with. I guess those individuals who forced their will on these trusting critters would be called PET-o-philes.)

If you had an irreconcilable difference you just couldn't work out "man to man," as a last resort you could call in an arbiter from the county courthouse.

Everyone did their part during the war. Rationing of selected commodities was the order of the day and all were issued ration stamps. For example, tires and fuel were in short supply. Many things we needed were just not made during the war. Many U.S companies were told what they could make for local consumption; the rest was for the military effort. The Studebaker automobile company made trucks for the Army; Ford made military Jeeps and liberty ships, and so on.

Some food items like sugar, coffee, and wearing apparel (especially shoes), were almost impossible to get.

We farmers were lucky. We grew a lot of food items that were scarce in areas outside of our local communities. Farming families, of course, had been planting gardens and preserving produce for generations. Now, their urban cousins got into the act. All in the name of patriotism.

Magazines such as the *Saturday Evening Post* and *Life* printed stories about victory gardens. Women's magazines gave instructions on how to grow and preserve garden produce. Families were encouraged to can their own vegetables so the commercial canned goods could be given to the troops.

According to the above magazines, in 1943, families bought 315,000 pressure cookers (used in the process of canning), compared to 66,000 in 1942. The government and related businesses urged people to make gardening a family and community effort.

The result of victory gardening? The U.S. Department of Agriculture estimates that more than 20 million victory gardens were planted. Fruit and vegetables harvested in these home and community plots was estimated to be 9 million-10 million tons, an amount equal to all commercial production of fresh vegetables. The program made a difference in the war effort.

Some folks got creative with their gardens and planted them in patterns that depicted different patriotic phrases and symbols. My sister and her husband Audry always planted a garden laid out like the American flag. They consistently had the best-producing and most well-kept garden in town, and still do, although they are in their 90's.

So-called luxury items like chocolate, nylons (this material was used for parachutes), some spices, cheese, cigarettes, candy bars, things containing rubber, sheets and pillowcases, and linens were in short supply. Used flour sacks were utilized in place of milled cloth.

We would have "blackout" drills; at certain times we would put heavy dark curtains over the windows to block out all the light from escaping. The government would send aloft airplanes and balloons nationwide at these times to see how effective this program was against a potential airborne attack and how it could be improved. In school, we would have regular "air raid" drills.

After the war they discontinued the rationing stamps, but people never got tired of licking stamps. Most all the retailers in our and surrounding towns switched to S&H green stamps. The stores bought the stamps from S&H (*Sperry & Hutchinson*) and gave them as bonuses with every purchase based on the amount you bought. The more you bought the more stamps you got. Every store that participated in the giveaway had free catalogs showing the items that you could get by licking and sticking the stamps in books. Eventually you saved up enough stamps to toddle down to the redemption center with a sore tongue and trade them in for merchandise.

I had my usual chores on the farm and my assorted odd jobs in town. I could work at my friend John's beer joint any time I wanted to. He always had something for me to do.

My most regular job: All the bottles from the beer he sold in his establishment would go into a big barrel under the bar. All the bottles he redeemed from those customers who took the beer home to drink would be stored in a different area until I or someone else would retrieve them, put them in cardboard cases and stack them in the shed to be picked up by the brewery's bottling company in Lincoln. I remember the redemption fee was two cents per bottle.

Once in a while I would deliver buckets of draft beer to the Catholic priest's rectory and other shut-ins. I could have become an alcoholic very easily and no one would have noticed, because I smelled like beer most of the summer.

The farmer my dad rented our little farm from was pretty well off. He owned several farms and leased additional land to his renters to farm and to pasture their cattle. He also had a trucking company; he hauled grain and livestock to market for the smaller farmers.

He always needed help in some form throughout the year. He raised a lot of corn so periodically he would hire any kid who wanted to work to remove sunflower plants (the farmers considered them weeds) out of the crop rows. The small weeds would get pulled up and the larger weeds would get cut out with a "corn knife" that looked like a jungle machete. I wish I could have foreseen the future need for sunflower seeds being used for snack food. Can you imagine having a corner on the sunflower seed market for the baseball industry? Wow!

Removing these weeds was a hot, dusty and nasty job. The corn was always high when we were working in the field. I don't know if you know it or not Corn leaves are sharp.

I would wear a long-sleeved shirt with a bandana

tied around my neck and a billed hat pulled low over my eyes. If you didn't do this, you would get cuts on your exposed extremities and your sweat would make it burn like heck. You really didn't want to get any cuts around your eyes because they would usually become infected right away.

This type of job paid $6.00 per day (cash, no withholding), which was great pay back then. The wealthy farmer usually had a lot of kids working, so the jobs didn't last more than a few days.

Politically, my parents both voted a straight Democratic Party slate. I am not sure they knew who the candidates were, or cared. My dad always said the Democrats were for the "little man" and the Republicans were for the "rich man." My parents always voted.

They felt it was their "patriotic duty." You picked up your ballots at the post office if you didn't get rural delivery. Before they went to the polls, my dad would mark his ballot and also my mom's (so they wouldn't cancel out each other's vote). I don't think my mom ever knew who she was voting for, or that it mattered.

Chapter Thirteen

Journalism

Advertisements contain the only truths to be relied on in a newspaper.

— Mark Twain

Another great opportunity presented itself. It was a job that would enlarge my already sizable savings account.

The local paperboy in town was moving, and his boss was looking for someone to take over the job. I didn't know what the route paid, but I was sure it had to be a lot! I told my parents I'd like to have the job.

My dad told me all the downsides of a paper route: you had to do it every day (sort of like milking the cows); people would be counting on me so they could read their daily news. The papers had to be picked up daily from the railroad depot and delivered before Mom got off work, so I would have a ride home. I had to get up early on Sunday mornings and someone would have to take me to town so I could get everyone their paper before 9:00 am. I said, "*No problem!*" I met with the man whose responsibility it was to find someone to fill the position. I must have made a great impression on him (probably my eager personality and "good looks"), because the next day he contacted my mother at the store where she worked and told her I had the job. Later I found out I was the only one who applied.

One of the prerequisites of the job was, you had to have a bike. I had part of the money saved to buy a bike and mom said if I would promise to stay with the paper route for at least a year she would pay the difference. This enterprise was coming together nicely!

My mother and I looked in the Sears, Roebuck catalog and I picked out a new model made by Schwinn, red and white in color. We liked the Schwinn bicycles because they had all the right stuff: balloon tires, chrome fenders, a horn, simulated gas-tank, whitewall tires, head and tail reflector lights, spring fork, deluxe saddle (seat), and it was guaranteed for life. It was one of the first civilian bicycles Schwinn made after the war. Between 1942 – 1945 they made military bicycles.

The base price of the bike was $19.00 delivered, Sears catalog showed all the accessories you could put on the bike to customize it. My mom had more than the necessary amount of money saved in her Jefferson nickels jar. She said she would buy the bike, and I could buy all the accessories I needed for the paper route.

That was a great deal—I was on my way to financial independence. I decided on the extras I felt were *essential* to the operation of my new paper route: I ordered red, white and blue saddlebags with buckle-down flaps to carry the papers (they would keep the papers dry in bad weather); handlebar grips with red, white and blue tassels; a siren that hooked to the front forks and when you pulled a wire it pushed the siren against the tire and made a noise like a police-car. (the faster you went the louder the siren); front fender brace clamps that held playing cards against the spokes and made the sound of a motorcycle (again, the faster you pedaled the louder it was); an aerial that hooked to the back of the seat, which was going to hold a raccoon's tail from a raccoon my dad killed because it was raiding the chicken coop. I was going to be the most "decked out" paperboy in town, which shouldn't be too difficult since I'd be the only one. We decided that I would leave my bike at my sister, Lucille's house after my route each day, and pick it up when I started my deliveries. That way I would always have the bike available no matter what the weather conditions.

It took almost two weeks for the bike to be delivered (I don't know why everything ordered from catalogs took so long to be delivered, the waiting was shear torture.) It arrived at the train depot in a big box. It was all assembled with the exception of the handlebars and the kickstand, not like today's unassembled items that require an engineering degree to put them together.

The accessories came in a separate box. We tied both boxes on the top of the car and took them home. My brother helped me install the handlebars and the newly patented folding kickstand—I was ready to go. I wanted to unpack the rest of the accessories and put them on also, but my brother said it would be better to not install them until after I learned to ride the bike because I would probably crash a lot. *Dead silence* . . . I have to *learn* to ride a bike? . . . *How did I miss that?* I thought you just got on it and rode away!

How do you learn to ride a bike? The word *learn* indicated someone had to *teach* me. There were only three people besides me living in our home and two of them, Mom and Dad, I knew didn't know how to ride a bike, and my brother never owned one. I had less than three weeks before my paper route started. How was I going to pull this off?

Being the eternal optimist I figured, *"How hard can it be?"* I had seen other people riding bikes and they didn't look any smarter that I was, so I devised a plan. I started out by pushing the bike and jumping up with my left foot on the left pedal and coasting. I got to where I could go pretty fast and balance fairly well. I did that for a couple days, then it came time to put my leg over the seat. Every time I tried I fell. Obviously this method was not going to work. Fortunately I was doing all this practicing on the lawn so when I fell I didn't scratch the bike up (much).

We had a big oak tree in our front yard. I decided to use it to steady myself while I got on the bike. I would then start to pedal slowly, keeping one hand on the tree for balance. I could make several laps around the tree, but I still had to keep one hand lightly intact. After a couple of days I would try to balance myself and let go of the tree periodically, but still using it for a safety net in case I lost my balance. Once in a while I would overcompensate and steer away from the tree and crash, but not too often. I was starting to get the hang of this.

After another couple of days, I could make several revolutions around the tree without touching it. I got better and better going to the left around the tree but I was a hopeless mess when I tried to turn right or go the other direction. I would lose it completely.

I was running out of time before my route was going to start. I obviously had learned bicycle riding the same way Indianapolis race-car drivers and horserace jockeys did. I have never seen an oval racetrack that had right-hand turns. Either I had to master complete control of my bike and the ability to turn *both ways*, or map out my whole route with only left-hand turns. I got braver and braver and finally got completely away from the tree, and once I could go straight I found it was just as easy to turn right as left. I had mastered riding a bike, and the bike didn't look too worse for wear.

Now was the time to unpack my accessories and turn my already sleek-looking bike into a *classic*! I put on the new handlebar grips with the red, white, and blue tassels, attached my red, white, and blue saddlebags over the rear luggage carrier, mounted my siren on the front fender brace and making sure it touched the front tire just right when I pulled the wire. I mounted the whip antenna with the raccoon tail behind the seat, and clipped the playing cards on the front fender so they would touch the spokes and make the "motorcycle noise." I stood back and admired the masterpiece. I was going to be the coolest dude in town, maybe even in the state.

I could hardly wait to show my work of art to my mom, dad and brother, I was sooooo proud! My dad's reaction was: *How much did all that stuff cost.* My mom wanted to know *if I could even ride the bike with all the extras on it—would it even roll?*

My ego was deflated a little because of my parents' negative reactions. Obviously my parents were just old-fashioned and not up on all the latest trends.

Surely my brother would appreciate the classy look I

created. After all, he was one of the *modern generation*. Lloyd looked at my bike and just shook his head. He said, "*Why in God's name did you put all that crap on a perfectly good-looking bike?*"

I was devastated. What's wrong with these people?

I asked my brother, "Are you just jealous that you don't have a bike that looks this good? Come to think of it, you never even had a bike, so what do you know about anything?"

He said, "That monstrosity looks like a Patriotic Clown-Mobile (whatever that was) and I'd appreciate you not riding it anywhere near me in public. I don't want anyone to know I know you."

I wasn't quite sure how he could pull that one off because everyone in town knew we were related.

Now I was mad. I figured I'm just hanging around with the wrong people! These "hillbillies" wouldn't recognize class if it bit 'em in the butt!

My mother had gone to work, my dad was in the fields and my brother had gotten in his car and left. Now was my chance to ride into town and show this beauty off to the town folks. I knew they would appreciate it. So off I went. I imitated my classic Roy Rogers flying start (that's where I would get a running start, hop on the left pedal with my left foot and swing my leg over the seat and *into the saddle*, just like Roy did it). *Disaster*!

To do it right you have to make sure the pedal you are jumping on is at the *bottom* of its traveling arc. If its rotated past the bottom of its traveling arc toward the rear wheel when you jump on it, you actually apply the rear brake. To make matters worse, I forgot about the whip antenna mounted behind my seat. I caught my foot on it as I was swinging my leg over. I did a 180 degree flip over the handlebars and the dang bike *ran over me* and crashed in a heap.

Now a lot of people wouldn't survive a crash like that, so I figured I had to be hurt pretty bad. My mind flashed back to the radio programs and the comic books. When a car crash or some catastrophic accident occurred, the medics would always tell everyone "Don't move the injured party." The victim could have broken bones, severed arteries, brain damage . . . or worse.

I couldn't recall any of the radio or comic book incidents wherein the injured party was alone. After I had lain there for a while, I figured that sooner or later I'm going to have to move.

I was hoping I would be conscious long enough to drag myself to the "BIG (medical) BOOK" and be able to apply some first-aid remedies until help arrived. I could see my mom boiling dozens of eggs and using the skin on the inside of the egg shell to close up all the open gashes I must have.

I slowly tried to sit up, thinking *that at any minute*

I would be overcome by excruciating pain, but . . . so far so good. I felt myself all over and didn't feel any sharp bones sticking out of my clothes. So far, so good. I slowly got to my feet looking for something I could use as a crutch because I was sure I wouldn't be able to walk, but—so far, so good!

I was looking myself all over and, *unbelievably*, nothing was wrong. I'm thinking, *Come on . . . after a crash like that I gotta' at least have a skinned knee?* I pulled up both pants legs and . . . nothing. Not even a hangnail. I had mixed emotions: On one hand I was thankful I wasn't hurt bad, but on the other hand, when I told people how bad this crash was no one was going to believe me. The only damage I could find was a torn pocket on my bib overalls where the handlebar ripped it.

Unfortunately, my bike didn't fare as well. When I picked it up my handlebars were pointing in a different direction than the front wheel, the right-hand grip was scraped up and the red, white and blue tassel was still lying on the ground. The mount on my siren broke off and bent the fender brace that it was attached to and it was just hanging by the control wire. The whip antenna with the raccoon tail on it was bent at a right angle. It looked like a *fuzzy* turn signal. The clamps on one side of the wheel that were holding the playing card "motor" were bent and wouldn't hold the cards on that side any longer.

The only item of the cool accessories I had installed that wasn't trashed was my saddlebags. Which, ironically, was the only item that I *really* needed. Must be full moon!

I took off the custom handle grips and replaced the originals; undid the siren, removed the fuzzy turn signal, removed the playing card holder, went to the shed and got a wrench and straightened my handlebars, put all the damaged parts in a box on a shelf in the shed and rode to town.

My brother saw me in town and remarked he was glad I finally got some sense and took that crap off my bike.

I said, "Yeah, I realized you were right."

Some days it just doesn't pay to get out of bed.

Funny, no one ever asked me why I took that stuff off my bike. I guess they were just glad to see it go and wouldn't have to be embarrassed by my "Patriotic Clown-Mobile" any longer.

I kept my promise to my mom and stayed with the paper route for over a year. I had to admit, my parents were right: There wasn't much difference between having a paper route and milking cows other than I got paid for the paper route and only had to do it once a day, not twice. I still had to work every day and there were a lot of days I just didn't want to make the deliveries, especially in bad weather. The downside was I had to pick up the papers at the train depot, fold and put them in my saddle bags and ride my "very plain vanilla" bike on my route no matter what the weather conditions were.

I had about thirty residential customers. I took fifteen to twenty papers to the drugstore daily. They were the only store that sold reading material. I would also drop off a few papers to a couple of businesses in town so they could give them to their walk-in customers.

All my residential customers had porches on the front of their homes. If the weather was good, I would just ride by and toss the paper as close to the porch as possible and everyone was OK with that process. I usually made my deliveries between 3:00 p.m. and 4:00 p.m. some of my customers didn't get home until after 6:00 or 7:00. If it rained during that time span and I didn't get the paper on the porch, under cover, I was screwed.

If that happened and I knew about it in time, before I went home for the day, I would have to go by the telephone office and call the publisher in Lincoln (the buffalo horn lady would let me call for free) and have them send me some extra day-old papers with the regular train delivery, the next day, and of course they charged me back for those replacements.

If I didn't get replacements ordered in time, I had

an unhappy customer and I had to adjust the bill when I collected at the end of the month. That happened to me on about a half a dozen occasions, so I either had to get off my bike at each stop and place the papers on the porches or get better at throwing them more accurately. I mastered the latter.

I learned a lot about responsibility. I must admit there were a few times it was really tempting to just tell everybody. "*The train didn't leave the papers today. Sorry!*" But I figured I couldn't pull that off since the guy that ran the depot was one of my customers. That was one of the good things about living in a small town, it kept you honest. You couldn't get away with anything.

Another Business 101 entry in my memory log: before you go into business, find out what the time demands will be and decide if you are willing to make that commitment before you start. You won't always have your mom and dad around laying a guilt trip on you to do your job.

CHAPTER FOURTEEN

Hunting and Fishing

Hunting is not a sport. In a sport, both sides should know they're in the game.
— Paul Rodriguez

G un safety was closely monitored by my father and adhered to by my brother and me except . . . for that one time.

My paper route and odd jobs kept me busy during the summer, but I had fun, too. My dad hunted a lot, in what little spare time he had. It was a good way to get extra meat for the table. When I got older he started taking me with him so I could learn the art of tracking game. At first I just went along to learn the basics. Later he taught me how to handle a gun, to shoot and actually stalk prey.

He constantly stressed gun safety, he would drill my brother and me on loading and un-loading the firearms.

You always "assumed" that a firearm was loaded, and you handled it accordingly. When unloading the family's firearms, my dad would insist that after you were sure the gun was empty; you always point the gun in a safe direction and pull the trigger. This would release tension on the trigger spring, reason being, he felt the gun should be stored "un-cocked."

One day, my brother was unloading the Remington .22-caliber pump rifle after hunting rabbits. On this particular occasion after the hunting trek, my brother followed the proscribed unloading procedure, as he had done many, many times before, but omitted two *very important* steps. First error: He dumped all the bullets out of the magazine but, for some unknown reason, didn't pump the live ammunition out of the breech. Second error: He didn't point the gun in a safe direction when he pulled the trigger to release the trigger tension. Unfortunately, these two steps he eliminated just happened to be the most important ones. He was on the summer porch (a screened-in portion on the back of the house where we processed the milk and also where we stored our coats and overshoes when not in use). Lloyd was sitting on a chair next to the closet where the coats and outside clothing were kept when he pulled the trigger on the unexpectedly loaded gun.

The ammunition we used to hunt rabbits was as "high powered" a charge as we could get for a .22 caliber rifle because we often had to fire long-range shots to bag some of the wary prey. The rifle slug went through the closet door (behind which my dad's favorite rain-slicker was hanging), through both my dad's *favorite* (new) "galvanized" milking buckets, through the back wall of the closet (which was a common wall with the stairwell from the upper level of the house), through the wooden stair-railing banister, through the door into the downstairs guest bedroom and hit the ball on the brass bed post, and fell at the foot of the bed.

My brother, devastated, ran into the house, praying no one had been in the line of fire. My father's first reaction on hearing the gunshot was one of consternation. He knew a shot had been fired inside the house. After determining that everyone was safe, his follow-up reaction was one of anger at Lloyd's negligence, which could have been critical.

When the gravity of the careless act sank in, and my brother realized what might have been, he broke down and cried. My dad's anger subsided when he noticed that Lloyd was punishing himself more harshly than anything he could ever inflict. However, some of Dad's anger was *slightly* rekindled when he examined his (nearly new) rain slicker hanging on a nail behind the door. Even though only one bullet slug was fired, it made about a dozen holes in the raincoat. Then he noticed the two neat holes through the bottom portion of each of his two new milking buckets. Needless to say, conversation was almost nonexistent at the supper table that night.

Our family hunted mostly rabbits and squirrels because there were a lot of them and the season was open all year long. We hunted pheasant (Chinese ring necks), ducks and geese when in season. Ducks and geese were harder to bag because you had to have decoys and a dog that would bring the birds out of the water.

My dog Spunk would go into the water and get them, but then he would eat them. He thought it was great fun—we did all the work and he got the meal. He only went with us once. We didn't feel like killing *his dinner.* The whole point was, *we* were supposed to get to eat what *we* shot. He could do his *personal* hunting on his own.

My dad hunted rabbits and squirrels with the .22-caliber rifle. Most folks hunted with a shotgun. Dad said he was intending to eat everything we killed and he didn't like a lot of shotgun pellets in his food.

He used a shotgun on pheasants and ducks, but only a 410-gauge gun. This meant less pellets in his food, but you had to be a heck of a good shot to bring down a bird with a gun that small. He didn't miss many.

Living on and around our farmland there was always a lot of feed for rabbits, squirrels and varmints. The "cottontail" rabbits got pretty big and the jackrabbits were huge, but they were tough to eat. Mom would fry up the cottontails like chicken but the jacks would have to be stewed. My dad always had the reputation of "eating anything that wouldn't eat him first."

We hunted on foot so if you shot four or five rabbits you had a load to carry with you until you got back to the house. My dad taught me a trick that I have used many times since. This is a procedure that has won me many bets along the way. About 35-40 percent of an animal's weight is entrails, the part you are not going to eat, so why carry it around with you all day.

Pay close attention I don't usually give this information out for free. You take hold of a rabbit (works better with a dead one) right behind the front legs with both hands and start squeezing and working the entrails toward the tail end until you get a tight ball, hold the rabbit over your head with both hands, give it a quick downward snap between your legs toward the ground, and *guess what happens . . .?* Right. It cleans that rabbit out slicker than a whistle. The only thing you have left is the *good part*!

The trick is to know when to stop the snap. You want the entrails to land on the ground behind you. You golfers may have a problem if you try to "follow through" with your swing.

Instead of the entrails landing on the ground they will affix themselves firmly *to the back of your head*!

Now that you have lightened your load, all you have to do is make an incision with your pocketknife between the tendon and the bone right above one rear foot and insert that foot behind your belt and slip the other foot through the slit and voila', you can now carry five to six rabbits with your hands free to shoot some more at half the weight. Pretty cool huh?

Hunting squirrels is a different story; the squirrels we hunted in Nebraska were big fat Fox squirrels. They were usually 18 to 24 inches long (including the tail) and weighed about two pounds. Some people liked to eat them, but the only one in our family who would eat them was my dad. Mom would cook every one we brought home just for Dad. He really loved them.

These critters were pretty wily. You almost had to hunt in pairs to have any luck. They lived in trees of course. The trick was to try to sneak up on them before they saw you or otherwise they would always position themselves on the opposite side of the tree that you were on. If you had two people you could do pretty well, bagging one or two of them without too much trouble.

After Dad and I hunted together for a couple years he was comfortable in letting me hunt on my own. Dad *really* liked squirrels, so anytime I wanted to get something *extra special* out of him, I would go out and shoot a couple of squirrels. It worked like magic.

You are wondering how I was able to consistently kill squirrels by myself, right? There was a stand of big old oak trees not too far from the house and there were always squirrels hanging out in them. Remember, I'm hunting alone, so this is not going to be an easy task, unless you are creative!

Mom had made up a scarecrow out of Dad's old overalls and shirt. She had it looking pretty lifelike with a hat and everything. She kept it stored in the barn during the off-season when we didn't have a garden. When the crops were starting to bloom she would bring it out and set it up on a pole in the middle of the garden. Its presence would hopefully keep the crows and other birds from eating everything before we could harvest it.

The best squirrel hunting was fortunately in the spring and winter, when the scarecrow wasn't in use. I had the idea to take the scarecrow out to the oak grove and prop it up on one side of a tree and camp out on the other side and wait for the squirrels to show up.

I could do a pretty good squirrel imitation by puffing air in my cheek and patting it with my hand. I could hear the critters coming out of their holes to see what was going on, but no matter how still I sat they still seemed to see me and scurry around to the other side of the tree. It was very frustrating . . . *I needed a better diversion.*

I needed to make the scarecrow move, so I went back to the barn and cut a length of bailing twine off the big ball Dad kept there and went back to the grove. I tied one end to one of the arms of the scarecrow and held onto the other end where I was hidden on the other side of the tree.

I made my squirrel sound, he came out, he saw me, and went around the other side, I pulled the string and moved the arm and he came running back on my side—and he was heading for the frying pan. I got one more and went home and put the scarecrow back in the barn. I figured I would only take a couple of squirrels now and then so I wouldn't deplete the population that was closest to the house. That way they wouldn't get wise to my ruse right away, besides I didn't want to lug that heavy scarecrow any farther or more often than I had to. It was my ace in the hole when I needed a favor from Dad in a hurry. I wondered if that was the way Daniel Boone got to become a great squirrel hunter?

Mom and Dad were really impressed by how I could consistently bring back a couple of squirrels most any time I wanted to. I never told them about the scarecrow. I just said, "I must be part Indian with unusually crafty skills." Luckily, I never had to bag a squirrel when Mom was using the scarecrow in the garden.

My dad didn't like to fish but he loved eating the fish. So I used to go fishing with my brother-in-law

Audry (my sister Lucille's husband) and also my friend John who owned the busiest beer joint. He always took me with him as a fishing buddy. We usually fished in the local ponds, lakes and creeks. Catfish and bullheads (a miniature version of a catfish) were the main catch of the day. Some of the lakes also had carp.

All of these species of fish were "bottom feeders" (trash fish) as the locals called them. Most people liked the catfish and bullheads, but almost no one liked the carp because it was a very bony, strong-tasting fish, but you know my dad—he *especially* liked the carp (I don't know how he got that way). I loved to fish but I didn't like to eat them. I heard the story of someone getting a bone caught in their throat and choking to death. I figured there were too many other better forms of *safer* food. My dad and I had an agreement. I would catch the fish if he would help me clean them and I didn't have to eat them.

We were a good team! My dad and I always had a variety of wild game animals, birds and fish to keep my mom busy cooking the local fare. She would always come up with different ways to cook everything so it was never a boring menu. Personally I preferred the beef, pork, chicken and vegetable meals. They were a little more civilized and a whole lot tastier.

Nice string of bullheads from a local pond

CHAPTER FIFTEEN

Coyote Ugly

Whenever the pressure of our complex city life thins my blood and numbs my brain, I seek relief in the trail; and when I hear the coyote wailing to the yellow dawn, my cares fall from me—I am happy.

— Hamlin Garland

I had no idea as to the extent of the carnage I would be involved in and the lasting burden I would have to bear!

On the farm we had our own *"organic"* security system for varmints and scavengers. Every animal on a working farm had its place and its purpose. We didn't feed the farm cats because their job was to keep the rodents and egg thieves in check and their kill was their food reward. We only kept the female cats because they were the best "mousers." The toms were almost completely wild but always "Johnny on the spot" when it was time to "service" the ladies. At night you would hear some of the most god-awful howling, growling, and fighting in the area when the ladies were "in season." I guess this is where the term "caterwauling" came from.

What really ticked me off—some of the wild toms would come around after the kittens were born, before their eyes were open, and kill the newborns and sometimes even devour parts of them.

One year, I took it upon myself to be the protector of a new litter of kittens. After supper I would take dad's 410-gauge shotgun and hide in the proximity of where the kittens were and watch for the tomcats to come around. One evening I spotted a tom sneaking in close to the area of the newborns and I blew him away. My dad heard the gunshot and came out to the barn to investigate jus as I was taking the dead cat off to be buried.

He asked me why I shot that cat and I told him. I thought he would be proud of me for protecting the kittens. He sat me down and explained why it wasn't necessary to protect the kittens. He said, "We have to let nature take its course," and "The natural order of things shouldn't be altered unnecessarily."

If we needed to replace one of the older farm cats, for whatever reason, we would keep one of the kittens (and he would let me pick it out). Otherwise, we would let the neighbors know that we had kittens and when they were weaned they could come and get as many as they needed (no charge).

I asked, "What happens if we don't need any and nobody else wants any?"

He said, "They would have to be destroyed."

I asked, "How do we do that?"

Dad told me, "You don't need to concern yourself with those details."

I learned that my concern for the safety and well-being of the kittens was creating more problems than I was trying to solve.

As I matured and experienced life's trials and tribulations, I came to the conclusion that most of the bad conditions that existed were caused by someone trying to alter nature's scheme of things "to make things better." Once when my friends and I were playing in one of the swimming holes in the creek, we discovered a couple of burlap bags filled with drowned kittens. At first we were stunned at the discovery, but after the initial shock we resigned ourselves that the technique was probably one of the most practical, humane methods of disposing of unwanted cats. . . . *Such is life.*

The most prolific small game we had to hunt was rabbits. They were easy to hunt and if cooked right rather tasty and they were everywhere. The downside of having so many rabbits around was, they brought in a lot of coyotes. My dog Spunk's job was simple: He was supposed to keep the foxes and coyotes away from the chickens. Spunk was a German shepherd mix (with what I don't know) and he was a great watchdog. Nobody came around without your knowing it. He was good at keeping the foxes away, but he had a problem with coyotes, reason being they were a lot smarter than Spunk.

Coyotes run in packs and they work in packs. They would come in close and yip and cry like babies (it would sound like a hospital nursery with a lot of dirty diapers). They did this to lure the guard dogs out from their post and, while they did that, others would sneak in and get the chickens.

Spunk couldn't handle it. He would hear them serenading him and off he would go. I could just imagine him thinking, *"I'll get those chicken thieving so'n-so's. Let me at them."* They would lure him out and then the rest of the pack would gang up on him and just beat the living crap out of him. We always knew when it happened because we would hear the chickens raising 'you-know-what.' Dad would go out with his gun and fire in the air. He couldn't really see anything to shoot at with that "piece of crap" flashlight we had. Dad would yell, *"Where is that damn dog when you need him?"*

The next morning we would go out to see what damage was done. There were always a lot of loose feathers and usually at least two chickens missing. You know, come to think of it, they never got "Killer the rooster" or any of his cohorts. I could just imagine them hiding behind the ladies and pushing them out in front towards the coyotes.

We would go out and try to find Spunk, who usually made it back as far as the neighbor's haystack before he would lie down and not budge. We never knew if he was too weak to make it home or was too embarrassed to admit he had screwed up again.

Now this may sound harsh, but when you live on a farm and raise animals for food and income there is a priority in discretionary spending of limited resources. The animals that produced food or aided in producing food came first. Second came the animals that produced income or aided in the process of producing income.

Dogs and cats are way down on the food chain. No self-respecting farmer would be caught, or admit to, spending money on a veterinarian to fix a dog or a cat. There were too many of the animals around and they usually were free. So Spunk got fixed up by the "BIG (medical) BOOK" or he went to that big *coyote killing* heaven in the sky. Spunk had been down this road before, and he knew what his chances were when he took on the coyote gang.

Mom had more compassion than Dad, but they both would do their best to nurse him back to health. If the truth be known, it probably was more for my benefit than Spunk's. They treated his wounds and bites with disinfectant. He would get the bread and milk poultice treatment on the infected areas. They would put axle grease on the wounds to keep the flies away. Dad would then give him a dose of his *magical cure,* kerosene with a pinch of sugar, and put him in the barn, and he was on his own.

By some miracle, Spunk always seemed to get better, in a manner of speaking, but always with a few extra scars and an even deeper hatred for coyotes.

For a time after this last encounter, we tried tying him up at night when we heard the coyotes howling. But Spunk would howl and bark until the coyotes would finally give up trying to entice him outside the confines of the farm complex. I can remember my dad yelling out the window and throwing his shoes at the dog to try to get him to shut up. It wasn't a pretty sight.

At times the coyotes would become so plentiful that their quest for food caused them to become extra daring. Some would find easier prey and start killing young calves and baby pigs. When they did that it was the last straw. Something drastic had to be done. The first thing the county authorities would do was put a bounty on them. That would put a sizable dent in the population, but when that wasn't enough they formed *coyote roundups.*

I had heard of these hunting roundups by word of

mouth, but had never witnessed one. It sounded like fun (sort of like the Old West roundups). Well, the time had come and we were going to have one. Every able-bodied man and almost-grown boy was expected to participate. I was excited, but I still wasn't sure how they worked. I knew they were designed to significantly thin out the coyote population.

I thought this was my chance to get even for what they did to Spunk, so I begged my dad to let me participate. I was invited—my dad decided I was old enough—I was ready.

It took a while to organize the roundup. Someone had to decide where to concentrate the hunt to take out the most critters. Everyone had to have a gun; the organizers (at first light) would station us in a huge circle. We were to be evenly spaced around the target area. At a predetermined time we would all start moving toward the center of the circle. The idea was to trap all the coyotes inside the circle as it tightened and then blow them all away.

The image of this event was starting to materialize more vividly in my mind . . . *What's wrong with this picture?* You have a bunch of angry, excited farmers with guns walking towards each other and when they get in nice and close they start shooting at a bunch of scared, wildly darting coyotes trying to get out of the circle.

I asked my dad, "How many people have been killed doing this?"

"I don't think anyone, but I'm not sure," he said.

Hmmmmm—he didn't *think* anyone had been killed? All of a sudden I wasn't so sure I wanted to do this. What happens if in the frenzied execution of the coyotes someone accidently shoots the guy on the opposite side? And the guy that's shot gets really pissed off and shoots back? Didn't the Civil War start like that? Or at least some life-long feuds?

I couldn't back out at this late date. It would look real bad if I came down with some rare disease at the last minute and had to go home. How could I live it down?

As stated earlier, my dad was a really proud guy, and you didn't publicly embarrass him. He wouldn't take it kindly. After all, he had gone out of his way to get me invited. No, quitting wasn't an option.

I began trying to find the up side in this venture. It couldn't possibly be as dangerous as I was imagining. Surely all these folks were too smart to involve themselves in something that could cause someone to get shot . . . *weren't they*? While looking at the faces of those who were taking part in this fiasco, and I feared I may have overestimated their intelligence quotient—just a little. At least we were only using shotguns, not automatic combat rifles. Getting shot with a shotgun had to hurt.

I got shot with a B-B gun once and it hurt like heck. I couldn't imagine getting hit with a whole bunch of B-B's at one time.

I thought the name "Coyote Roundup" was a misnomer. It should have been "Coyote Massacre." (the vision of the demise of General Custer and his troops came to mind). In addition, we wouldn't just be killing the marauding adult animals but also their children.

OK . . . I had to get a hold of myself. I was going to have to do this—just as well make the best of a bad situation! I finally came to the conclusion that I would do the only intelligent thing a guy in my situation could do. When the shooting started I would get behind my dad. That may not be the manly thing to do but *hey* . . . he got me into this, I'm sure he wouldn't mind taking one for his kid!

The hunt began and progressed with an occasional coyote trying to sneak through the circle and getting shot. As the circle tightened, more and more coyotes exposed themselves because the cover was slowly diminishing due to the volume of animals trying to hide.

As I had imagined, it was a bloodbath. Whole coyote families (including the pups) were slaughtered. This event was not one of the more marvelous moments in my life.

I know the hunt was necessary to preserve the livelihood of those farmers who participated. Life wasn't always fair but it was equitable. Nature's imbalance created untenable problems for those who caused it: Beginning with the farmers who planted all the crops that fed the prey (rabbits) of the coyote. The solution fell to the coyote, whose job (appointed by nature) was to control the rabbit population so they wouldn't overrun crop growth. As this vicious cycle spiraled out of control, someone had to step in and correct the situation. Unfortunately, the coyotes had to take the hit! Sounds cruel, but necessary. It was swift, efficient justice—nature's justice.

The party at my friend John's beer joint after the hunt was also a necessary step in healing any shortcomings of the "roundup." We all had a lot of good food, the older participants had a few beers, the younger participants enjoyed a variety of non-alcoholic beverages (my favorite being a large Pepsi with planters peanuts [I would drink it to half-full and then pour in the peanuts] yummy). We all exchanged a lot of experiences (and a few lies). No one needed to know I had never fired a shot. Exempting the coyotes, a good time was had by all.

My dog Spunk as a puppy.

CHAPTER SIXTEEN

My Hero

A hero is a man who does what he can.
— Romain Rolland

My sister Lucille was married a year after I was born. Audry, her husband, drafted into the Army, was stationed in Belgium during the latter part of the war. He never saw action on the front lines but he was called up just prior to the surrender of Germany, ending the war. He used to tell me the Germans heard he was coming and decided to give up. I'm pretty sure he was kidding.

After the war ended he came home and for the remainder of his tour of duty was stationed at an Army Air Force base near Schyler, Nebraska. He worked in the Fire Department and Crash Crew on the base. They had a rented house off base. Because he had to work a 24-hour shift, he had to stay on the base several nights a month. Lucille didn't like spending those nights alone with a young son. Lucille and Audry had two boys: Gary, born in 1941, and Richard (Rick), born in 1946. Her kids were younger than I was but I enjoyed visiting and playing with my nephews.

When Audry was discharged, the Army kept the base open and let the Fire Department and Crash Crew personnel stay intact even though they were now civilians. It was a great job for him, with increased pay as a civilian. Audry and Lucille decided to move the family back to Valparaiso because that was their real home, even though he had to drive a fair distance.

They rented a nice brick one-story corner house on a large lot with a garage, utility shed and chicken house.

Everyone was excited when they got a TV. It was black and white; color wasn't available until much later. Because of Audry's work schedule, Lucille was home alone a lot of the time, so I would come by often to help her with her chores. I didn't mind because they had the TV.

Their family ate a lot of chicken. Lucille would always ask me to come over after school to kill the chicken. That was one thing she refused to do.

My brother-in-law Audry was really a neat guy—he was a great role model for any kid. A good husband and father, also a good athlete. All the surrounding town's high school alumni had what we called a "town league." They played basketball and baseball. When the competing high schools would have an intercity league game, the school teams had their games first and then the town league teams would play.

The town league basketball games were always fun to watch. Some of the older guys were still in good shape, but most weren't. At times the games got pretty rough. Audry was always the star of our team; he was the guard and the ball handler. He had the best behind-the-back pass I had ever seen. Pete Maravich could have taken a few tips from him.

Audry also was a great baseball player. He threw right-handed but batted left-handed, which was unusual in those days.

A couple years after Audry was discharged from the Army, he started developing severe shoulder pain. He went to a medical specialist in Lincoln and was diagnosed with polio.

Shortly after World War II ended, epidemics of polio occurred in the U.S.—an average of more than 20,000 cases a year from 1945 to 1949.

The doctors said his shoulder could be paralyzed in a very short period of time. He handled the bad news bravely. Audry swore the immediate family to secrecy. He didn't want his employer at the Fire &

Crash Department to find out about his ailment for fear of losing his job.

The accepted treatment at that time for paralysis polio was immobilization of the affected limb by actually putting it in a cast. Audry went to the government library on the air base where he worked and researched everything he could on the disease. It was a well-discussed topic in several medical journals, because of the debilitating effect it had on President Franklin Roosevelt.

A practicing nurse, named Sister Elizabeth Kenny from Australia, had other ideas on how to treat the virus. Her methods were very controversial. Her solution was to vigorously exercise the affected limb. She took a lot of flack from the established medical authorities for this plan of action.

Audry read about her treatment theory and figured if he accepted the conventional treatment and let them cast his shoulder the results would be completely out of his control—and that just wasn't his nature. He decided to pursue the Australian nurse's procedure. He made himself a set of weights out of window sash counter-balances (counter-weights were used to ease the opening and closing of older-style windows), and he started a rigorous workout schedule.

I would watch him from time to time and I could see it was very painful, but he never missed a day and he never lost hope. It was an inspiring feat considering no one *ever* knew about his problem. Everyone just thought he was on a body-building program. His regimen even inspired a lot of his friends to try to duplicate his workout commitment to improve their physical conditions and well-being. Believe it or not, he eventually beat the virus and has not had any recurrence or ill effects of the disease to this day and he is in his mid-90's.

Audry loved his job at the Fire & Crash crew where he worked, and would tell me stories of the fires he had to fight and the airplane accidents that occurred on a fairly regular basis. He told me, that if I ever had a chance to get on a Fire Department or an Airport Crash Crew, to take the job because the position had *real* job security. I told him I would always remember that.

My sister Lucille was the family historian. She always kept mementos and pictures and recorded family events and experiences. She showed me some of the souvenirs Audry had saved from his Army and Fire Department experiences. One of the more memorable ones was a real German Luger gun with a wooden holster that could be used as a shoulder stock and shot like a rifle. He had an authentic German helmet plus a few other items of interest from the war.

I remember one time, my nephew Gary and I got out the German helmet and wore it out in a hailstorm. The hailstones were about the size of golf balls and it sure was noisy with the big hailstones hitting the helmet. I wished I would have worn something like that on my hands too because I got smacked on my wrist by a hailstone. My mom thought it was broken the way it swelled up.

Along with the war souvenirs there was a small box in with some other items that she wouldn't show me and, of course, that's the one item I really was hoping to see the most. She would just say, "You don't need to see that". . . *I had to see it*! I asked Audry one day when we were alone to please *show it to me*. He said he would if I would promise to not tell my sister Lucille. I quickly promised and he took out the box and opened it. It was a piece of something that looked like a bit of broken pottery from an old clay pot. "What is it?" I asked.

He told me that it was a piece of a man's skull that he picked up after the guy had walked into a propeller of a running airplane. I guess that was one of the bigger pieces that were left of him.

My sister was right, although I have seen many worse things in my lifetime. I was a little too young to see that at that time because I never could quite get the picture out of my mind of a young man walking into that kind of horrible death. How could something that horrible happen?

CHAPTER SEVENTEEN

Modern Conveniences?

*Any sufficiently advanced technology is
indistinguishable from magic.*
— Arthur C. Clarke

I would often do my homework at my sister Lucille's
house because it was so much easier to see with
electric lights. Growing up on the farm, we only had
kerosene lamps, which were difficult to read by. You
had to sit right next to them to see anything, and they
gave off a lot of heat and smelled bad. To make the lamp
brighter you extended the wick with a little control, but
if you turned it too high it would start smoking and
turn the chimney black with soot. Then you couldn't
see anything. When that happened you would have to
extinguish the lamp, wash the chimney and trim the
burnt part of the wick with a pair of scissors and start all
over again. The thing was a pain in the butt. You always

had to have backup lamps so you weren't completely in the dark.

Later, someone invented the Coleman Lantern, (probably by a guy named Coleman) Golly! What an improvement . . . *it was truly a miracle.* The lantern burned "white gas." They called it *Coleman fuel* (what marketing geniuses) and you could buy it at the gas station.

It had the same purpose and function as the kerosene lamp, except it didn't have a wick and a burner. To get it to work, you pumped air pressure into the fuel chamber and the pressurized gas was fed to a pair of mantles. These mantles were nylon or rayon bags coated with a "rare earth" compound, which, once lit, the fabric would burn off, leaving a fragile oxide residue ash structure that would glow brightly when the pressurized gas flame was introduced.

You had to have a lot of spare mantles because if you bumped the lantern the ash mantles would disintegrate and have to be replaced. What a difference in the light given off between the Coleman lantern and the kerosene lamp—it was like night and day!

A few years in the future, when I was thirteen, we actually had electricity installed in our house. In addition, we erected a "yard light." The yard light was mounted on a tall pole right outside our house and it illuminated the housing compound and the barnyard, including the outhouse. No more trotting to the toilet in the dark. What a difference. It was amazing! I remember going through the house and flipping all the switches on, and my dad going behind me flipping them off, telling me, "Electricity costs money."

The lighting and the conveniences that were available because of the electricity were truly a godsend. After we got electricity and used it for a while, I couldn't imagine how we ever got along without it, and neither could my mom.

The main problem though was that it wasn't that reliable. The slightest thing would cause the electricity to go off. When it was off, being without it was almost unbearable. Even with the Coleman lantern and the battery-operated radio as backup, being without electricity was like going back to the dark (no pun intended) ages.

What was adequate in the past was totally unacceptable now. I swear sometimes I felt as my dad would say, "We were better off before all the *newfangled* improvements!" But, thankfully, that foolish feeling would pass quickly.

Shortly after the electricity was installed, Dad bought a Zenith black and white TV and radio combination. We were almost like regular folks you would see on TV.

By then the TV channels had increased to two main ones, CBS and NBC. The programming was a little more diverse, which presented another dilemma—who got to decide who watched what and when.

Dad didn't have much time to watch TV, but he insisted on tuning in on wrestling at least two nights a week. He was addicted to it, and if you *ever* suggested that it might be just a *little bit scripted* he would come unglued. Dad had his favorite "good guys" and hated the villains. He would shake his fist at them and would call them "dirty bastards" (that's about as profane as my dad ever got).

I enjoyed watching wrestling also but I took it with a grain of salt. Sometimes (just to see how Dad would react) I would pose the question: why had they never bled after taking that kind of a beating? He would just ignore me and turn up the volume.

Mom hated wrestling. She said it was too violent and that I shouldn't watch it because I was too young, but I would just ignore her and turn the volume up . . . *worked for Dad*!

Mom loved to watch the shows like: "The Ed Sullivan Show," "The Arthur Godfrey Talent Show" and "I Love Lucy." That was about it. She was always busy and tired. Both Mom and Dad went to bed early most every night with the exception of Wednesday and Saturday nights. Those were the nights when the town was open later and Mom had to work at the store.

Other than those few shows my parents liked, I just

about had the pick of the programs as long as I got my schoolwork and chores done. I particularly liked "The Red Skelton Show," "Jack Benny," "Amos and Andy" and "Dragnet." Some of the Saturday morning shows like "Flash Gordon," "Buck Rogers" and the cartoons were my favorites.

Mom did a lot of cooking and entertaining on the weekends. Hardly a week would go by when we didn't have someone in the family over for a Sunday dinner and a visit. In addition to our immediate family members who lived in and around our town, my mom had several relatives (brothers, sisters, nephews and nieces) in Lincoln and surrounding areas. She would get up at daybreak on Sundays and cook until noon, when everybody would start showing up, and they would stay until late afternoon and often into the evening.

I enjoyed most all the company with a few exceptions. Sometimes my cousins from Lincoln were a little "uppity," coming from a big city and all. Often, they would treat me like the illegitimate child of the Hillbilly Yokum family (aired on the radio). I wasn't as "cool" as they were. I may have been a little jealous, because I didn't know what they were talking about all of the time when they referred to the things they did and places they went in the "Biiiig City." They probably never hunted or shot anything in their lives. I know they couldn't bag a squirrel if they tried—so there!

Since Mom did all that cooking, she insisted on my dad getting her an electric refrigerator. She said she would pay for it, if he would get one for her and hook it up. He did and she did.

We tried to talk her into also getting an electric stove, but she said "the wood stove cooked better." How would she know—she never used a modern electric one? Go figure. We never had indoor plumbing or running water the entire seventeen years I lived there. That might have explained why I enjoyed attending school as much as I did.

CHAPTER EIGHTEEN

Holiday Antics

I once wanted to become an atheist, but I gave it up—they have no holidays.
— Henny Youngman

We often got together as a family, especially for holidays. They were always special for me. Christmas at our house was sort of a nonentity. As far as decorating our farmhouse, all my mom would do was get out the fake Christmas tree, which was about two feet tall and made out of wire with green crepe paper wrapped around about four branches. Her adornments consisted of a colored glass ball hung on the end of each branch. That was the extent of our festive decor.

I looked forward to the whole family celebrating Christmas at my Sister Lucille's house because they went all out for their kids, Gary and Rick. We would arrive early on Christmas Eve and bring all the presents and put them under their tree . . . *a real live Christmas tree!*

A big Christmas dinner would take place around lunchtime, and then everyone would sit around and visit until early evening. Then we'd have a traditional light supper, consisting of *oyster stew* with several side dishes including *minced-meat pie* for dessert.

Where the heck they came up with a traditional meal of "oyster stew" and "minced-meat pie," no one seemed to know or remember why . . . or even cared. I don't think anybody really liked the two menu items . . . I know I didn't.

What is it with minced-meat pie? Why do they call it that? There isn't any meat in it . . . thank god! It's just a bunch of raisins, grapes, brown sugar, cinnamon, green tomatoes and some other spices ground up to look like meat—*WHY?* It must now be extinct because I never see them advertised at Marie Callender's during the Christmas season.

All the kids were anxious to open presents, but the grownups always took their time after supper. They had to clear the table, wash the dishes (until they were spotless), and meticulously dry and polish every dish and utensil. They cleaned up like they were going to have a surprise military inspection at any moment. Having to wait like that to open presents was pure torture for us kids. I swore that when I had a family we would never do that to our children.

Another traditional occurrence took place prior to opening gifts. We would get a visit from Santa Claus, who was Mr. Schmidt (the owner of the store where my mother worked) in a tattered red suit and a really bad Santa mask. He would come in, stumble around, give each of us kids the wrong present, and made sure he hugged all the ladies. He would then run outside, stomp on the porch, ring some sleigh bells, simulating reindeer I suppose, and disappear into the night. He wasn't very convincing as Santa Claus, but he was consistent. He did the same thing every year without fail.

Our family had an unusual "gift-giving" procedure. Everyone would give a gift to the kids. The grownups would all draw names and give one gift (**one** gift only) to the recipient. There was a limit on how much you could spend for each gift, so everyone would give and receive value for value. Sounds like something that Vladimir Lenin or Mao Tse Tung would have come up with.

I guess this course of action was necessary since no one had much money, but at least the kids got a lot of presents. I later found out that some of the adults would tell the people who drew their name what they wanted, and on some occasions would just buy the gift and give it to the other person to wrap and then act surprised at Christmas Eve. Can you imagine? Where was the Christmas spirit?

When I was older, I loved buying and giving the gifts *almost* as much as I did getting them. One year when I was in high school I had worked a lot over the summer and saved my money. Come Christmas time I bought a present for every member of my family and *I* decided how much *I* would spend for each gift.

I was so excited, because I had kept the plan secret and had hidden all the presents until the last minute. I couldn't wait to see their faces when I surprised everyone . . . *OH MY GOD* you would have thought I had just committed a capital offense—*I had the nerve to break tradition*. When I passed out the gifts I told everyone that I picked every gift out myself, had thrown away all the receipts so they couldn't take them back or know how much they cost. I told them, "I made the money, and planned this all year." This was probably the worst Christmas the family had ever experienced to date because of my blunder.

At first I was upset and disappointed with everyone because they didn't accept the gifts in the spirit in which I gave them, but the more I thought about the situation I had created I realized I was the one that was wrong. I had embarrassed and caught my family off guard. I felt a need to apologize to everyone that night, telling them *I wouldn't ever do that again.*

At Easter, everyone would dye eggs for the kids, have a big picnic dinner (weather permitting) at the park in town, conduct an Easter egg hunt, and at night we would all go to the evening service at the Methodist Church. That was the extent of our family's annual religious commitment.

I wasn't a very religious person, and I didn't know a whole lot about the Gospel principles, but I did believe in a higher power in some form, and I *usually* tried to be a good person. Personally I had attended all three churches in town, mostly as a guest of my friends. The Catholic Church was the most demanding. You had to be in good shape to survive their services with all the standing and kneeling. The priest conducted the services in Latin so I didn't know what was happening, *or why*.

Sometimes, I would spend the night with my Catholic friend Jerry. He always said the same prayer when we ate and before we went to bed, but he said it so fast I never knew what he was praying about. One time I asked him what he was praying for and he thought a moment and he said, "I'm not quite sure but I'm supposed to say the same thing each time." That philosophy didn't impress me.

The Christian church was less structured than the Catholic Church. It was OK.

Whenever I attended church I picked the Methodist

Church. I had a few friends who went there and everyone kinda' did as they pleased as far as doctrine was concerned. The pastor was really laid back. They admonished you to follow Christ's teachings but didn't condemn you if you fell a little short. The best part of attending that church sporadically was, they had some great parties and outings for the youth.

Of the holiday myths, i.e., *Santa Claus* and the *Easter Bunny*, guess which stayed with me the longest? No, not Santa Claus. I think Mr. Schmidt had something to do with that. It was the Easter Bunny, because *I saw him* . . . or her . . . or it . . . or whichever—really! *I did see the Easter Bunny.* One snowy Easter eve as I was going upstairs on my way to bed (there was a window in the stairwell that looked down on the first-story roof) as I looked out the window I saw a huge white rabbit sitting on the roof. Hey . . . I lived on a farm and I have hunted rabbits with my dad, I know what a rabbit looks like . . . That was a *RABBIT*! I ran and tried to get my mom and my brother to come and see it but they just laughed at me (citing my *weird* imagination), and said it probably was a cat and I was told to go to bed.

First of all, we didn't have any all-white cats, and none of the cats we had were ever that big. I went back to the window and it was still there, sitting on our snow-covered roof, just looking back at me.

From then on, Easter had a special meaning for me.

I couldn't tell anyone and convince them of what I saw, so I quit trying. But I know what I saw, if it wasn't the *Easter Bunny*, what else could it have been?

Memorial Day was a big event in our town. Everyone would go to the cemetery and take part in an impressive service. This particular Memorial Day would be the most memorialized one of my life—this one almost killed me.

Everyone participated in sprucing up the grounds of the memorial site for our fallen servicemen. In conjunction with the traditional Memorial Day festivities, those who had relatives and loved ones buried there would mow the grass and plant flowers on the graves of our dearly departed so they would be presentable to all who attended.

Both sets of my grandparents were buried there, plus a few relatives I never knew. They died before I was born or I was too young to remember them.

As a youngster, I usually went with whoever was designated to tend to the gravesites. I enjoyed going because I would take my lariat. I would play like the tombstones were wild horses and I would try to rope them and jump up and straddle them like I was riding a wild bucking bronco. Talk about a weird, morbid imagination—*tombstones are horses?* . . . Go figure.

Anyway, on this occasion, I had gone with my mom and my sister Lucille. While they were working on beautifying the graves, I roped and jumped up on a rather large tombstone and unbeknownst to me it wasn't cemented to the base.

With a loud" whump" it slid off the base, tipped over and fell on top of me. I was lying; face up, underneath this huge piece of granite covering all of my body up to midway between my waist and shoulders.

I started crying and screaming as loud as I could with what little breath I was able to expend. My mom and Lucille came running as fast as they could. They tried to lift the tombstone off me but they couldn't budge it. (Later it was determined it weighed between 300 and 400 pounds).

My mom was panicking. Lucille told her to stay with me and she would drive to town, about six miles away, to find my dad and her husband Audry. Luckily they were working together on a carpentry project for someone.

I remember it was really hard for me to breathe with all that weight on me, and my mom trying to stay calm so I wouldn't panic, hoping help arrived soon.

Later, Mom told me that I had told her, while lying under the tombstone, I really felt close to my grandmas and grandpas. I could indentify with how they must have felt lying in a graveyard with a big tombstone on top of them all this time. That was about as close to them I ever wanted to be . . . on this side of the dirt.

My sister finally came back with my dad and Audry and with great difficulty they all lifted the stone off me. They carefully loaded me up in the car and took me to the closest medical facility, which was the chiropractor's office about twenty-five miles away in Wahoo. The doctor took X-rays of my torso and determined I had no broken bones, although he was very concerned that the tombstone may have damaged my pelvis and maybe some internal organs.

He prescribed complete bed rest. He said we had to give it time for things to heal, just in case I did have some injuries he couldn't find.

My parents moved a bed into the kitchen where everyone hung out so I wouldn't be lonely in my bedroom by myself. I liked all the attention I got for a while after the accident. I got out of chores and everyone did their best to make me comfortable, even my brother . . . I think deep down, he really liked me!

Everyone said you could see the outline of my body in the grass when they picked me up off the gravesite; luckily it had rained prior to us going to the cemetery that day. The ground was soft and the tombstone *pushed* me into the ground instead of *crushing* me against it.

You are probably thinking that by having an accident caused by a un-cemented tombstone in a public cemetery, we surely would now own the cemetery because of the lawsuit we filed, and we are now in the burying business . . . *right*?

Not a chance. Folks didn't operate that way in the "Valley of Paradise." First of all, it was my fault, and it wasn't an attractive nuisance (as a sharp lawyer might claim) because who in their right mind would think some kid would mistake a tombstone for a . . . *horse!!* Or, that he would try to rope it and ride it like a bucking bronco. Second of all, no one knew of any attorneys, or why you would ever need one.

The cemetery folks did help with the medical (chiropractor) expenses and came by to see how I was from time to time. What more could we ask for? Besides, I was a "star" for a while. People would point and say, "That's the kid who had the tombstone fall on him and lived," at least I think that was what they were saying. Or maybe they were saying, "There's the dummy who mistook a tombstone for a *horse*" . . . What do you think?

Needless to say, my tombstone roundup and granite bronco riding days were over, so I didn't spend much time at the cemetery after that.

I think my favorite holiday was Halloween. We used to plan all year for things to do and pranks to play on people at Halloween. It wasn't just us kids, high school teenagers and even some alumni got in on the fun and games.

Most of the pranks were harmless, with nobody getting hurt or property damaged (too much) with one exception, and that was the Catholic Church's outhouses. All of the churches and most of the businesses had outhouses. Even when indoor plumbing was later installed, most of them still kept their outhouses in use. I don't know if it was due to tradition or if they were just easier to take care of, but for whatever reason they still used them.

"Outhousing," as we called it, was the most fun and the most traditional prank to play. There was a creek right behind the Catholic Church and they set their outhouses right on the edge of the creek bank so—what was the most natural thing to do at Halloween? That's right; you pushed them down the bank. What else? Of course this exposed the "poop pit" for all church members to see . . . *and enjoy.* This is where the charming expression of "Holy Crap" came from, I'm sure.

So *every year* the church members had to haul them back up the bank, repair them, and reset them over the poop pits. We never figured out why they didn't move them to a different location away from the creek bank— must have been a job security thing for the church's maintenance crew, or maybe they figured if that was the worst thing that would happen at Halloween it was worth it. If they made it easy for us to dump the privies, we probably wouldn't do anything else to them. Sounds reasonable to me.

If Halloween fell on a date during the week, everyone would go trick or treating on the actual Halloween night, but no one was safe from pranks until after the following weekend was over.

"Outhousing" was an art. Pushing the church's outhouses down the bank was simple and easy. Other tactics required a little more planning, i.e. *tip-overs*— the art of waiting in hiding until someone was in the toilet and tipping the outhouse over with them in it. With this method you had three options:

1. If you tipped it over backwards, the person could just stand up, and crawl out through the open door;

2. Tip it onto one side or the other, and again the person could open the door and crawl out, but it was harder because you had to roll out. You couldn't stand up;

3. The most effective option was to tip it over door-side down. You only did this to someone you didn't like very well because they couldn't get out. They would have to yell out through the hole (or holes, depending on the configuration) until someone heard them and came and set the outhouse upright again so they could escape.

Each of these methods had a certain amount of risk. If you used method number one or number two you had to do some pre-planning to make it work well, making sure you could get away before the person got out and saw you. You also had to be relatively sure the person wasn't fast enough to catch you before you could flee.

Technique number three was the safest from initially getting caught, but with this method you had to be realistic. You couldn't leave someone in there overnight. In all fairness, you had to go back in a couple of hours and check to see if someone had heard them calling for help and got them out. If not, you had a problem, and it could be a *big* problem!

It takes two to three people to set an outhouse upright again. Once it is upright, it is very easy for the person inside to get out. Put yourself in someone's place that has been trapped in a smelly toilet for several hours having to yell for help though a hole in the seat. What frame of mind do you think you would be in—hmmmmm? Here was the dilemma: We could try to convince the person that we just happened to be going by and heard him yelling and stopped to help, and then hope we could convince him of this before . . . *he killed us*! Or we could roll the outhouse on its side and run like hell. Either way was risky.

To be successful, to go undetected or not get beat up at "out-housing," you had to choose your tipping methods to fit the mindset of the person who was going to be inside the outhouse at the time of the tipping. See, I told you that "outhousing" *was an art*!

The safest method, but with the most devastating

effect, was to find an outhouse in an area that was really dark and move the outhouse back from the "poop pit" and *never, ever, ever* go back there again—let your imagination *flooow*.

We did this one time to the outhouse behind John's beer joint a rather large Polack farmer had purchased a hamburger and a beer and *then* decided to use the toilet before eating his dinner (some would consider the option of *reversing* this procedure, but you have to consider the person we're dealing with here). Everyone heard this awful yelling and cussing out back and when the folks went to see what was wrong there was a very irate individual standing waist-high in "deep doo-doo" (there is that coined phrase again . . . lest you forget), holding his hamburger and beer over his head. I hope that guy *never* reads this book!

We did the usual soaping of windows and screens to those who didn't give out treats. Of course we utilized the old standby of the *crap in a paper bag*, which was placed on a porch, lit on fire and then we would ring the door bell. In most cases we had to knock (no doorbell). It was a consistently funny prank, no matter how many times we repeated it. Year after year, people always tried to stomp the fire out—*some things seem to never lose their charm*.

We would shorten one side of the swings on the school playground and take the merry-go-around carousel off its spindle. We usually grew out of these *minor pranks* by the time we got into the last couple of years in high school.

Very rarely would we get caught or get into trouble pulling off the usual pranks at Halloween. There were six boys who lived in or close to town and were of the obvious ages to be suspects.

I guess they couldn't figure out who was doing these things because we always wore Halloween masks, also probably because there were so many of us.

When we got older we tried to think of more elaborate, *sophisticated* pranks. I remember one year about a dozen of us who were seniors in high school, in addition to some that had already graduated, contacted a farmer who had an old horse-drawn buggy and we talked him out of it for a small price.

Halloween weekend, we hooked it to a truck and towed it into town in the middle of the night. It took all of us several hours to hoist it on top of the awning over John's beer joint. We were excited to see his face the next day. We thought he would blow his stack.

Come to find out he loved it and it was still there the last time I was in town. You just never know how things will turn out. It wasn't supposed to work that way. His reaction took all the fun out of it.

Some of the things we thought up were borderline criminal. Sometimes we would go to other neighboring towns and wreak a little havoc. If things started to get out of hand, the following year the town council would *secretly* deputize someone to infiltrate our group. Then when we were pulling the caper the appointed cop would bust us and take us to the *one-room jailhouse* to spend most of the evening. This, of course, was all done in good fun. It got to be a great game to see if we could find out who was the spy and if we could still pull off the prank without getting caught. Nobody ever got hurt or had property damage to any great extent. It was a tradition most everyone looked forward to . . . that one Halloween weekend a year.

Another holiday was the Fourth of July. You couldn't purchase fireworks in Nebraska, but you could buy them though mail order from the neighboring state of Missouri.

My brother used to order firecrackers through a mail-order catalog. The catalog offered most every kind of recreational pyrotechnics available at that time. You could get all sizes of firecrackers from ladyfingers (they were real weak explosives that you could hold in your hand and they wouldn't hurt) all the way up to the real powerful M-80's. They were like a mini stick of dynamite with a fuse sticking out the side and that would burn underwater.

When I was smaller my mom wouldn't let me have anything but ladyfingers and sparklers. She would have my brother get me some extra when he ordered his. Some of my friends would do the same thing and we would have war games using the ladyfingers as bombs and hand grenades.

The older we got, the less fun the lady fingers were and we slowly graduated to the regular firecrackers like the Chinese brands, i.e. *Black Kat, Golden Dragon*, or the most reliable, *Zebra*. These types made the games more fun, but you had to make sure you didn't hold them like the ladyfingers. Every once in a while, in the heat of battle, someone would forget to get rid of the firecracker in time and it would do some real damage to their fingers.

I had it happen to me on one occasion and I made sure that would *never, never* happen again. The blast actually split the ends of two fingers and it was very painful. I was definitely a casualty in that war game.

That wasn't the worst wound I suffered playing war games. The only way to light the firecrackers we were using in the games was with a wooden match (the kind that lights anywhere, just strike it on any surface) or with a product called *punk*. We would light it and it would slowly smolder, and when we needed to light something we would blow on the smoldering end and it would glow hot enough to ignite a firecracker fuse.

That type of igniter was OK if you were setting off a lot of fireworks in one place but in our war games you didn't want to carry around something that was burning—you might grab hold of the wrong end. The punk wasn't safe and it wasn't fast enough if you had to get off a quick grenade lob.

When we were playing the games, I always had a pocket full of wooden strike-anywhere matches, *much safer* . . . right? I was running to get a better strategic position in which to conduct this particular tactical war game maneuver. I stumbled, fell and slid on the graveled road I was running on. The slide caused friction on the pocket. Where I was carrying about fifty wooden strike-anywhere matches in and guess what? . . . You got it . . . My pants were on fire. I had the equivalent of a good-sized campfire blazing in my pocket. I was beginning to look like that comic book character "The Human Torch."

The location of the war games we were playing was in town, on a Saturday night. There were a lot of people around watching while I frantically ripped my pants off and watched them burn up. Much to my mom's concern, I lost a pair of pants, scorched my undershorts and had a huge blister on my leg. It took me quite a while to live down the humiliation of that spectacle.

We got really creative in the art of exploding firecrackers. We would put them under cans and shoot them high in the air, and build little wooden ships and float them down the creek and blow them up with M-80's.

We would stuff several M-80's or cherry bombs in pipes and other containers to see how powerful an explosion we could make. *Luckily the FBI wasn't interested in that type of activity back then.* (I think they call them "pipe bombs" now.)

We would tie a weight to the M-80's and throw them in ponds and lo and behold, we discovered a new way to fish. The owners of the ponds discouraged that practice by running us off their property. We quickly figured that if we kept that up we wouldn't have any place to fish soon so we eliminated that practice from our repertoire.

One time we crossed the line, *big time*! I and my friend Jack lit some M-80's and flushed them down the toilet at the high school. That was not a smart thing to do for several reasons, the main one being my dad filled in for the regular custodian while he was on summer vacation.

When my dad worked at the school, I and a friend (my choice) could go with him and play basketball in the gymnasium all by ourselves while he did his custodial duties. I was really popular during that time because all my friends wanted to go with me and I got to decide who was to be the lucky one (I was drunk with power).

I would schedule my friends at different days based upon the criteria of "who most appreciated the privilege of using the gym all alone with me." But to be really truthful it was mostly based on "how and what they offered to demonstrate their appreciation!"

Jack (one of my best friends, the one I invited the most) and I pulled the dumb plumbing/M-80 stunt when he, I and my dad were *the only ones there*. Obviously we hadn't put a whole lot of planning into that caper. Deniability was not an option.

The only good thing (unintended, but fortunate) about the damage to the plumbing was, the toilet we put the firecrackers in was on the second floor, so the exploded drainpipe was in the ceiling of the first floor where it was easy to find and get at. And more importantly, no one was there to use the toilet so there was little water damage to the premises, caused by flushing the toilet multiple times.

My dad had to open the ceiling to expose the drainpipe, remove and replace the bad section, and repair the ceiling. Jack's dad said he would pay for the material if my dad would do the labor, which he agreed to. It was *strongly* suggested that Jack and I be present when the work was being done, reason being, we would do all the "grunt" work and clean up, which we happily agreed to without reservation.

The consequences of that dumb stunt were two-fold

(both bad). First; my dad was publicly embarrassed because I was *directly* involved in inflicting damage on school property, while he was entrusted with its well-being and safety.

That infraction encouraged and demanded an impromptu meeting with me and his famous razor strop. A whipping with a razor strop was standard punishment in those days—a penalty which he enthusiastically administered to the extent of his humiliation. (Actually he beat the crap out of me . . . *literally. I had the tendency to lose control of my bowels when he got really angry. Unfortunately this made my mom angry also because she would have to wash my underwear*).

As painful as that form of punishment was, it was preferred by me, since it was quick and it was over without any lasting effects, other than my doing a lot of standing for the next couple of days.

The second, the worst, longest-lasting consequence was, I wasn't allowed to play in the gymnasium for the rest of the summer.

My friend Jack was mad at me, again, because for some reason he had tried to convince himself, and probably his dad, that the whole episode of putting the firecrackers in the toilet was *my idea*. His dad, probably (adhering to tradition) had applied the same razor strop *get-together* that I experienced.

I doubted that Jack's dad would buy into the "he

made me do it" excuse. I know, because I tried the same thing, blaming him, and my dad didn't go for it either.

Jack figured he got punished twice, because I wasn't allowed to use the gym for the rest of the summer and he didn't get to either. Soooo, he didn't talk to me for a while *again*, and made that same dumb request *again* as he did, on several other occasions, to not include him in anymore of my hare-brained ideas. I don't know what that guy's problem was?

Another important business 101 principle learned: "The downside side of taking bribes and favors for services rendered is—*you better darn well be able to deliver the services.*" That summer, I was pretty lonely.

Getting back to fireworks displays, as I got older and made more money, I started buying more assorted types of fireworks. Plus they were coming out with bigger and different firecrackers each year. They always had the M-80's, which were the best firecrackers, but they also had cherry bombs, torpedoes (you didn't have to light them, you just threw them against a hard object and they exploded on impact) and buzz bombs, which rose into the air like a helicopter and then exploded. My last couple of years at home, I was ordering the deluxe assortment, which had everything they had in their catalog. The deluxe package cost about $20.00, which was several days' pay for me.

I was getting a good reputation for the fireworks shows I put on for the family. It was getting to the point that some of our relatives came all the way from Lincoln (thirty miles away) to watch my extravagant exhibit each year. In those days, the fireworks company didn't have the spectacular types of pyrotechnics they have for the shows they put on today (for almost any occasion). The presentations I exhibited (working with what was available, and with my meager income), were so impressive that even some of our neighbors would drive by and park and watch from the roadway.

My mother would always caution me not to spend so much money for other people's enjoyment, saying that I should save my money. I told Mom that I probably enjoyed putting on the display more than those watching it. Whatever it cost, the excitement it created was well worth the effort and expense.

My parents were very, very practical people. They believed you only spent money on the essentials and saved the rest *for a rainy day*. I could understand this concept, considering the hardships they both went through, but it led to an extremely dull, uneventful life that I didn't want to participate in. Besides, it *rained way too much* in Nebraska (too many rainy days to save for).

CHAPTER NINETEEN

Getting Even

Life being what it is, one dreams of revenge.
— Paul Gauguin

My brother Lloyd had graduated and moved in with my sister, Dorothy, they resided in the city of Lincoln. Until that time he lived at home with my parents and me. Most of the time we got along, but at times he would tease and pester me unmercifully. He was nine years older than me, so I couldn't get even with him by "beating him up" or anything like that.

One day when he was in one of his more torturing modes, his teasing was in overdrive. Later in the afternoon he decided to go out on the lawn and take a nap. I had had enough. It was time to stand up and be counted so I devised a plan to retaliate. I was small but I was a pretty fast runner. If I could sneak up on him and get in a few good whacks while he was asleep, I could

189

make a run for it a get to where my mom was working in the garden before he could wake up and catch me. If I made it to where Mom was, she wouldn't let him punch me out.

I realized that all he has to do is wait until another day when Mom isn't around and then he would beat the crap out of me, but that would be . . . another day. It would be worth it if I could get him good right now.

I found a good-sized stick and snuck up to where he was lying on the lawn, on his stomach. I figured I could get in two or three good licks before he would be able to realize what was happening and by then I would be well on my way to my mom. It was now or never.

I drew back the stick and let it fly. I hit him once on his butt and twice on his back, and took off at record-breaking speed, looking over my shoulder to see how he was reacting. He must not have been as sound asleep as I had figured, because he was up and running after me, yelling out all kinds of cuss words. He was really mad. I was about halfway to the safety of my Mom. I risked another look back over my shoulder and saw he was gaining fast. I never remembered him being able to run that fast—it was going to be a close race.

One important thing I hadn't factored in my escape plan was, my dog Spunk deciding to relocate his position on the lawn at this critical time. While I was looking back he had taken up a new lounging position and had lain down directly in my escape route. When I turned back around to see how far I had left to go to reach the safety of my mom, there was Spunk, sprawled right at my feet. I couldn't avoid him and, you guessed it, I tripped on him and did a nosedive into the grass.

My brother was on me in a flash, and all hell broke loose. He was beating the tar out of me and I was yelling for Mom to come and save me. *Finally* she did. She yelled at Lloyd to leave me alone but it was too late—the damage had already been done.

Well, just like they say about the chain-of-command in the military, and a public sewer system—punishment and crap ran downhill. My brother beat me up; *consequently* the only living creature below me on the food chain was . . . Spunk. He caught the full force of my ire. After all, it was his fault for moving. While I was punishing him, he's looking at me like, "What the heck did I do? Whatever it was, it must have been terrible."

CHAPTER TWENTY

Another War (Police Action)

I'm fed up to the ears with old men dreaming up wars for young men to die in.
— George McGovern

When the Korean War broke out, President Truman put out the call to arms in late 1950. Between the Korean War outbreak in June 1950 and the year 1953, the Selective Service inducted 1,529,539 men. Another 1.3 million volunteered. Most joined the Navy and Air Force. My brother Lloyd and all of his friends rushed to join the Air Force. Lloyd didn't know or understand much about the conflict with the North Koreans or why he was going, but he knew he had to go because it was expected of him. His president had asked him to serve and all his friends were signing up. That was reason enough.

All Lloyd's lifelong buddies passed their physicals

and were accepted, the only exception of the group was my brother. Lloyd was diagnosed with high blood pressure and hypertension, and was rejected out of hand. He was devastated. They all had made a pact to enlist and go off together.

Lloyd filed a grievance with Selective Service and was allowed to retake the medical exams, but to no avail. Each time he tried to pass the physical, the Air Force turned him down.

He couldn't stand having to stay home while all his friends went off to war to defend their country. He made one last attempt to serve: He tried to enlist in the Army instead of the Air Force and for whatever reason he passed his physical with flying colors and was accepted.

Congress passed the Universal Military Training and Service Act in 1951 to meet the demands of the war. It lowered the induction age to 18½ and extended active-duty service commitments to a minimum of 24 months.

There were some draft-age individuals granted deferment for *unusual* circumstances, and a few young men in our area took advantage of the exemption. There were rumors that if you paid off the right local politician, your son was not drafted. But I think those were mostly just rumors. Anyway, those individuals who didn't go to war for whatever reason were not as highly esteemed, at the time, as those who did serve.

Despite some early combat failures and later stalemates in Korea, the draft has been credited as playing a vital role in turning the tide of war. A February 1953 Gallup Poll showed 70 percent of Americans surveyed felt the SSS (Selective Service System) handled the draft fairly.

Lloyd had turned twenty-one years of age, enlisted and was heading off to war by himself instead of with his friends. He was a member of an Army battalion that was almost assuredly heading into the thick of the fighting. He went through basic training and was, as expected, on his way to Korea.

All of the family were very worried for his safety, especially my mother. She had brothers and relatives that served in the first and second World Wars. Many of these individuals related stories of the horror and dangers of combat. This was waaay different for Mom— this was her child and he was going to a faraway land she could barely find on a map to fight for a cause she couldn't understand. My dad was worried also, but very proud of his son, who answered the call of his country in its time of need . . . without reservation.

I cried when he left. I had taken a lot of teasing from my brother. Oftentimes when someone would ask me what I wanted to do when I grew up I would say,

"I want to beat the crap out of my brother." But I really loved him dearly.

It truly broke my heart when he told me, "Donnie, you're probably the one I will miss the most." To top it off, he gave me his extensive comic book collection, which he took great pride in owning.

This was my big brother going off to war, and I might never see him again. It was a sad day when he left all by himself. He looked so lonely boarding the train. I was thirteen when he left. At the time, I wished I could take his place, so my mom wouldn't have to be so sad, worrying about his safety.

Lloyd went through basic training and then onto heavy artillery (105 howitzers) training at one of the Army bases. He came home for a short leave and then he was on his way to the frontlines in Korea. A funny thing happened . . . on the way to a war. When he arrived in Japan, the Army randomly chose ten guys from his company to be mail couriers. So for the next one and a half years (the rest of his enlistment), he rode a mail train, as a guard, from Yokohama, Japan to several coastal cities and back. It was incredibly good luck on his part and a real load of worry off his family at home. Every letter my mom wrote to him while he was there ended with, "Don't bring home one of those Japanese girls!"

CHAPTER TWENTY-ONE

A Journey to the Outside World

*Focus on the journey, not the destination. Joy
is found not in finishing an activity but in
doing it.*

— Greg Anderson

My brother Lloyd and my sister Dorothy were rooming together in Lincoln when Lloyd enlisted in the Army. The deal they made was, she would take care of his car (a 1941 Plymouth sedan) and make the payments while he was away and in turn she would get to drive it.

My mom was feeling sad after my brother was on his way to Korea. She called Dorothy and asked if my sister could get some time off for a short vacation. Dorothy said she would ask her boss, but wanted to know where Mom wanted to go.

Mom had just found out that one of my older sisters,

Wilma, had moved to Idaho. She had married a man, named Arch, from Lincoln. He was working in a bar for his brother who owned the establishment in Idaho Falls. Wilma had written Mom and suggested that we should come and visit them.

Mom said she would pay for the trip if Dorothy would drive Lloyd's car. My mother and Dorothy made all the arrangements for a two-week excursion. As soon as they were sure everything was going to come off as planned, I was informed of the trip, I guess they didn't want to disappoint me in case things didn't work out. I was really excited. I was 13 years old, and it would be my first time out of the state, the farthest I had been from home was about fifty miles.

The AAA auto club mapped out the best round-trip route. The club gave us a booklet outlining all the points of interest along the route (complete with pictures), both going and a different route returning. We decided to take the route to Rock Springs, Wyoming, and turn north and go through Grand Teton National Park and into Yellowstone National Park at the south entrance. We would exit the west gate of the park and then head down to Idaho Falls. The length of the outgoing leg was about 1,200 miles. I couldn't imagine how far that was because on a map it was just a few inches.

The terrain we traveled through after leaving Lincoln was all the same, flat farmland until we reached Rock

Springs, Wyoming. We turned north from that point and proceeded up through Jackson Hole and into the national parks.

The landscape changed drastically. The mountains were beautiful; the parks (Grand Teton and Yellowstone) were breathtaking. We were fascinated with the geysers, the bubbling mud flats, and waterfalls. There are approximately sixty species of mammals in Yellowstone Park, including the gray wolf, lynx and grizzly bears. Other large mammals include the bison (I always thought they were buffalo,) black bear, elk, moose, mule deer, mountain goat, pronghorn antelope, big horn sheep and mountain lion.

I remember the signs saying "Don't touch or feed the bears!" It never occurred to me that you would need a sign warning people not to fool with bears, seemed pretty obvious to me.

One day we were talking to one of the park rangers and he was telling us that just the other day they had to ask a tourist to leave the park because he was trying to get one of the bears into the driver's seat of his car so he could take a picture, go figure.

The only contact I had with the bears was when I spotted two baby bear cubs feeding alongside the road. I wanted to stop and take a picture of them. We had one of the new Kodak Brownie cameras; they called it that because it looked like a plain brown box. The way it worked was: the lens was on one end of the box and it had a little window on the top that you looked down into to see what you were going to take a picture of.

It didn't have a focus control, so the way you changed your field of vision was to get either closer or farther away from the object.

I was trying to get the cubs entirely in the picture and in focus, but I was having trouble. Just as I was ready to snap the picture they would get bigger and I could only see one. I kept backing up, but they would still get bigger. Finally I heard my sister yelling at me, "Get in the car quick!" When I looked up I knew what the problem was. The mother bear had showed up and was protecting the kids. She was going to make sure I wasn't going to hurt them, and was moving toward me at a rapid pace. I jumped into the car just as she got to where I had been standing. From then on, I admired all the wildlife from the interior of the car.

I never realized there was so much to see and to explore. I was consciously making a personal commitment to myself to see as much of the world as I could in my lifetime.

On our way from Yellowstone Park down to Idaho Falls we stopped by a place called Heise hot springs, close to Idaho Falls. It consisted of a lodge and a large swimming pool fed by local hot springs. The water stayed at a comfortable, natural 92 degrees year-round.

They also had other mineral pools that maintained an invigorating 105 degrees.

This is where I taught myself to swim (at least dog-paddle). I discovered, after watching other people who obviously knew how to swim, that I could dive down in relatively shallow water, control my ascent and stay on top at will. I gradually ventured into deeper and deeper areas of the large pool, applying what I had learned in the shallows with the same success. I was accomplishing these feats, all the while trying to ignore the warnings of my sister and mom, neither of whom would even wade in the pool, because they were afraid of drowning. I remember the deeper I would dive in the large pool the hotter it got. I never forgot that experience.

The other incidents I had involving water, prior to the hot springs, were at home. A few of us boys would go to one of the local swimming holes in the creek (Oak Creek) that ran though the countryside. The swimming holes were nothing but washed-out areas that were of various depths depending on the local rainfall. These holes all had mud bottoms. Sometimes you would sink up to your knees in the thick, oozy stuff.

None of the guys I went swimming with knew how to swim, so we would try to stay in water depths that weren't over our heads. We would tie ropes onto the trees that overhung the creek, so we could swing out and drop into the pools of water.

I recall one time my friend Jack decided he was going to dive into one of the pools. I don't know what prompted his hare-brained idea, but it happened shortly after we had been to see a Tarzan movie at the Wednesday night "free show." As I said, none of us could swim, but here is Jack climbing up on one of the overhanging trees and diving head-first into the water. The rest of us (the *sane* ones) watched Jack. After he hit the water his feet were still sticking out above the surface and he was kicking frantically.

Now Jack had a habit of often taking a deep breath, and standing on his hands under the water with his feet above the surface and playing like he was drowning. We all thought he was playing the same trick, but this time he wasn't coming up. We decided we had better help him before he *really did* drown. We grabbed his legs and pulled him up out of the water, and much to our surprise, we discovered that he had stuck his head into the muddy bottom and would never have gotten out by himself. I had to clear the mud from his nose and mouth so he could breathe. This whole episode could have ended tragically had we not reacted quickly. The incident certainly cured Jack from ever playing like he was drowning again.

On another occasion we were on a school outing at one of the many ponds located on the local farms. The new principal of the school took the ninth and tenth grades on the outing. Unbeknownst to him, most of the students didn't know how to swim with the exception of his son Bob who was in the same grade as I. We had a bunch of inflated truck tire inner tubes that we were floating on.

For some reason Bob thought I could swim (I don't remember if I had given him that impression or not—probably so). Anyway, he tipped my tube over as a joke. The water was well over my head. I can vividly recall sinking to the bottom and pushing off with my feet to the surface and taking a breath while floundering around trying to stay afloat. I did this for what seemed like forever until I tired. I was standing on the bottom looking up at surface and thinking: *This is it—it's all over!* Suddenly a pair of strong hands grabbed me and pulled me up so my head was out of the water. It was the principal, floating on a log—he couldn't swim either. Bob had seen that I couldn't swim, panicked, and swam away to get his father.

When we arrived in Idaho Falls, Idaho, we were met by my sister Wilma. She was fourteen when I was born. I hadn't been around her that much. She had developed a medical malady right before I was born and had to go away for extended treatment. After that she only returned on rare occasions.

As it was told to me over the years, when I was growing up, cases similar to her type of disease would crop up from time to time throughout the county, not of epidemic proportions, mind you, but it did happen and it only seemed to afflict young girls. The treatment applied was always the same and each case required an extended stay at a remote facility or home. It must have been a persistent virus because it always took eight to ten months to cure. I never understood the technical term for their condition but it rhymed with *pregnancy out of wedlock*, or something like that.

I know you won't believe this, but people back in those days actually believed it was a family disgrace to have a daughter who was pregnant before marriage. They tried to hide their shame by sending the young lady to a remote relative, or home for *wayward girls*, to give birth to the baby, who was then promptly put up for adoption.

Since there was obviously no cure for this chronic sickness, the trick was to keep the event secret, to preserve the integrity of the family. It seemed to work. I know I didn't tell anyone. I don't think *anyone* ever figured out what was really going on. I guess back in those days everyone just minded their own business . . . yeah, right!

Wilma's new husband, Arch, was her second one. She was first married to a neat guy named Robert. I met him once when she brought him by the farm. He said he was part Indian—I don't know what tribe he belonged to. He took me hunting with him on several occasions, and taught me a lot of hunting and stalking techniques that I have utilized on numerous hunting trips.

Wilma had a habit of showing up when she got married and again when she got divorced. Each time she would stay awhile and then take off again, to parts unknown.

Wilma's new husband had an entirely different personality than Robert. Arch was a masonry laborer by trade and, while they lived in Idaho Falls, he was a bartender. I was fascinated with the theme of the bar in which Arch worked: It looked like the old saloons in the western cowboy movies. It had the traditional long wooden bar with the huge mirror behind.

The patrons who frequented the establishment were mostly cowboys and ranchers. They looked like the "Old West" cowpunchers—without the guns and holsters. The place served steaks and hamburgers and several side orders, had a long shuffleboard and a pool table. We hung out and ate there most of the days while we were visiting.

We took a different route home to Nebraska. This itinerary took us though Colorado, where we stopped in Colorado Springs to visit the Cave of the Winds. My sister Dorothy and I took the tour way down in the bowels of the earth (Mom wouldn't go, she said people weren't meant to venture inside the earth), into these huge rooms and caverns. We saw huge mineral icicle-like things hanging from the ceiling of the caves and the same things growing up from the floor called stalagmites and stalactites. I don't remember which was which.

The ones growing from the floor reminded me of our outhouse. Let me explain. One of my chores during the winter was "crap knockdown duty" —I'll try not to be too graphic. When it was below freezing and you went number two (I'm sure everyone knows which one that is), the frozen crap would freeze solid and stack up in these long tall columns, which would get so tall that I would have to take a stick and knock them down so they wouldn't grow up through the hole. This was not a chore I relished, but it seemed that it always fell to me to administer . . . maybe I was good at it. . . I don't know.

After we left Colorado, we were back to the monotonous flat farmlands the rest of the way home. I liked reading the "Burma Shave" signs along the highways (these were real catchy phrases and poems written on small red signs . . . a few words on each sign, they would go on for miles, and at the end the last sign would give you the punch line and say *Burma Shave*).

Every once in a while we would see signs advertising various attractions ahead. I always insisted that we stop at each one, but my mom said her funds were running short so we had to save our money for the couple of motels we were to stay at along the way.

We kept seeing the signs promoting the oddity called, "*The Thing.*" The signs said, "It was from another world," it was the "only one of its kind," a once-in-a-lifetime opportunity. It sounded really exciting, and I kept pressuring my mom and my sister to stop and see it. Finally they relented and we stopped. It wasn't very expensive to see the attraction—it was only fifty cents per person. I guess they worked on volume. They really promoted the exhibit, the signs were displayed for probably 100 miles on either side of its location, and it reminded me of the *carnival hype* when the show came to town.

When we finally stopped, my mom said she didn't want to see it, so my sister and I went into the tent where it was displayed. "*The Thing*" turned out to be some kind of a mummified Indian they had displayed under glass in a coffin. We looked at it for about ten minutes and left somewhat disappointed. It didn't live up to the advertising—like so many things in life.

We returned home, tired and sore from all the sitting in the car. I told my few friends in school about our trip. Most of them were envious. They too had never had the opportunity of actually venturing outside the state during their childhood. Again I vowed I would see as much of the United States and the world as possible in my life's journey.

CHAPTER TWENTY-TWO

Educational Punishment

All pain is a punishment, and every punishment is inflicted for love as much as for justice.

— Joseph De Maistre

My time in seventh grade was passing quickly; I had one more year before I could go into high school. I was really anxious to get into the higher grades—then I could start to really have some fun. My grades were good, usually all straight A's, I took my schooling seriously—*then*. I never got into any *real* trouble, until this kid named Paul moved into the area.

Paul and I were both in the seventh grade. I liked him from the first time I met him and we hung out together a lot. We had a lot in common, with the exception that he lived in town (He was a "townie"... I was *almost* a "townie.")

We liked to do the same things most of the time, but there were a few key concepts we just didn't see eye to eye on. He thought he was a better athlete than I was, so he wanted all the best positions when we played games on the playground. When the games required choosing up sides, he always wanted to be the one who did the choosing.

The only problem with that logic was that I wanted the same thing, only with a different leading man—me. After about a month of playing together, we got into an argument during recess, and it resulted in a fight. The teacher saw us, broke it up, and sent us to the principal's office.

This was a new experience for me; I had heard of kids getting sent to the principal's office (my brother warned me of this *dreaded* course of action when I started kindergarten) and sometimes they even got a paddling. I always vowed that was never going to happen to me, but there I was. I didn't know what to expect, and I was feeling apprehensive.

We didn't actually go into the main office; we were in the reception area. The principal met with us and gave us a stern warning and told us the school did not tolerate fighting, and if it happened again we would be punished and he would have to tell our parents. We both promised we would never do it again, and went our separate ways.

My dad was a quiet, easygoing guy most of the time, but you didn't want to cross him. If you made him mad, you quickly found yourself bent over a chair with his razor strop laid across your butt. It had happened to me on more than a few occasions and they were memorable encounters which left lasting impressions in the form of welts on my posterior. Luckily, when my mother would see me getting close to crossing the line with my dad, she would bravely run interference for me and distract him—until I came to my senses.

Anyway, the unspoken law was, "Don't cross him and don't embarrass him, in any way, in front of other adults." Those were his rules and as long as you adhered to them everything was fine.

Paul and I made up and got along pretty well for a while until one day he did something or said something that I couldn't tolerate, so we went at it again. The teacher tried to break us apart but we wouldn't have any of that and we kept fighting. Before we knew it, we were back in the principal's office again.

We were hoping for another warning, but the principal stayed true to his word. We were told to stay after school and report back to his office for disciplinary action.

That was the longest school day of my life, worrying what exactly had he meant by "disciplinary action." We weren't positive but surely we wouldn't get a paddling, would we? We would, and we did.

We went in to see him one at a time. The principal selected Paul first, which I was grateful for. I had to wait just outside his office and, much to my anguish; I could clearly hear *everything* that went on inside the office.

I heard Paul getting smacked and him crying. As usual, there went my imagination kicking in again. I could visualize him hanging by his wrists from the ceiling and being flogged like the sailors in those pirate movies. I broke out in a cold sweat. I could feel my bowels getting loose and I thought I would go to the bathroom right there. I thought seriously that this would be a good time to quit school and go to work—*full time.*

After what seemed like hours, Paul came walking out, head down and shoulders slumped. He had been crying (which I clearly heard from where I was sitting). He was thoroughly dejected.

The beating must have been terrible to make him look like that. Paul was a tough kid, I thought. I was terrified. If he couldn't handle the ordeal, how was I going to hold up under similar punishment?

Finally the principal appeared and motioned for me to follow him back into his inner office. I had never been in the "actual" principal's office before, I expected the place to be a dark dungeon-like place with weird organ music playing in the background. To my surprise the office was bright and cheery.

The principal asked me if I knew why I was there and if I knew what was going to happen to me. I told him I was pretty sure, after hearing what had just happened to my friend Paul.

He told me he didn't enjoy punishing students, but as principal, he had to maintain order. He couldn't tolerate fighting on school grounds. I felt like telling him if he felt so bad about paddling students I would be willing to help him out and we could call the whole affair off. "Are you ready for your punishment?" he asked.

I replied, "I guess . . . I'm as ready as ever."

He pulled this paddle out of his drawer. It looked like a large Ping-Pong paddle. I was worried, based on the way Paul had been carrying on. I thought the thing must have nails sticking out of it. He told me to drop my pants and bend over the chair. He said he was going to give me six whacks with the paddle. Considering some of punishment I had seen meted out in the pirate movies, six whacks with that funny-looking paddle would be waaaay better than fifty lashes with a "cat-o-nine-tails"!

I did as he told me, and bent over the chair and braced myself for some excruciating pain. The principal laid on the six whacks with the paddle and I'm thinking: *That wasn't so bad.* My dad's whippings were ten times worse than that, even the ones when I knew he wasn't really mad, but he had to go through the motions to make his point.

I didn't want the principal to think that he hadn't given me a good-enough thrashing and feel like he had to do it all over again, so I tried to shed a few tears.

He restated his regrets for having to do that and made me promise I wouldn't do any more fighting on the playground, which I readily agreed to. I kinda felt sorry for the guy; he was more upset about this incident than I was. It was all very confusing. My dad never showed any remorse when he gave me a whipping.

What really disillusioned me was the way Paul acted when he got his paddling. He was screaming, crying and carrying on like it was the end of the world. Either he got a worse beating than I did or the guy was really a wimp. Maybe he never got a whipping at his home and didn't know what a "real" paddling was.

I didn't want to feel disrespectful toward Paul, because I always thought of him as a tough kid. I knew when we fought, we were evenly matched. He was still waiting outside the school for me to come out. I just had to ask him what his story was, and why he reacted like he did.

He told me his strategy, "I figured, if I really yelled and cried a lot, maybe the principal would feel sorry for me and cut the punishment shorter." I thought about it for a while and came to the conclusion that *what he did was brilliant.* We thought alike! It restored the faith I once had in him.

I also filed that strategy of his about faking his emotions in my memory bank to use in a similar circumstance if the need ever arose again.

After I left the school grounds, I went into town to the store where my mom was and waited for her to get off work.

I reflected back on the unpleasant incident. All in all, I felt pretty good, having survived the traumatic event relatively unscathed. This was all behind me and my parents would never have to know because the principal said he wouldn't tell them . . . "this time."

The main thing I would definitely do differently if this scenario ever happened again: I would volunteer to be punished first instead of waiting my turn while someone else got their discipline. The waiting and my imagination caused me way more grief and worry than the actual punishment ever could.

I was in relatively good spirits on the way home. In fact, I was feeling a little cocky. I had just been sent to the principal's office for fighting, gotten a paddling (like the ones my brother warned me of when I started school) this whole affair was "a pretty big deal" in the general scope of things. I decided I would tell my other friends the next day in school about my experience.

When they heard the story with all the gory details I would probably be considered *a hero*.

When we got home, I went in the house and dropped off my books and went outside to start my chores. I was in the process of pumping water for the livestock when my dad approached me and told me to go into the washhouse and wait for him. He sounded mad, but *why*? I couldn't think of anything I had done wrong to make him angry. I hadn't shirked my duties around the farm lately. What could it be? If I could only come up with the problem, I could have an excuse ready when I was confronted. Here was that dilemma again . . . the waiting . . . the anticipation . . . the agony . . . *why me?*

Finally Dad showed up where I was told to wait, looked at me sternly and stated, "I understand you were fighting at school again, and this time you got a whipping from the principal." I was stunned and caught completely off guard thinking, *how did he know?*

My dad and mom both worked all day, the incident had just happened a couple of hours ago, the only people who knew what actually happened were the principal (he said he wouldn't tell, this time), Paul (I knew he wouldn't say anything), and me. Even if the principal changed his mind and decided to tell my parents, he couldn't have let them know that fast! We didn't have a telephone, and he couldn't have driven to our farm that quickly. My mom couldn't have found out either, as I went straight from school to the store where she worked and I was with her until we got home. It was impossible for him to know, but here I was being angrily confronted and he knew all the details. There was no use denying it . . . "I'm dead."

You remember my telling you the rule was to "never embarrass my Dad?" If I got into trouble, it was a direct reflection on him, and he didn't like that one bit!

My quickly formed plan was to admit to the crime and relate what had happened at school, emphasizing that I had already received a paddling as punishment. Surely the worst retribution I would get from my Dad would be just a good talking to! Boy, was that the world's greatest *underestimation* of the year.

I was relating the circumstances of the fight between Paul and me, the involvement of the playground teacher, and the ensuing trip to the principal's office. I hadn't even gotten to the paddling part yet and my dad was getting madder and madder by the minute. He was getting red in the face. He was *furious* (I hadn't seen him that angry in a long time).

I was scared to death. Then he suddenly said, "*Bend over that chair!*" His famed razor-strop miraculously appeared in his hand (to this day, I don't know where he had it hidden), and he then began to wail on me with that darn strop. That was, without doubt, the worst beating he ever administered to me. As he was smacking me he was saying he would have to go see my teacher and the principal and apologize for my behavior. While contemplating each of these embarrassing chores, he would increase the intensity of the whipping accordingly.

After the first couple of whacks I thought this would be a good time to initiate the strategy that Paul used with the principal earlier. I began to bawl and plead for mercy and begged him to stop, but after the fifth or sixth whack I had a feeling that this plan wasn't going to work. The bawling and begging quickly became genuine; it was getting out of hand. At the time, I didn't know which was going to give out first, my butt or Dad's swinging arm. So far my butt was running a distant second.

Finally after what seemed like hours (actually it was only a few minutes), Dad quit and abruptly turned and went into the house, I don't know what made him stop but I was sure glad he did.

My mom came out to the washhouse and said, "Let me see your behind." I pulled my pants down and she looked at the damage. She made warm compresses from towels and hot water. She told me to hold them on my butt for a while, and she then turned and marched into the house to confront my dad over the severity of the whipping.

I heard some loud discussions between the two of them over my situation. My dad was contending that the punishment fit the crime. My mom was arguing that the punishment was overkill. I remembered, at the time the word "overkill" seemed a little overstated, but I must admit that while I was getting punished the word "kill" did cross my mind as a possible outcome of the whipping.

I had mixed emotions about this whole event. I could see my dad's side. He had been publicly embarrassed and he had to go see the principal and the teacher to clean up my mess.

My mom was my hero. She took my side and tried to step in and mitigate the carnage, but . . . was that a wise thing to do, to confront my dad (in front of me) for doing something he thought was, the correct handling of a grievous act on my part?

I reluctantly came to the final conclusion that it was nobody's fault but mine. If I hadn't gotten into the fight with my friend Paul this whole situation could have been avoided. My parents wouldn't have had the argument and would still be speaking to each other, instead of employing the silent treatment demonstrated at the supper table that night.

I vowed I would do better from then on. I would try my best to not fight with Paul, or at least not get caught next time. I *almost* kept my vow over the next one-and-a-half years: Paul and I only got caught fighting twice more! I don't know what it was about our personalities; we were good friends for over two years. But sometimes we just had to test each other like two old roosters vying to see who was going to rule the roost.

The results of these ensuing conflicts had pretty much the same outcome as the first episode. On both occasions we were taken to the principal's office and with our past record intact, each visit ended with a paddling. The only exception was that the school had changed principals between the second and third incident. We thought we might catch a break with the new principal, but like I learned later, the penalty phase for violation of the law was administered by *precedence*. In our case we were "three strike" offenders.

The thing that puzzled me the most through all three of these episodes was that, on each occasion, my dad always knew about the offense before I would get home, and I could count on the same punishment to be waiting for me. As usual the home whipping was always worse than the school paddling. Just goes to show you, you don't need a college education to be an effective disciplinarian.

To this day, nearly sixty-two years later, I don't know how he did it, even my mom didn't know. "*How did he know?*"

The only conclusion I could logically come up

with was that he had "Ant Intelligence." You know that's where this one lonely ant (the scout) breaks into your house, travels down a long hallway, goes through three bedrooms, down a flight of stairs, through your living room, into your kitchen, through your door to the garage and finds one *little piece* of dog food that accidently fell out of the bowl. Within a *very few minutes* 10,000 of his buddies follow his same trail and are consuming the dog-food, en masse. Just like my dad, they didn't have a telephone, telegraph, or even a Navy flag semaphore. *Think what has to happen here.* The first ant (the scout) has to let the rest of the gang know he's found something. *How does he do that?* . . . Without going all the way back the exact way he had come. I can sorta understand how he could follow the same trail (it's probably got to do with his scent, or bread crumbs . . . or something similar).

Once he gets back to the main party he has to convince them he's found something worthy of the long grueling trip back. You would think that would take some time to convince everyone (they may even have to vote on it). But, as fast as these guys get there after the discovery, it's safe to say *he doesn't have time to make that round-trip—that fast*, unless the guy they send out (the scout) had trained with the Olympian Jesse Owens.

There has to be some other form of communication

which is . . . "Ant Intelligence!" This had to be what my dad had. There is no other explanation!

Why couldn't this "intelligence" be bottled or put into pill form? Think of the possibilities. The military benefits alone are mind-numbing. Relatively thinking and put into perspective, if you consider the size of the ants (compared to humans) and the distance the first ant (the scout) had to travel to find that *tiny-little bit* of dog food and to send the message back to his buddies. Comparatively, a human (Army scout) could summon a whole Army from halfway around the world in a matter of minutes . . . *without a walkie-talkie*! Wow! I wondered if anyone else had thought of this infinite potential. Hmmmmm? There must be millions of other applications if you just put your mind to it.

As an afterthought, what if the ant (the scout) sends the message, and convinces the tribe that the prize at the end of the long trip is—*in fact*—worth the effort of the trek and, lo and behold, when they get there the treasure doesn't measure up to the horde's expectations, *you see where I'm going with this?* What do they do to the scout that made the snap judgment as to the quality of the find? I'm sure after all the trouble of the mass migration that the disappointment of the group is not going to be satisfied with *just* a change of his job description. This guy is going to be in real trouble.

I am going to pay more attention to ants from now

on. I always thought when you saw a large number of ants around a small bit of food; at first glance they all seemed to be frantic to get at the food, when in reality I'll lay a wager *it's a riot*. Next time, I'm going to stick around until they all leave and I bet I'll find one lone ant (the scout) firmly attached to a tiny cross.

Chapter Twenty-Three

On the Job Training

Creative minds have always been known to survive any kind of bad training.
— Anna Freud

I was finishing up the eighth grade and about to start high school. My dad really wanted me to be a farmer and follow in his footsteps. None of the other five children, with the exception of my older sister, Evelyn, who married a farmer, turned out to be farmers either, so I was his last hope.

Dad filled in for the janitor at the school, when the real janitor was on vacation, so he had time to ask around about high school courses that would steer me into farming. He found that certain biology classes were tuned to the farming industry. He suggested I take a class in, animal husbandry. Animal husbandry? What the heck was that? At first mention, it sounded like counseling for an immature bull who was conflicted about his role as the dominant male in his relationship with a young heifer. Later, I found the class was about the breeding and caring for farm animals, which sounded a little more interesting.

Dad was showing me the intricacies of raising row crops of all kinds. He even offered me a deal: he would buy me my own yearling steer. For you city folks, a steer is a young bull with his male reproductive capacity irretrievably altered. I could feed-out the new steer until it was ready for market and I could keep all the profits. The only part of that last conversation I heard was "profits." Being the ever-attentive capitalist, in training, I was thinking, *that's a heck of a deal.*

Part of my chores were feeding and watering all the stock, anyway. It really wouldn't be any extra work, on my part. Then I get to sell the steer and keep all the profits?

I could buy whatever I wanted. This just sounds too good to be true—what's the catch here? As expected, my dad dropped the bomb. He said I should take the profit and reinvest it by buying two more yearlings for next year.

"When do I get to stop this cycle and spend the money?" I asked

He said, "That's entirely up to you. It will be your calf. You can handle the raising and selling of the steer

223

anyway you want," *but*—if it was *him* (here comes the guilt trip) *he* would keep rolling the profit into more cattle each year. When I accumulated a certain amount of animals, I could start breeding them until I had a small herd.

On paper this sounded good, but the downside was, I would have to make a long-term commitment. First of all, I wasn't sure I wanted the responsibility of a "small herd" of cattle to care for. Secondly; I was about to give up my paper route because I still had four years of education left and I wanted to play sports in high school. And thirdly; I just wanted to have some fun!

After the trip to Idaho, I had gotten a taste of the world outside Nebraska, and I liked it. I definitely did not want to be a farmer. This was another "poser!" Not wanting to hurt Dad's feelings, and knowing he was doing what he thought was best for me, I agreed in principle—I would give it a try.

He told me the rich farmer, whom we rented our farm from, had some young "white-faced" steers he was getting ready to sell to the feedlots. White-faced meant that the cow was either purebred, or had dominating Herford genes in its bloodline.

The purpose of the feedlots was to take the cattle off pasture and put them on a grain-supplemented diet for about five to six months. During that interval, the steer increases in weight from about 800 pounds to approximately 1,250 pounds, the ideal market weight.

The grain diet is what gives the marbling of fat and the good taste of Nebraska beef. My buying the young cow at this stage of its life meant I would be replacing the concept of the feedlot and eliminating the middleman with, hopefully, a higher profit point.

Dad said we could barter the purchase by working on the guy's farm in exchange for the price of the steer.

The following week we were going over to pick out the steer. At that time we would agree to what kind of work and how much we would have to do to complete our share of the barter. We were doing this together, and it sounded like fun. My dad worked all the time. I very rarely saw him idle, that was another reason I didn't want to be a farmer.

The following Monday we got up early and drove over to our landlord's place (his first name was Weldon). He lived about another three miles farther from town past our farm. He took us out to look at the small herd of cattle he was getting ready to ship to the feedlot. My dad reminded him of the bargain they had arranged the previous week.

Dad told Weldon that I had consented to raising the steer on my own until it was market "prime." Dad was beaming with pride that I had decided to take on some responsibility and learn the trade, so to speak.

Weldon shook my hand and said he was also proud of me, that he had always liked me and knew I was going to amount to something.

They discussed the terms of the barter and what the resulting work requirement on our part was to be. Dad would plow a forty-acre section of the landlord's land (using the landlord's tractor and plow); in addition to some extra chores he would perform, as time permitted.

In the meantime, Weldon would bring the steer over in one of his trucks when he was ready to haul the rest of his steers to the feedlot, which should be in the next couple of weeks. He told my dad that if he delivered the steer before dad had a chance to do the plowing and other agreed chores not to worry about it, he would trust him to complete his part of the bargain. They shook hands and the deal was done.

Now came time to pick out the steer. Dad said it was my steer so I should pick out the one I wanted, but to make sure I got a good one. OK . . . *no pressure*. Other than verifying that they had the correct amount of legs and all the other standard appendages I was pretty much at a loss as to what else to look for.

I didn't have enough time to get to know the animals to be able to judge their personalities . . . what should I do? I turned to my dad and said, "You are a much better judge of beef cattle than I could ever be, would you do me the honor and pick one out? I'll trust your decision!"

Dad puffed out his chest, gave the landlord a big grin and said, "I'd be happy to, son." He then walked in among the herd, ran his hands over six or eight animals, stood back contemplating, then circled the bunch and finally pointed at one of the steers and said, "We'll take that one." Weldon had a pair of crooked pliers and a tag. He walked over to the animal and clamped the tag to its ear and we started home.

On the way home, I asked Dad, "What were you looking for when you picked out the steer?

He replied, "I looked into their eyes, to see if they might have the malady "pink eye." I also looked at their confirmation, and lastly I felt the firmness of the flesh around the back and the rump. All these areas will determine what price the beef will bring when they go to market. You have to feed them all the same, but if you start with a good sound animal, you will get the most reward at the end."

I answered, "Sounds good to me!" (All the while secretly thinking, *that he had picked the ugliest one in the bunch . . . it had a bent ear*).

I also asked him, "Why did you decide to perform all the labor for the barter yourself? I thought we were going to work together."

He said, "I didn't think it was right for you to have

to do any of the work since I said I would buy the steer as my part of the bargain."

I really appreciated the gesture and I told him so. When we got home we started to build a pen to keep the new steer separate from the other livestock because he was going to be on a separate diet.

A couple of weeks later, here came Weldon driving one of his trucks with my steer in the back. He backed up to the new pen we had just built, dropped the loading ramp attached to the back of his truck, and *my* new steer (bent ear and all) calmly walked down the ramp and right into his new home. Piece of cake. Dad must have picked out a smart one.

For the rest of that year, Dad began to include me on even more of the "behind the scenes" workings of the farm. You are probably wondering why I wasn't more involved in the intricacies of farm work. I was old enough—why I didn't do more things other than the mundane, brain-dead chores that had been expected of me. You have to understand, Dad was the type of guy who liked to do most things himself. He was a perfectionist. I don't know if he just didn't trust me or if he just wanted to make sure everything was done right. With the financial condition we were in, there was no margin for error. He was making this last-ditch effort to convince me that farming was a noble, and at times a profitable, venture.

He often told me, "You can always count on the land to provide!" He was right, to an extent. All in all I was a happy kid. I had great a family, a few *good* friends, and we always had plenty to eat. At that time in my life my motto was, "What else do you need?"

Getting back to my involvement in dad's daily routines, some of the necessary chores were very interesting. One of the more memorable was the time Dad took me with him when we had our milk-cow bred. This cow was my favorite milk-cow, named Bess. She was the Jersey breed, the one with the big brown eyes and the floppy ears, the one I told you about riding.

She was slowing down on her milk production. This meant she had been too long without having borne a calf. If you wait too long between breeding a dairy cow, their milk quantity tends to diminish, the terminology is: She is "starting to dry up." When this happens, you have to have her bred again. When she gives birth to a new calf, the whole milk-giving process recycles and returns to normal.

My dad seemed to be a lot more apprehensive about me witnessing this *shotgun wedding* than I was. I guess this was the farmer's adaptation of having the dreaded *sex talk* with your son. The process of getting your cow bred is not like joining your local "Lonely Hearts Club" to find a compatible soul mate. You have to use what's available—it's not like the two cows have to date for a while. The only endearing quality you need from the male participant, in this case a bull is sperm. The sperm can be reassigned to the cow by one of two ways: It can be done "au naturel." This method involves some foreplay, which is a lot more fun for the participants, but is not 100 percent foolproof. The success of the mating depends a lot on the *experience* of the bull. He has to know what he is doing, as the saying goes.

The cow's contribution to the transfer of sperm is minimal. She has to be willing, but in the grand scheme of things she just has to be ready, and *there*! According to Dad, the success of this mating depended almost entirely on timing. The bull has to do all the important work. If he gets too excited and is too quick, or if he is too slow and the cow loses interest, the whole episode is a flop.

I don't mean to make this sound sexist, but that's a lot of pressure on a dumb animal, especially a guy animal. That reminds me of a joke I heard. There are two bulls standing on a hill, with a herd of cows below them. The young bull says, "Let's run down there and make love to one of those cows." The other older bull says, "Let's walk down and make love to *all* of them!" This is the experience factor we were talking about, and puts everything into perspective about the "au naturel" method of breeding livestock.

Contemplating the experience factor of the bull,

over time I have given this perplexing subject more thought and I came to this conclusion: If a "good" bull is an experienced one, and they are the preferred sort used in the breeding process, how does a *rookie* bull become experienced? Another poser: He can't just go down to the local "Bovine Brothel," plop down a few ears of corn and have some loose heifer give him on-the-job training, can he?

This kind of selective treatment of these young animals could lead to the delinquency and ill temper of these frustrated juveniles! With a surly attitude like that they could end up in a Tijuana bull ring . . . *Ole!*

Witnessing the breeding act and the humiliation that my animal friend, Bess, had to endure was disgusting. Her exploitation was demeaning and just downright ugly. Also being an observer to the complete fool the bull made of himself (he acted just like an animal), I felt like I needed to go home and take a bath.

We didn't discuss the churlish event on the way home. I asked dad some pertinent questions regarding the mating later that evening. He replied, he "didn't want to talk about it right now," so we never did.

The second method of transferring sperm is a lot more effective and foolproof. The sperm is removed from the bull—artificially (I'll leave that to your imagination) and placed—again artificially (you figure it out)—into the cow. That's it. The mating is consummated. The two participants don't even have to be introduced; the whole thing is very impersonal, and as far as I'm concerned, *inhumane*. It's like two little kids being put into a playpen but someone took out all the toys! It just ain't right.

Another thing my dad wanted me to help him with was cleaning out the corncrib. This chore is tackled in the springtime because the corncrib is empty after all the corn has been fed to the livestock over the winter. That sounded like a rather easy, pleasant chore and it met my usual basic criteria, "How hard can that be?"

Dad had a bad habit when he described an upcoming event. He only told you about the good part of a chore. I soon found out the *downside*.

I figured the way this would go was, we would each take a broom and a shovel and we would work together and have the place cleaned out slicker-than-a-whistle in no time flat. Then I could get onto something fun.

Instead of handing me a broom he gave me a *club*!

"What the heck is this for?" I asked.

Dad said, "The club is for the rats."

What he failed to mention earlier was, there have been *rats* (lots of rats) living in the corncrib, all winter, with an unlimited supply of food. With the corn gone they had to be dealt with because there was no telling what they would start to feed on, now that their main food source was exhausted. I asked, "how come you didn't tell me that part?"

His retort was, "Killing a few rats is a relatively simple thing to accomplish, so don't worry about it."

There were no places for the rats to hide inside the empty crib. Corncribs don't have windows, so even though it was daylight outside, when the door was shut it was almost completely dark inside.

Dad gave me instructions as to how this confrontation was going to take place. He was going to open the door to the crib and go in with our "piece of crap" flashlight and a club and start the bedlam. My job was to stand in the open doorway and keep them from escaping through their only means of egress. The final act of my participation was to smack'em when they tried to get out. The only source of light, to augment the almost *useless* flashlight, was through the open door,

I'm thinking, "*This might not be so bad. How hard could it be to knockout a few little rats?*" It might actually be fun to vent a little pent-up hostility. I said to my father, "Don't worry, Dad, I got your back!"

Everything is a go. I have my instructions. Dad turns to me and says, "I'm going in" and in he goes with flashlight in one hand and a club in the other (what a guy). I'm at my post in the doorway, my feet are spread at just the right distance to give the rats the least amount of opening to get through, I've got both hands on the club . . . "let the mayhem begin!"

Once inside, Dad shines his light around and starts whaling away on the rodents. I hear the *thuds* and the *screeching* of the wounded vermin. Every once in a while I can catch a glimpse of the rats in the shadows—*holy crap*! These weren't the little rodents I had expected to see, not like the ones we would catch in traps in the barn. These things looked more like bloated beavers! They were so fat from being on welfare all winter they could hardly run and they were everywhere!

To put it into modern terms (so you can appreciate the magnitude of this scenario), compared to what I was witnessing, the worst scenes from the evil rodent movie "Willard" would be likened to a Mickey Mouse cartoon. It was a creepy thing to watch the chaotic disarray of all these fat rats frantically trying to escape, with no place to go, and my dad swinging his club as fast as he can. *The passion . . . the pandemonium.*

One of the critters spotted the doorway and started towards me. I braced myself for the onslaught and started swinging my club at him as he got into my range. I connected with some part of its body and he went rolling away from me. I was glad the thing wasn't armed because it was big enough to hit back!

The critter I had just pummeled quickly got to its feet, looking no worse for wear, then went and told some of his friends that this was the way out, and here came six or eight of the beady-eyed creatures with teeth gnashing coming at me at a *full waddle*.

I quickly sized up the situation, realizing I had just given the last rodent my best shot and he shook it off like nothing had happened. What good was I going to be against the full charge of the "rat" brigade? Discretion quickly triumphed over valor and I deserted my post and ran.

Dad, seeing a few rats escape through the doorway and me not there, quickly ran out of the corncrib and shut the door before any more could break out. He came over to me, shaking his head in disgust. "Why did you leave the doorway?"

Drawing on all my knowledge of military tactics I had gleaned from comic books and the war movie at the last free show on Wednesday night, I answered, "Dad, they overran my position and I had to fall back to a better defensive area."

He said, "If you would have just stood your ground they probably would have turned around because they were afraid of you."

I replied, "I don't think so. It had all the earmarks of one of those Jap suicide *banzai* charges they showed on then newsreels. I think they would have gone for my throat!"

He looked at me, still shaking his head, and said,

"There are still a lot of them left in there. I have to have the door open to see. Got any ideas?"

I suggested, " I'll go get Spunk (my dog) and send him in." I figured that since he could almost hold his own with the local coyotes, if they didn't gang up on him, he ought to be able to take out a few obese rodents.

Dad said, "I don't think that's a good idea. He might get bit and infection would surely set in. It also wouldn't be good if he bit one of them because rats carry diseases."

Now I love and respect my Dad and value his opinions and his courage, *bu*t sometimes he just gets his priorities all screwed up. He is reluctant to risk the health of the family dog to the dangers of the disease and pestilence caused by rats, but he is willing to place his only "last born" son in harm's way, making me susceptible to the same perils, knowing all along he is too old to *make another one*, if something should happen to me. It just ain't right!

After thinking about our problem, Dad walked over to the machinery/junk shed and came back with an old wooden door he had taken off one of the outbuildings for repair, when he had the time.

We went back to the corncrib and he explained the new plan. He was going to go back in after the rats and the door would still have to be open so he could see

(I'm cringing, God, he is going to make me guard that doorway again). But this time would be different. He placed the old door turned on its side, so it only covered the lower portion of the doorway opening. I was to hold the door in place. This way, the critters couldn't get out, Dad still had light from the half- open doorway and I had something substantial between me and the rats . . . *that's the way to solve problems.*

After Dad was satisfied he had brained all the critters, we got two shovels and went out to the edge of a plowed field (where the ground was softer), dug a big deep hole and buried over thirty *big* rats. I logged another mark on the negative side of the ledger—*against* the virtues of farm life.

A momentous juncture in our daily lives was taking place. As I mentioned earlier, in chapter seventeen, we were finally getting our farmhouse and grounds wired for *electricity*! This was going to open up a whole new environment involving our living conditions. We were finally moving into the twentieth century.

This modern improvement meant television, decent interior and exterior lighting, outside lighting so I could finally see to go to the outhouse at night, possibility of a decent cooking stove for my mom, refrigeration, an electric radio (it was going to be great not having to haul those heavy car batteries for the radio back and forth to the garage for charging), and lastly a vast array of electrical appliances and, most importantly to me, *electrically powered toys.*

What an *electrifying* time in all our lives.

The new Sears, Roebuck catalog arrived the following week. I was shopping through the catalog with a whole new purpose. The inevitability of electricity opened up a lot more possibilities.

I spotted a new Lionel electric train set. None of my friends had one and it looked like it would be a lot of fun. The set I liked had a steam locomotive, just like the one that came past our house every day. The engine had a headlight, an authentic whistle, and you could put little pellets in the smokestack so it would actually puff smoke, just like the real thing.

The coal tender had the train whistle built-in. The set came with a caboose, boxcar, and two automated cars: a refrigerated milk car with loading dock and a flatcar loaded with logs that automatically rolled onto a dock. The layout consisted of two oval tracks with two switches, a lighted depot, an operating crossing gate and miscellaneous signs.

I sent off to Lionel's home office in New York for a complete detailed catalog showing all their packaged layouts.

I had about a month and a half left of feeding my steer and he would be ready for market. One day I casually asked Dad, "About how much money would I be making on the sale of my steer?"

"The market fluctuates daily, but it has been holding steady for the past weeks, he answered. Your steer is looking good." He guessed at the profit after, of course, deducting the cost of all the feed and any medication I had used while raising my steer. He said, "When all is said and done, you'll probably have enough profit to buy two more yearling calves, like we planned. Why do you want to know?"

"Oh nothing . . . just wondering," I answered.

For the next few weeks every time I went to feed my steer, I imagined seeing a big **L** branded on his hindquarters (**L** . . . for *Lionel train set*).

The profit I expected to get from the sale was almost exactly the price of the train set, but maybe not enough for all the accessories I wanted. I was starting to regret letting Dad pick out that particular steer. I kept thinking, *I could have gotten a lot more for him if he didn't have that darn bent ear.*

I made up my mind. I was going to *magically* turn that animal into the electric train set I had always wanted. Now that I had made that decision, how was I going to break the news to Dad and convince him to go along with it?

That task was going to take the full power of my creative thinking. Thankfully I had some time to work out the details. I agonized over different reasons I could come up with that were logical and believable scenarios for the decision I was contemplating. One solution I dwelled on and thought had some merit was: I could tell Dad that I had been sneezing a lot lately while feeding my steer—maybe I was becoming allergic to cattle and should get out of the business! The more I played that concept over in my mind, the more I knew it wouldn't fly. Why would I just be allergic "just" to that animal? None of the other cattle ever bothered me, and why just now at sale time? Nope, that one wouldn't work.

I had another medical malady solution hatching in my brain. By my dad's own admission, prices and conditions in the market fluctuated daily, coupled with the fact that there was the possibility of the cattle I would be accumulating over time coming down with some life-threatening disease. It was all just too much pressure for someone my age—I'd probably contract an ulcer before I graduated, therefore I probably shouldn't be in this kind of business.

Pondering this scheme, I didn't think this excuse would fly either. I had to be careful of espousing these health malfunctions too much or I might end up on the receiving end of one of my parents' undesirable home remedies: The sulphur and molasses treatment, the dreaded mustard plaster, or Dad's turpentine cure. They could even come up with some new type of organic torture. This problem was going to require a lot more thought and planning. *I had to have that train set!*

The time was fast approaching when I had to sell my steer. I still hadn't come up with a good-enough excuse, so I went to Mom with my dilemma. I told her, "I don't want to hurt Dad's feelings, but I just don't want to be a farmer for the rest of my life and furthermore I didn't *really* promise him I would *definitely* carry this steer-raising experiment past this initial phase. I told him I would give it a try."

But conversely, I didn't want him to think I was going back on our agreement. But he said it would be my steer, my responsibility, and my profit from the sale to do with what I wanted . . . *he did say that.*

"Mom, what should I do?" I asked.

She looked me in the eye, smiled and said, "Just tell him the truth. He'll understand." Now there was a novel concept that never occurred to me. "Do you really think that will work?"

She answered, "It's better than you trying to make up some cock-and-bull story, and expecting him to swallow it. Besides—*you aren't very good at it.*" Mom can really come up with some great solutions at times. I told her I would try it sometime in the next couple of days, when the opportunity was right.

The opportunity presented itself on a Saturday morning. We had just finished a great breakfast, and

Dad was always more amiable on a full stomach. I helped Mom clean up the dishes and joined Dad on the front porch. I related my feelings about farming as a vocation, the decision I had made about disposing of the profits from the sale of my steer. I showed him the catalog with the Lionel train set and waited for his reaction.

I could see in his face that he was *grudgingly* becoming resigned to the fact that none of his progeny were ever going to follow in his chosen profession, with the exception of my oldest sister, Evelyn.

He was very quiet. I was apprehensive. I didn't know just how he was going to react to the news. He said, "I appreciate your being straight with me. This train set, any idea how much electricity it will take to run it?" he asked.

"I have no idea, but it couldn't be much, it isn't that big." I answered,

He inquired, "Where do you plan to set the thing up?"

I told him I hadn't thought that far ahead. *This conversation was going much better than I envisioned it.*

Dad said, "Your mother is not going to like it sitting where she has to work and clean around it." He thought awhile longer. "If you are going to get it *we* need to set it up right." Did I hear him right? He said *we . . . we* were going to set it up right!

Dad asked to see the catalog again. There was a picture (with dimensions) of the track layout, and he started planning. His solution: We were going to get a 4-foot x 8-foot sheet of plywood and lay it on the dining room table. We didn't use it all that much anyway (only on special occasions), and all the track would be attached to the wood. He was even picking out extra accessories (which I hoped he was going to buy), like scenery, more signs, buildings, and so on.

Dad was really starting to get into the spirit of this project. He said, "If we attach everything to the sheet of plywood, then when *we* aren't playing with it *we* can slide the whole thing under the guest bed."

The project of raising and selling the steer was turning into something I was beginning to look forward to. It was going to be a joyous occasion for all, except for the steer of course. I didn't believe this was going to be a memorable occasion for him.

The buying and the setup of the train was one of the few things my dad and I were really going to do together other than hunting. I may have to rely on this *truth-tellin'* thing more often if it turns out like this.

The sale came off as planned, the profit margin was as expected, and the ordering of the train with all the accessories was a joint effort by both of us. Dad had his usual poker face on and wouldn't let on that, in fact, he was almost as excitedly anticipating the arrival of the train set as I was.

The assembly and creation of our miniature railroad community, established on a sheet of plywood, inspired a newfound camaraderie for quite some time. It was one of the rare times I saw my Dad participate in something frivolous just for the fun of it. Something that didn't have to produce a result from a hard day's work.

CHAPTER TWENTY-FOUR

Up in Smoke

I tried marijuana once. I did not inhale.
— William J. Clinton

The terrain in our county was mostly flat, with various agricultural row crops and pastures laid out in sections like a patchwork quilt. These sections were bordered with various kinds of trees, mostly perennial hardwoods.

The farmers of our era learned valuable lessons from the near-catastrophic farming mistakes back in the Thirties. The devastating Dust-Bowl scenario had played out in the past because the farmers of yore unwittingly cut down *all* the trees and plowed under every available square inch of arable soil to afford themselves the greatest amount of tillable land. Consequently, the relentless Plains winds literally blew the topsoil away.

The remedial solution was bordering each section

with planted trees to quell the fury of the winds. This, coupled with sensible growing practices and systematic crop rotations, resulted in the rebuilding of the top soil.

In addition to the intentionally planted flora, we had many various weeds that grew wild around the edges of agricultural fields, creek beds and railroad tracks.

It was a constant battle to control this persistent parasitic growth from choking out the productive plants. The most prolific weed was hemp. Also mixed in with the hemp was similar-looking plant called stinging nettles.

While hunting rabbits one day, I had to go to the bathroom (number two). If you are wondering why I continually refer to the category of bodily waste excretion as a number, it was required in our grade-school classrooms. If you needed to go the bathroom you would hold up either one or two fingers, denoting the method of waste emission you planned to expel . . . you figure out which is which.

I digress. Not having anything handy to wipe with, I tried using the large, soft-appearing leaves of the stinging nettle family . . . *bad idea*. The term *stinging* is grossly understated. The ensuing pain, itch and rash that resulted from my misguided application caused me many days of conducting my daily activities in the upright position.

Anyway, back to the weeds, namely the hemp

variety. The farmers were doggedly trying to eradicate this unwanted foliage by any means appropriate.

The railroad company periodically would go down the railways with a self-propelled railcar that had big fuel tanks on it (it was a gigantic blowtorch). Their job was to burn back the tenacious hemp weed a good distance from the tracks.

This rolling torch would be followed by another self-propelled section car that carried a few workers called section hands. Their job was to make sure the fire didn't spread too far.

The railroad company had many section gangs, manned by local and regional labor, that performed many different functions, i.e., minor repair of the railbed, the wooden ties, and the tracks themselves. For some strange reason, the weed-burning gang's duties always seemed to be the *choicest* job to have. There was constantly a waiting list among the workers to serve on this particular crew and no one seemed to know why. All you baby boomers know why, don't you? Burning hemp . . . happy workers (see where I'm going with this?). Can we all say *cannabis*, boys and girls?

If the people of these destitute rural Midwest counties had only known what kind of a cash crop they were doing their best to destroy, the Depression era would never have lasted as long, at least in rural Nebraska.

As kids, when we were first experimenting with smoking we couldn't *legally* buy cigarettes until we were eighteen years of age, but even if we had been allowed we couldn't have afforded them at 20 cents a pack.

However, anyone could buy the 'fixings' (little cigarette paper packets you would use to roll whatever you wanted to smoke into a cigarette), but not the tobacco. You still had to be eighteen. (The most popular tobacco, *Bull Durham* brand, came in a little bag with a drawstring on it.)

Without the real stuff, we kids had to innovate. We tried to smoke corn silk (the stringy stuff on the end of the cob that turns brown when it dries out), coffee grounds, used tobacco from old cigarette butts, and so on. Luckily, or unluckily (depending on your point of view) we were still ignorant about the hemp.

CHAPTER TWENTY-FIVE

Hostile Invasion

Our relations with the Indians have been
governed chiefly by treaties and trade, or war
and subjugation.

— Nelson A. Miles

You remember my saying that the only way to make a living in these local counties was either by farming or working for the railroad?

The regular railway workers (section hands, laborers composed of mostly local and regional folks) made up the various section gangs, those handling the minor repair work on the rail-lines themselves. The real heavy-lifting, which entailed replacing or adding sections of the entire roadbed and track, was accomplished with a Native American work force mostly provided by the Navajo tribe.

This work force traveled as a whole separate train

system; the engine, tender, caboose, several flatcars with heavy equipment including replacement material and parts, bunkhouse cars with restrooms and showers, and a cooking/dining car.

At rare, unscheduled intervals this repair train would come through our town and stay for various durations, depending on the scope and vicinity of work needed.

The city fathers and businessmen were alerted a few days in advance when this work-train was coming so they could stock up on supplies that would be consumed by this large work contingent. Most of the business owners looked to this visit with great anticipation because the railroad company was going to spend quite a lot of money resupplying their stores and living supplies and equipment while they were in town.

In addition, the working Indians themselves would spend money on various personal items not provided by the railroad company. The only *restricted* item forbidden to the Indians was alcohol. At that time, there was a federal law banning the sale of alcohol (in any form) to any Native American. Other than that, the sky was the limit. It was a festive time for the merchants while the train was in town. The exception to the anticipated visit was *the local residents*! Generally, the local folks didn't like this invasion of their tranquility. Some had experienced this incursion before with mixed reactions; for others this would be their first encounter.

The railroad company parked the lodging railcars on the edge of town. Each workday they would hook up the engine and tender to the flatcars, which contained the equipment, tools and materials. The Indian workers would occupy the personnel cars and they would proceed to the work area.

At night, after their return, some of the Indian workers would eat in the railway cookhouses and some would eat at the local establishments. The Indians were usually tired after the long days and bedded down early in their bunkhouse railcars. This schedule prevailed during the week, but on the weekend when they were not working, the Indians liked to "roam" (I don't know if they were looking for buffalo or what,) you would see them walking everywhere in town and the surrounding countryside.

Some Indians spoke broken English, but most spoke only their native tongue. They were usually very private, quiet people and didn't mingle well with the local population. Human nature being what it is, some folks were afraid of what they might do, what they might steal or what harm they might inflict on the populace.

The townsfolk started doing things they had never done before, like locking their doors and windows (those that actually had locks), putting their chickens and domestic animals up during the weekend, and making sure they knew where their children were at all times.

I happened to be in high school when this latest migration came through and it was fun to contemplate all these "wild" Indians roaming around. Being the ever-inquisitive youngsters that we were, we would try to interact with them, with mixed results.

I and some of my older friends managed to meet and isolate a couple of younger braves who could speak fairly good English and we talked with them for some time. We asked them questions like where their tribe lives, how they liked working for the railroad, and if they still wore war paint. You know, the *real important* information.

One of the main topics we were curious about was why they couldn't buy firewater (liquor or beer). They told us that some of their brethren got kinda' crazy when they drank booze so it wasn't allowed on or around the train, but now and again a few of them would find a way to get a couple of bottles and have a little private party. They said it was fun.

My friends and I could identify with their plight: we weren't allowed to buy or consume alcohol either, but once in a while we would find someone to procure a couple of bottles for us and have ourselves a little party too and it *was* fun.

The more we thought about it, the more we felt it just wasn't right that these hard-working fellas weren't allowed to have a little enjoyment after a hard week's work.

A plot was forming. . . .

I and three of my friends were gathered one particular evening of the week, which was a Wednesday, the only evening other than Saturday night when the businesses stay open later (past six o'clock).

This was one of the nights that the rural farmers would come to town to let off a little steam and pick up supplies. We as underage "townies" had trouble getting locals to buy us some adult beverages—too many people in town knew us. But we could usually find some inebriated farmer who would help us out. Therefore we had a few regulars we could always count on.

We didn't have any money, so we went to some of our esteemed high-school alumni who worked for the railroad on the aforementioned section gangs. These guys usually had some discretionary funds earmarked for a good cause and we told them our plan.

We wanted to raise enough money between Wednesday and Saturday night to buy several cases of beer. There were about twenty-five to thirty Indian workers on the work train. There were 24 bottles of beer in a case, so if we got at least five cases that should be enough to give the braves the start of a nice little party.

Little did we know that there was animosity between the regular section gangs and the Indian work crew. (I never knew just why that was but, for our purpose, it didn't matter.) This dislike was just the motivation we needed. They thought it would be a good joke to play on the Indians and maybe hassle the Railroad Company a little too. The local section gang friends, with the money, were committed to the idea but none of us were twenty-one, so all we needed was someone of age to buy the beer. It wasn't unusual for the farmers to take a couple of cases home with them on Wednesday and Saturday nights to last for the rest of the week.

We would have to spread out our purchases so as not to draw attention to us. We would buy a portion of the beer this night (Wednesday) and the rest Saturday night. We also would have to have two or three people buy it so it wouldn't look suspicious with one person buying that large a quantity of beer.

Our plan: we would buy two cases this night. One of my friends volunteered to store them until Saturday (in an old unused shed behind his house). We would have to buy the rest Saturday and then figure out how we were going to distribute it to the tribe. *This was really going to be fun!*

We talked to one of our buying sources and got a commitment from him to purchase two cases this night and contacted another source to purchase three more on Saturday as planned. Everything was a go until one of my conspiratorial friends asked a very important question:

"Are we going to get into trouble for this?" After all, it was a federal law we were planning to break.

We thought about it for a while and decided the only people actually breaking the law were the three farmers who were purchasing the beer. We hadn't told them what we were planning to do with the beer. I'm sure they thought we were just going to have a big party. Other than me and my friends, the only other guys involved were the ones putting up the money and we were sure they wouldn't say anything or they could get in trouble with the Railroad Company. All in all, we thought we were reasonably safe from discovery and the risk was worth the adventure. This one could go down in Valparaiso's annuals of history as *the* best-planned enterprise *ever*. We all shook hands . . . *We were committed!*

On Saturday afternoon, we contacted the two Indians we had talked to earlier in the week and told them of our plan of getting them the beer. They were excited about the anticipated revelry later that night. They asked, "How much beer are you going to bring and how much is it going to cost us?

We looked at each other quizzically. We told the two Indians to wait a few minutes as we had to discuss something and we moved off to the side where they couldn't hear us. Our scheming little group was always looking for ways to pick up a quick buck and it was tempting to take the free beer, paid for by the railroad workers, and resell it to the Indians. But we agreed that would be pushing the envelope too far. After all, this whole idea was hatched because we felt the Indians were being exploited and taken advantage of so if we did the same thing it would be a little hypocritical of us.

We went back to the Indians and told them there would be no charge to them, to just consider the gift as a gesture of friendship between the white man and our Indian brothers (sort of a "peace treaty").

The Indians were really happy and excited; they shook our hands and thanked us. We made arrangements to meet them at their campsite after it got dark. One of my friends borrowed a pickup truck to make the delivery.

All that was left was to make contact with the two farmers who were to purchase the other three cases later that evening, and get them the money . . . *This was coming together beautifully*!

We picked up the three cases, just recently purchased, went by for the two cases we bought on Wednesday, and off we went to rendezvous with the redskins. The transfer went smoothly—no one saw us. All we had to do now was wait for the *fruits of our labor to develop*—not knowing for sure what to expect.

About ten o'clock that evening, things started popping. We noticed some bonfires outside the train cars at the campsite. We began to hear a lot of laughter and a few whoops and hollers coming from that area. Soon they had the drums out and the dancing around the fires began. The revelry got louder and louder as more Indians were participating.

Hearing the commotion, people were coming out of the beer joints and other places of business to see what was happening. The residents peeked out of their houses and the townsfolk that were out started to huddle together.

Someone in the crowd said that the sound of the revelry reminded him of a John Wayne movie he had recently seen, and added, "The Indians in that movie sounded just like this group, just before they . . . *attacked the white settlers!*" Needless to say the folks were getting antsy and a little concerned. Being one of the white settlers, I felt we had them outnumbered, so we stayed together and just observed until about midnight, when things started to calm down. Soon the drums stopped and the fires were put out and once again everything was all quiet on the Midwestern front.

The next day a lot of the local people congregated at the Railroad Company's depot and encouraged the telegraph operator to send a complaint to those in charge of this Indian repair crew. They didn't want a recurrence of last night's incident.

On Monday, a representative from the Railroad came to town to get to the bottom of the disturbance.

He found out that someone had provided the Indians with alcohol and interrogated the owners of the two local beer joints to see if they could shed some light on the crime. The bar owners couldn't recall anyone purchasing a large amount of beer.

The Railroad detective spent a couple of days longer in town investigating the misdeed and came up with nothing. Nobody that was in on the plot talked. I guess we covered our tracks pretty well.

From then on, when the Indian work crew came through town, by request of the town leaders, they parked their sleeping cars farther outside of the city limits. I don't know if we hurt or harmed relations with the Indians. I guess it depends on whom you are asking!

You are probably wondering why I would admit to being part of a scheme as serious as this. The good thing about writing a memoir at the age of seventy-two is that most of the eyewitnesses have moved onto a *happier hunting ground*, the statute of limitations surely has run out on any culpability on my part by now, and lastly, no one's going to give a harmless old fart like me a hard time at this stage of the game *anyway*.

CHAPTER TWENTY-SIX

More Creatures

*Human beings are the only creatures on earth
that allow their children to come back home.*
— Bill Cosby

Going back into the annuals of the local country
lore, I remember a story that always stood out in
my mind. It has always been told and repeated without
deviation and what makes it even more eerie is, I knew
the people involved, none of whom were crackpots (you
know, the ones that get picked up in space ships). In
fact, one of the main players was my dad, and as I've
told you before, he was not one that knowingly would
be part of anything frivolous or fake.

To set the scene: It was common practice for most
people who lived around us to hunt. It was a cheap
and easy way to put an abundance of food on the table.
The prey of choice was rabbit. They were plentiful and

considered a pest for the farmers. The rabbits were relatively easy to bag and not bad eating, depending on how you cooked them. Since most of the hunters were "meat" hunters, as opposed to sportsmen or trophy hunters, this meant they killed as many rabbits as they needed in the most expeditious (not necessarily sporting) methods available.

One of these methods was employed when there was snow on the ground, the rabbits were then easy to spot. In conjunction with that stalking edge, if you shined a bright light on them at night they wouldn't move, they just sat there looking at you while you shot them (so much for "Bugs Bunny's" intelligence).

Everyone who was inclined to hunt in this manner had a spotlight (like the cops use now) installed on his vehicle. The usual practice was to pick up a six-pack of beer, drive the country roads until you spotted a rabbit, turn your light on it—and then blow it away.

I know what you are thinking. By today's standards, us country bumpkins have just broken at least half a dozen laws; drinking while driving, having an open alcoholic container in a moving vehicle, shooting from a public roadway, trespassing, taking game out of season, etc.

To be completely honest, you could on most occasions add drinking beer underage, hunting without a license, driving without a license (some of the farm boys learned to drive tractors and autos when as young as twelve or thirteen), littering, and on and on.

On this fateful night, an individual (of good character) who happened to be of legal drinking age was driving down our country road looking for rabbits to spotlight. About a mile past our house the road came to a 'T', and at that particular intersection there was a nice flat field next to a grove of cottonwood trees, a perfect spot for rabbits to congregate, and easy to see, especially since there was over a foot of snow on the ground.

The aforementioned individual had parked his truck on the shoulder of the road, opened a bottle of beer (his first one of the night—this is important), turned on his spotlight and began searching for rabbits. He noticed out of the corner of his eye, someone or . . . *something*! It was moving out of the grove of cottonwood trees, standing erect on its hind legs, and it was *huge*!

The guy tried to reposition his spotlight in the direction of this—*thing*, but as soon as the light shown on it, it was startled. It raised its arms (or front legs) and started running towards his car. The hunter was horrified . . . *what the heck was it?* He knew it was nothing like he had ever seen or ever heard of before, and it was quickly running towards him. He had to get out of there *fast*.

He dropped his beer bottle, which landed in his lap; he started his car, threw it in gear and sped away.

While he was retreating, he was looking over his right shoulder to see if it had stopped or if it was still coming after him. He didn't see it *now*. He was having second thoughts about if he had, in fact, actually seen *anything,* so he started to slow down. He turned back around to see where he was going, he noticed movement outside his driver's door. He turned further and peered out his side window (remember it was dark). "*My God,*" the thing had been running alongside his car all this time, *bending down looking in at him through the window.*

Later in town, while breathlessly relating his experience, he said he didn't know how fast he had been going when he first noticed it running alongside, but when he floored the accelerator, the speedometer reached *forty miles per hour* before the thing stopped chasing him. He recalled that during the entire chase, the creature had to bend down to peer into the driver's-side window of a full sized pickup truck which meant it had to be quite tall. The hunter has always sworn that he only had that one partial beer the entire evening.

Between our farm and the 'T' intersection was another small farm that had been owned by an elderly couple for many years. Recently the husband had passed away and his wife was in the process of selling the place and all the stock. She was going to move in with some of her kin in another state.

Until she was able to actually make the move, my

dad had volunteered our family's assistance to help her with her chores and took care of her livestock.

The next morning after the sighting of the strange creature, the neighbor lady walked over to our place and asked my dad if he would come help her find one of her horses. She told him it must have gotten out in the night because she heard it trampling around her bedroom window last night.

Dad finished up what he was doing and walked her back to her place. Our neighbor went in the house and he went to the corral to see where the horse might have escaped. But lo and behold, both her horses were in the corral with no obvious breaks in the fence. He then walked around to the rear of her house and saw a bunch of strange-looking tracks in the snow outside her window. Dad assured the neighbor lady that her stock was secure and that he would be back later in the evening to finish her chores. He didn't want to alarm her about the strange tracks he had discovered.

Now dad is pretty savvy when it comes to identifying tracks of the indigenous and domestic animals that inhabited our area. These footprints he saw matched none of the known species he was familiar with.

Later that day, he went into town on business. And while visiting one of the stores he overheard a small group of townspeople recounting the confrontation involving the rabbit hunter and something strange on our road last night. Dad shared his experience about the strange tracks he observed earlier in the day. The concerned townsfolk decided they should call the neighboring county constable and report the findings.

The constable showed up later that day. There had been too many vehicles down our road to pick up any tracks on the road where the rabbit hunter had described the chase. My dad took the constable to see the tracks around the farmhouse. He took pictures and measurements of the strange tracks and told everyone he would get back to us.

The frantic description of the creature given by the rabbit hunter was that it was very tall (it had to be if it had to stoop down to look in the window of a pickup truck), it's body was covered with shaggy, hair with a humanlike face, and it could run like hell.

We never got a satisfactory answer from the county authorities as to what it may have been. From my dad's description of the tracks and the pictures taken by the authorities, there were rumors that they were checking around to see if a large animal (of the primate variety) had escaped from a zoo or a circus, but to no avail . . . *What Could It Have Been?*

Speaking of scary events, in 1951 they came out with a science fiction (I hope it was fiction) movie called *The Thing from another World*. It was a story about a U.F.O. spacecraft crash-landing in the frozen Arctic wastelands. The authorities had found a huge alien pilot frozen in the ice. They cut him out still encased in a block of ice and took him back to their military weather-station facility. They unintentionally thawed the *"Thing"* out and he started wreaking havoc on the inhabitants.

This seven-foot-tall bald guy (James Arness played the alien, one of his earliest roles in movies) from outer space turns out to be created from vegetable matter instead of flesh and bone. The sled dogs tear off one of his arms and it grows back. The *"THING"* multiplies through seed spores and he and the spoors thrive on human blood.

The whole story plot is the two entities (the alien and the military) trying to destroy each other with the military winning out in the end . . . *this time*!

Anyway, this movie was being touted on TV as one of the all-time great thrillers. We didn't have our television yet but my friends did and they were all abuzz about this flick. Some of them were trying to talk their parents into taking them to a theater in Lincoln, thirty miles away, which was the closest location where it was playing.

I started working on my mom to take me to see it. It was no use trying to get my dad to take me as he was always too busy. My mom didn't want to go because it was so far. She was a good driver but was short and had to sit on a couple of pillows so she could see over the hood.

I was a very persistent, stubborn eleven year old. Mom finally relented and we planned the trek. We were going to go the first day she had off from the dry-goods store where she worked. I offered to pay for the gas from my paper route money but she wouldn't hear of it. She made me save every penny I earned.

I found out from one of the newspapers I delivered where the movie was playing in Lincoln and the show times. We decided to go to the matinee, which started at noon. That way Mom wouldn't have to drive home in the dark.

I was excited. I told my friends we were going and invited a couple of guys to go with us but their parents wouldn't let them go that far without them being along.

So it was just my mom and I off together one morning on a thrilling trip going to the theater —the anticipation was mounting.

We arrived at the movie theater in plenty of time to get seated in the theater prior to the start of the flick. My mother didn't want to buy any food or drinks at the movie because it was too expensive. She said, "We'll get something to eat on the way home." I think deep down my mom was kind of looking forward to getting away from the farm and her job for a day.

We found our seats and shortly the action began. First, they had a cartoon, just one (at home at the Wednesday night free shows they always had two). Then unexpectedly they ran a short serial movie about Superman. We discovered they did that at all the movies in Lincoln at the matinees. It was a good marketing ploy to get people to come out during the daytime.

The movie was beginning. The build-up was riveting. The movie was in black and white, they played scary music in the background, and I was getting chills already.

Like I described earlier they had this huge alien in this block of ice and they placed a guard with him. The guard doesn't like looking at him and throws a blanket over the block of ice, but unbeknownst to him it's an electric blanket and the *"Thing"* thaws out, gets up and runs outside in the blizzard. The sled dogs attack him and rip an arm off. Then the *"Thing"* starts killing everyone. They eventually trap him in the greenhouse where *"The Thing"* hangs people upside down and drains their blood.

This isn't anything like I thought it would be. I'm terrified. I leaned over and whispered to my mom, "I don't like this. Let's go home!"

Mom turned to me with a startled look on her face and said, "What did you say?"

"I don't like this I want to leave."

Mom said, "You begged me to come all this way and pay all this money, you are going to stay and see it."

I said, "I can't." I got up and left the theater. I sat out in the lobby and waited for Mom. She didn't come out for sometime. I guess she finally realized I wasn't coming back. Out she came, mad as a wet hen!

She took me by the arm and we marched outside to the car and off we went on our way home.

I told her I was sorry but I just couldn't watch any more of the movie, it was way scarier than I expected. "I don't want to talk about it," she said.

I waited a few minutes into our return trip and asked, "Are we were going to stop and get something to eat?"

She emphatically said, "No!" It was a quiet, hungry trip home. I guess I had pushed the envelope a little too far on this one. It took a couple of days of silent treatment before things got back to normal. Thankfully, my mom didn't tell anyone about my behavior, not even my dad, so I could spin the story any way I wanted to with my friends without looking like a complete wuss. Needless to say, my Mom and I had no further bonding mother-and-son trips to the movies.

Chapter Twenty-Seven

High School Sports

As you walk down the fairway of life you must smell the roses, for you only get to play one round.

— Ben Hogan

E ntering high school was a memorable time in my life. I came through grade school almost at the top of my class, grade-wise. I didn't seem to have suffered any problems by skipping a lower grade other than being a little young and immature for the grade level I was in.

A lot of scholastic changes were about to take place. I would no longer be lumped in the same classroom with other grade-levels; my curriculum would be less 'general' and more specific. We were assigned a guidance counselor to help us work towards our career goals (I didn't have any occupational goal yet, I just knew my future wasn't going to be in Valparaiso), and we had elective courses like woodshop for the boys and home economics for the girls. The most important (for me), was organized sports.

I tried to stay on top of all the sporting developments, especially the outstanding stars in baseball. I loved professional baseball. My favorite team was the Brooklyn Dodgers (the Bums). All the players on that team were my heroes, especially Jackie Robinson. It took a lot of courage in 1947 to be the first black player to play professional baseball. I remember listening to his inaugural game at Ebbets Field on April 15. Even though he didn't get a hit that day, that dude could really play the game. Many times I would skip a class and sneak in some listening time during the World Series playoffs. I really loved the national pastime.

I was avidly looking forward to playing all the sports offered in our school. Basketball and track and field weren't a big deal at that time in my life, so I didn't have any heroes in those activities. Baseball, basketball and track were the only sports offered for boys at that time in our high school. When I was in grade school, I attended most all of the home games and track meets so I knew all about the different games, but I wasn't able to participated until now . . . hopefully.

One of my favorite professional sporting events, which I loved listening to and later on watching (after we got our TV), was boxing. I guess it was because I liked the Joe Palooka comic books. My favorite boxer was Joe Louis; I can remember sitting next to the radio listening to the championship bouts from Madison

Square Garden, Boston Gardens, and the Polo Grounds. One of the best fights Joe Louis had after the war, I can remember, was the rematch with Billy Conn at Yankee Stadium in 1946.

I was eight years old. My dad, brother and I were glued to the radio. Everyone thought it was going to be as exciting as their first fight was in 1941 at the Polo Grounds. In that fight, Joe knocked Conn out late in the 13th round after a really close battle.

This rematch was a disappointment because Conn mostly ran from him for eight rounds before Joe caught him and knocked him out.

In 1947 Jersey Joe Walcott almost beat Joe. Walcott knocked him down twice in the first four rounds, but Joe won the bout in a split decision. The last two fights he fought after coming out of retirement (because he owed back taxes) were with Ezzard Charles in 1950 and lastly Rocky Marciano in 1951, both of which he lost. It was heart-wrenching; I actually shed tears after the Marciano bout. Joe Lewis was a great fighter and a great man.

My freshman and sophomore years were my prep years in all the schools' sports. I played on the reserve teams in baseball and basketball. In basketball I was too short to be taken seriously, so I subbed most of the time. The tallest guy we had in the reserves was only 5 feet 10 inches. I was only 5 feet 6 inches my first two years in high school, but I was fast.

Front row; left end – number 00 (fitting)

273

I don't know if the difference in size between athletes back then and present-day teenagers was caused by the water we drank, the food we ate, engineered genetics, or whatever. In my day a guy who was six feet tall was a giant and automatically the designated center (whether he was any good or not). Nowadays you would barely be considered as a player if you weren't at least six feet tall. In my junior year I was finally designated the sixth man on the varsity team.

My mom wasn't a sports fan by any stretch of the imagination, but my dad was starting to attend games, especially the ones in which I participated.

About midway through the basketball season I and another team member, along with two non-athletes, were caught smoking off campus behind the Christian church. One of the guys had pilfered some Chesterfield cigarettes from his dad's supply and we were experimenting with "tailor-made" smokes (not the homemade crap we usually were resigned to).

Obviously someone ratted us out and the school principal just walked right up on us. He alerted the coach of our transgressions and the coach decided to make an example of two of his lesser-talented team members, I being one of them. The punishment was banning us from playing basketball for the rest of the season. I and my teammate felt that was pretty harsh treatment for first-time offenders. My team-mates appealed for leniency but to no avail. The coach had a hard and fast rule and he stuck to it.

I was devastated to be thrown off the team after it had taken me over two years to get on it. My main concern was how my dad was going to take the news. Remember, you were never to make a spectacle of yourself and embarrass him.

I was preparing myself for some serious retribution but Dad never ceased to amaze me. For some astonishingly unknown reason he took my side and agreed with me that the coach's action was way over the line, and he was adamant about letting the coach know his feelings.

I had mixed emotions about his reaction. I was happy he decided, for whatever reason, not to severely punish me for smoking. I was worried he was making such a big stink that it might endanger any chance of my getting back on the team in the future. After all, it was my fault I got thrown off the team; I knew the rules and the consequences if I got caught.

I went to my brother-in-law Audry who was good friends with the coach, and told him my problem and he talked to the coach and my dad and got everything ironed out. The coach told me and my dad if I kept my nose clean for the rest of the season he would reinstate me on the team next year when I was a senior.

We lived in a small town, consequently there were

no secrets. Everyone knew about this and it seemed most everyone took sides. My mother, being a clerk at the local dry-goods store, constantly was asked about the controversy. She usually replied that the problem was I had fallen in with the wrong crowd—*what was that all about?* Her explanation was ruinous. It made me out to be a whiner hiding behind my parents—not a reputation to aspire to.

I don't know how Mom could say that. The three other guys I was with could hardly be classified as a "crowd" . . . if fact, if you included the entire pool of potential associates available to me to choose from, you would still be stretching the definition of a crowd. Anyway, after the situation was resolved, the whole incident, luckily, just went away. Like it never happened.

I went out for the track and field team all four years of high school. I participated in the short sprints (the 100-yard and 200-yard dashes) the high jump, broad jump and the discus throw. I wasn't outstanding in any of the events, although I could usually place in the top three finishers in the sprints.

My nephew Dayle, who was two years ahead of me in school, ran the longer races (880-yard run, and the mile). He was really good, and his practice regimen was brutal—he ran all the time. Personally, I never figured there was any sense running *full speed* for more than 200 yards—unless someone was chasing you.

Pole vaulting always interested me. I recalled hearing and reading about Reverend Bob Richards who held the record at that time. I saw him a couple of times in the newsreels at the free shows. I was considering trying out for that event at school but I didn't want to make a fool out of myself in front of my schoolmates so I decided to practice at home. I had watched the technique applied by others at track meets, so I thought I had the theory down pat. The problem was I was missing two important items to practice with: a pole and something to vault over.

My dad had a wooden pole about ten feet long that he used to move loose hay around in the barn loft. I thought it would work just fine. The only thing that came to mind to vault over was Mom's clothesline. It was only about six feet high off the ground—perfect. I dug a small square hole in the yard in front of the clothesline. I'm thinking; *This is where I will plant the pole as I am running toward the clothesline.* Mom had two rows of clothesline parallel with each other. There was about eight feet space between the two lines. I figured that was more than enough room for me to land between.

From the memory of watching others athletes (who, supposedly, knew what they were doing). I had a mental image of how I was going to do this. I was going to run as fast as I could toward the clothesline wire holding onto the end of the pole, lower the end into the hole I had dug and hang on. My momentum would carry me up and over the wire and at that time I would turn and push the pole back toward the direction from which I had come . . . *piece of cake!*

Here we go. I raise the tip of the pole and start running. I had a hard time holding the end of the pole off the ground— it was heavy. As I'm nearing the hole I try to drop the end of the pole in the hole, but I missed and all I did was continue running under the wires. I needed a bigger hole (target) into which to plant the pole. Once that was accomplished I was off again for my second try, only this time I didn't run as fast so I could be more accurate hitting the hole. I hit the hole, and was airborne. Hanging on for dear life, I raised my feet into the air and rose above the height of the clothesline. When I was at maximum height. I hung there (balanced) for a few seconds and then fell back to earth, but on the wrong side of the wire.

OK, I had the hang of it now. I just needed more speed to carry me over the wire. I started out again and this time I'm flying toward the wire. I lower the pole and it hits the hole dead center. I'm hanging on and soaring well above the clothesline and then—*I get a brain lock*. I didn't let go of the pole. I'm crashing down still hanging onto the pole across both sets of clotheslines, which fortunately breaks my fall, so I didn't get hurt. I get up to assess the damage. I noticed both clotheslines are sagging down so low, the middle portion is only about three feet off the ground. *Oh–oh!* I'm initially thinking: "*Maybe Mom won't notice.*" C'mon dummy, the only way she would be able to use these things now is if she starts taking in laundry from dwarfs.

When Dad got home I told him what I had done. He shook his head (both my parents did a lot of that when I was around) and told me that on Saturday he would help me fix the clotheslines. He suggested it would be a good idea to forget the pole vault event, to which I readily agreed. As we were walking to the barn to start chores, he asked, "How'd that hole get in the middle of the lawn?"

"I don't know . . . must have been the dog," I said.

The other sport I participated in was my favorite, baseball. I played reserves as a freshman and sophomore and made varsity as a junior and senior. As a reserve I played the outfield but I didn't like that position because it was too lonely out there. I wanted to be in the infield where the action was and I had someone to talk to. I was pretty good at fielding ground balls but I didn't have a strong-enough arm to play third base or shortstop so they put me at second base. I loved it.

I was a fairly good hitter and I had a good average

until my senior year—*then it happened*. No high school baseball pitchers, in my time, were encouraged by their coaches to throw a curve ball. For that matter, I doubt if many *could* throw one if they were allowed. The theory was, you would ruin a young teenager's arm trying to get them to throw a curve ball too soon. We played this one small town named Weston. They were in our conference and they had one of the exceptions to the unwritten rule. They had this kid who could throw a wicked curveball with ease, and to make matters worse he could throw it *hard and fast*.

His coach wanted to win the conference. So he allowed his pitcher to throw the curveball much to the condemnation of the rest of the coaches in the conference. I don't know if the other coaches' motives were noble and they were truly worried about the pitcher's arm, *or* if they were only concerned about their own win-loss records.

It didn't matter. Nobody could hit this kid's pitching when he was on.

Our coach had hit against curveball pitchers in college. He tried to counsel us on the best technique to use against the pitch. There were very few left-handed pitchers or batters in our league. The curveball pitcher we're talking about threw right-handed against predominantly right-handed hitters. This meant his curve ball would start out coming right at you and at the last moment bend right over the plate for a strike. No one on our team had ever faced anything like that before so our first reaction to a pitch like this was . . . *self-preservation*!

Like I said, he threw extremely hard. Your first reaction would automatically be to duck out of the way, then look like a fool when the umpire called it a strike. Our coach told us the only way we had any chance to ever get a hit off this guy was to stand in there and not back away.

The following week we were scheduled to play the curveball pitcher's team. I liked my coach and had confidence that he knew what he was talking about and I definitely wanted to knock one of these *sissy* curveballs over the fence.

My first time at bat against this joker resulted in a strikeout. Three straight curveballs, and I had backed away from each one. He made me look bad. I was bound and determined to stand my ground and not get fooled my next at-bat. He took his sign from the catcher, wound up and let fly. The ball was thrown hard and as expected it was heading directly for my left rib cage.

I ignored the rational, *urgent* recommendation my brain was sending to my feet (get the hell out of the way . . . or you're gonna die—soon!) and stood my ground. It was then I found out he didn't throw a curve ball . . . *every time*!

This time, he had decided to throw an extremely hard inside fastball to move me off the plate. I like a fool, took it in the ribs. I thought someone had *shot me from the bleachers*. I had to be taken out of the game in excruciating pain. My dad was at the game and came over to the bench to see how I was. I was doing my best not to cry but I was slowly losing the conflict. The coach suggested my dad take me home to rest and let him know how I was the next day. I spent a painful night. I couldn't lie comfortably in any position where it didn't hurt and it was hard to take a deep breath.

My dad related my condition to the coach the next day and he suggested Dad take me to the doctor (chiropractor) in Wahoo. My prognosis came after an X-ray (which I was reluctant to be exposed to after my episode with the shoe machine). I had a fractured rib. The only treatment was to wear an elastic bandage wrapped tightly over the afflicted area and just tough it out.

I couldn't play baseball for a couple of weeks. When I did start playing again I found out I had a real problem. I was never as good a hitter as before the broken rib. I was always pulling out of the batter's box no matter what pitch was thrown. I was *almost* a good baseball player.

In my senior year our athletic conference decided to start a football league. I never paid much attention to the game and didn't even know how it was played. We had a school meeting with the principal and the coach. All the interested high school boys and their parents were in attendance.

At the meeting there was a representative from the athletic conference explaining the pros and cons of the impending sport. He explained the exceptions to the rules of the game that would have to be incorporated to accommodate the size of our countywide conference.

The problem, as he explained it, was that the game was normally played at most high schools and colleges with teams made up of eleven players. Our small conference wouldn't support those numbers (we didn't have that many kids); therefore our conference teams would be made up of only six players per team. The conference representative said, "Your coach will explain how these organizational changes will affect the rules when we started forming our teams." He also pointed out that our coach was instrumental in bringing this sport to the conference and that he, himself, was an outstanding player in his college days and knew the intricacies of the game quite well. We were fortunate to have him.

The representative stressed the benefits (pros) of adding football to the curriculum but he also mentioned the downside (cons), i.e., it was a violent sport and injuries could occur but every precaution would be taken and initially the best equipment (pads and helmet) would be provided by the conference to assure its quality.

He adjourned the meeting and asked those in attendance to discuss all the contingencies with our coach and principal. He said he would need a list of all eligible and interested potential players as soon as possible, so he could be assured that enough schools in the conference were able and willing to participate.

As soon as the words *violent* and *injuries* were mentioned in the same sentence, some parents were already making up their minds whether their sons were going to play or not. Much to my dismay, my mother was one of the more vocal *against* introducing the sport into our school.

This activity sounded like something I would definitely enjoy participating in, but I knew that the way the discussion was going I had my work cut out for me. I had to convince my parents to go along with it. I knew trying to convince my mother was going to be a tough sell and I needed some allies.

I approached my dad from the angle that he was a "real man's man." I said, "Dad, the coach said if we played, we would be in the best shape of our lives . . . I think it would really be good for me physically and I know you would enjoy going with me to all the games. I will make you proud."

How is any self-respecting "manly" father going to

counteract that logic? It worked. He was on board! Next stop on my ally list was my brother-in-law Audry.

As I mentioned before, he was good friends with the coach and was also convinced it was a good sport for me to take part in. The three of us bombarded my Mom with so much positive input that she finally relented, but firmly stated she would *never* attend any games. She wouldn't be able to stand seeing her "baby" maimed on a football field.

The game of football was successfully initiated into our conference. We managed to recruit seven kids to play the first year (my senior year) and it quickly became our school's most popular and largest-attended sporting event, nosing out basketball.

Six-man football was a fast running game with very little, if any, passing. All the players played both ways on offense and defense. The team positions were three linemen (a center and two ends). The backfield was a quarterback and two running backs.

The main rule to adhere to was: You had to have a complete, obvious clear handoff behind the line of scrimmage before you could run, which meant the quarterback was strictly the field general who called and executed the plays. He couldn't run the ball unless it was a reverse or some kind of trick play, which you usually didn't have time to complete. It all boiled down to— if you had a good quarterback and three good sized linemen who could block, you usually won the game.

The first part of the season I played halfback and I also called the plays from that position because the starting quarterback couldn't remember them. The second part of the season I switched to quarterback because I could handle the ball better and I could execute the one pass play we had.

I really loved the game. I loved the hard work we had to do to get in shape, I loved the physical aspect of the sport and I loved to tackle, and I didn't mind getting hit (the harder, the better). When I was a running back, I loved scoring touchdowns, and running back the kickoffs and punts. Finally I enjoyed a sport where I was the one of the better players.

That year I set a record in football that can *never* be broken (how many athletes can say that). I scored the very first touchdown in the history of Valparaiso High School.

I loved the hero worship that came with being good at a sport, however short-lived it was. I can better understand the ego trips some athletes develop over the years of this idolization. It can be intoxicating. I also can understand the devastation that an injury can inflict on you at the height of your career.

The last game of the year was a playoff game. My family had finally convinced my mother to attend since it would be her last chance to see me play. This particular game was to be played in the evening under lights.

Most all of the fields we played on were baseball diamonds, converted to football fields (depending on the season) which meant that half of the playing field was dirt.

It had been raining most of the day but had stopped prior to the game. The field was a quagmire. We were designated the visiting team so we were wearing our practice uniforms, which happened to be white (at least when we started).

Early in the second quarter, I had called a simple reverse from about twenty yards out and scored a touchdown, but in doing so I had taken a vicious hit on my left knee and had to sit out the rest of the game.

My mother was *apoplectic*. Here was her "baby" covered in mud being carried off the field and tended to on the sidelines, I could hear her screaming, coming from the bleachers "*I Knew It . . . I Knew It Would Happen . . . James I Told You So!*"

My dad got the silent treatment for about a week after that episode. I spent a lot of time at the chiropractor in Wahoo getting treatment for the knee and still till this day it bothers me when the weather isn't cooperating. But I don't regret any of it. Playing sports in high school is about as good as it gets.

Pretty basic uniforms-no face masks

Neither my mother or my father ever smoked, drank alcohol or cussed (other than a rare damn or hell). I don't know if they chose that way of life to set an example for their children or they just didn't like to indulge in those vices. Their example was rewarded by every one of their offspring drinking, smoking and cussing to some degree during their lifetime. Go figure.

As a typical teenager I caved under peer pressure and succumbed to most of the local vices that were available at the time. Luckily, our only choices was alcohol (mostly beer), smoking (in some form, either store-bought or something contrived, but remember — *we didn't know about the hemp yet*), or chewing tobacco (snuff or Redman, which almost always made me sick).

I and most of my friends couldn't afford any of the *objectionable habits* in any substantial quantities, so consequently we never got in *too* much trouble.

I mostly hung out with three guys who were two years older and a grade ahead of me (remember, I was so intelligent—I skipped a grade). Their names were Jack, Bill, and Ray, and because they were older they could drive and usually one of them had the use of their family's car for transportation for the rest of us.

On this particular occasion, one of my friends had gotten hold of a few bottles of cheap muscatel wine (I don't think it even had a label). I don't remember drinking an excessive amount of the stuff but somehow I did and passed out cold.

My friends didn't know what to do with me. They were all afraid of my father after some of the stories I had told them over time. They came up with the brilliant idea of taking me home and propping me up between the back entrance door and the screened door and wedging the screen door shut with a piece of wood. They then ran like heck to the car they had parked farther back on the road.

So dad gets up at the crack of dawn and starts to go outside to start his chores, opens the back door and in comes his favorite son, tumbling inside like a ton of bricks right on top of him (scares the h_ _l out of him). Sometime during the night I had gotten sick and thrown up all over myself, if you can imagine the stench of a mixture of one of John's, the owner of my favorite beer-joint's, greasy hamburgers and sour muscatel wine . . . yuck.

Can you envision my dad's frame of mind when he found me? He's probably still half asleep when he opens the door and all of a sudden he's being attacked by a foul-smelling wretched creature— *inside his own house.* It was a good thing he wasn't carrying something he could have used as a weapon.

I know what you are thinking. As soon as I came to, I was about to get the tar beat out of me . . . right?

That's what I thought was going to happen, but I guess my dad was mellowing in his old age (he was sixty-six at the time) because he sat down on the back step and laughed the hardest I had ever seen him laugh. I presume that seeing what pitiful shape I was, in his opinion, punishment enough. Plus he was probably relieved that he didn't get critically maimed by the strange creature that had attacked him. This incident happened almost sixty years ago and still to this day I get ill if I smell anything resembling the odor of muscatel wine.

CHAPTER TWENTY-EIGHT

Launching a New Career

*When you are asked if you can do a job, tell
'em, "Certainly I can!" Then get busy and find
out how to do it.*
— Theodore Roosevelt

The IGA grocery chain bought out one of the two general stores in town and turned it into a "pure" grocery store, that just sold groceries, produce and meat. The new owners of the franchise were two brothers, Harry and Elmer.

They remodeled the place completely, installed some new (state-of-the-art) rental food lockers and a modern butcher shop. Now back in those days a 'butcher shop' meant a live critter walked in the back door, was processed right there and served in a refrigerated meat counter at the front door.

The two brothers worked well together. Harry was

very personable, knew everyone in town and was a true salesman. He worked the retail store portion and handled the merchandising. Elmer, on the other hand, was the workaholic. He made everything functional, and he also was a heck of a butcher and meat cutter, so between the two of them they had an efficient, and promising enterprise.

This really impressed my mom. She would come by when she was not working at the dry-goods store (which was a really old drab building) and talk to the brothers about their plans and when they would be open for business. She had made a decision and informed Dad and me that she was going to apply for a job at the IGA store and leave Schmidt & Sons.

The main concern my dad had was, "What are the hours?" He said he wouldn't mind as long as he had supper at five o'clock, *no exceptions*!

I don't know if I mentioned it or not, but my mom (even though being small of stature) was pretty headstrong and probably wasn't asking Dad or myself for our opinion or input about her changing jobs. I think she was *informing* us what she was *going* to do, and if her new work hours should occasionally conflict with the preparation of supper, and we insisted on eating promptly at five o'clock, Dad and I better start brushing up on our culinary skills.

The next day she went in and informed Harry and

Elmer that she planned to be their new employee and proceeded to explain why they would be foolish to consider anyone else.

Her confidence must have worked, because they opened their store two weeks later and Mom was their new checker and stock clerk. I was really proud of her. She just wouldn't take no for an answer. I logged that employment tactic away in my business 101 file as a job procurement tool (which I probably wouldn't have the guts to attempt).

She gave her notice to her present employer, Mr. Schmidt, much to his chagrin. She wouldn't change her mind no matter how much Mr. Schmidt tried to persuade her to stay. He didn't like surprises or changes, and if I'm not mistaken I think that was the last time Santa Claus showed up at my sister's house on Christmas Eve.

Mom started working at the IGA store and of course, I started hanging around there after school. The grocery part of the enterprise was basically the same as Schmidt's grocery section, but the butcher shop portion, especially the slaughterhouse, was new and fascinating to me. I became good friends with Elmer and he would show me all the behind the scenes butchering and cutting of the different meats.

I had no idea you could cut up a cow or a pig so many ways. My dad did most of his own butchering and meat cutting at home. His theory on meat apportioning was, you had steaks (one kind), roasts (again one kind), and the rest he ground into hamburger with a hand-crank grinder.

Dad would wrap the meat portions in waxed 'freezer' paper and store those and other perishables in a rented refrigerated locker in town. However, the old lockers we used to rent weren't very efficient or reliable. If the power went off for any length of time the food would partially thaw and then refreeze, which caused "freezer-burn," and a lot of the products (especially the meat) had to be thrown out.

The lockers at the 'new' IGA store were more efficient and they had a gas generator as backup to supply the needed electricity.

The main thing I hated about Dad's method of cutting and trimming the meat was that he loved fat, so every piece had to have a lot of fat in it.

I must have had some of Jack Spratt's genes in my blood because I *hate* fat or gristle of any kind, in any kind of meat, and to this day if I get any of it in my mouth it makes me gag. The cardinal rule at home regarding eating was that you only took what you could eat and you better darn well eat everything you took (all of it)!

Being a growing young man I was expected to take some of everything whether I wanted it or not especially the meat (because it was good for you). I hated it when we had roasts because those cuts had so much fat they *jiggled* . . . like jelly. It was disgusting. I could feel the gag reflexes starting to activate just looking at it.

I can remember leaving the meat last on my plate. I took my time eating everything else hoping Dad would finish before I did so I could give the meat to my dog, Spunk.

Dad ate a lot so, unfortunately, he usually was the last one to leave the table. So there I was trying to pick out the fat, eating just the decent parts, but Dad would always catch me and tell me to clean my plate.

I had tried to reason with him at times but to no avail. I would always get the same response, "Food is hard to come by. There is nothing wrong with that meat, I ate it . . . you can too!" This oft-repeated statement was usually followed with some inane reference to "the starving kids in Africa." I felt like telling him I certainly would do my part and donate all my fat meat to their cause, but I didn't. I don't think that logic would resonate well with my father. As the years went on, I had to devise ways of disposing of the inedible fat meat. I tried to spit it in my napkin, or stuff it in my pockets and cuffs, even roll it up in my bread. I would on occasion hold a mouthful in my cheek and say I had to go to the outhouse and then spit it out in the dog's bowl.

My mom confronted me one time after she had done the washing and asked why my pants pockets and cuffs were always so filthy and why our cloth napkins were always full of meat?

I finally just came clean with my mother. I told her, "I just can't eat fat; it makes me sick to my stomach. At times after being forced to eat it I'd go outside and vomit!" OK," she said. "Here is what we will do: First, you have to stop putting the stuff in your clothes and napkins, it's too hard to clean, plus—it's disgusting." She said, "The plates we eat on are big, with extra wide brims. I want you to hide the fat you don't eat under the rim of your plate, and when I clear the table I'll dispose of it."

I gave her a big hug and said, "Would you? Thank you—thank you!" The things you sometimes have to do to keep peace and harmony in the family unit.

You know that piece of gristle that runs along the front part of the breast of a chicken? If you happen to bite into that you will find it's crunchy (just the thought of that sickens me as I am writing this).

One day mom fixed me a chicken sandwich and used meat from the breast because she knew the white meat was the only part I liked. She always made delicious chicken sandwiches and sometimes she would put pickles in them. I ate the sandwich, felt the crunch and assumed it was a pickle.

When I was finished, Mom asked, "How was the sandwich?"

I said, "It was great, as usual, especially good with the pickles in it."

Mom replied, "I didn't put any pickles in it." I promptly lost my sandwich and everything else I had consumed that day.

Getting back to the IGA butcher shop and meat department, Elmer would let me know when he was going to slaughter a cow or pig and I would come to the store and watch. It was captivating.

He was really patient with my requests for the reasoning behind what he did. We got to be pretty good buddies and one day he asked if I would like to assist in skinning a steer he was going to butcher on Saturday. I jumped at the chance. I was impressed that he trusted me enough to actually let me do some of the important work After all, this was his livelihood and maybe I could have screwed it up somehow.

I was there bright and early Saturday morning and he walked me through the entire process: He showed me how and where to shoot the animal to make the quickest kill, how to bleed it, skin it, disembowel it, what organs to keep and which to discard, how to cut it into two halves (sides), then into quarters. He said the quarters would go into the cooler for a prescribed time (to cure) prior to cutting it into the desired parts. This sounds morbid, but I really enjoyed this job.

As a side note, ninety-nine percent of his customers

were of the Bohemian persuasion. That being said, there weren't many parts or organs that were discarded. They used everything except the "moo" and the "squeal." When you finished trimming the carcass it looked like it had been lying out in the desert for a year.

I could go down a laundry list of the uses of animal byproducts used but—it may alter the way you consume your culinary delights in the future, I wouldn't do that unless, you want me to, heh - heh.

When we were finished, Elmer showed me how to salt down the cattle hides and stack them in his smokehouse to wait for the rendering company to come and pick them up. They purchased the hides and used them for all sorts of leather goods. If you were careful in the skinning process and didn't cut too many unnecessary holes you would get a premium price for the skins.

Pigs were the hardest to skin. They had a thick layer of fat under a relatively thin hide, so it was easy to cut unwanted holes in pigskin, and if you had too many the hide was worthless.

The worst part of the butchering process was the disposal of the throwaways (head, feet, skin, and entrails [filled with the food they had been recently eating]). The discards composed about forty-four to fifty-five percent of the *live* weight of an animal. We would load these parts (excluding the hides) into barrels and then into a pickup truck and haul them to the county dump, where for a fee they would bury it for you.

After we had the carcass in the cooler and properly cured, Elmer proceeded to show me how to cut meat into the different portions and how to grind the hamburger and sausage, and how to stuff the sausage into the casings (cleaned entrails) to make links. I learned how to prepare and present the various body parts and organs (you don't want to know the details . . . trust me) in the display cases, the way his clientele liked it.

Elmer was a really good businessman. He would barter the labor costs of butchering, handling, storage fees, cutting and wrapping, and finally the monthly fee for the storage locker.

If the animal was of "prime" or "choice" quality he sometimes would negotiate his fee by taking some of the meat in trade (in lieu of cash), and resold to his store customers. If he didn't butcher the quality of meat he wanted or couldn't agree on an equitable barter, he would buy his resale meat form a packing company in Lincoln, in the form of sides (halves). He was a good judge of the quality of meat, therefore they always sold the best meat in the county.

After I had helped Elmer a couple of weekends, he asked me if I would like to work for and with him when the slaughtering opportunities presented themselves and when things got real busy.

I told him I would have to think about taking the job. I discussed it with my parents. I had just quit my paper route. I was in high school and would be practicing and playing sports after school. I didn't want anything to conflict with that.

Mom made me save every penny I earned from the paper route and other odd jobs, so that money was like gone (I couldn't use it). I would need some money to do things that would surely come up from time to time in the pursuit of high school activities. Mom and Dad said they would give me a little spending money for the essentials but otherwise I would have to provide the necessary money myself. Elmer said most of the work he would need me to do would be on the weekends and only in emergencies would he need me during the week. I still had the part-time odd jobs with my friend John (the bar owner), but those were sporadic. It was up to me what and when I did those chores for him, so I could easily fit them in and still work at the butcher shop.

I really liked doing the butcher work so I decided to give it a try. Elmer was happy I was coming on board, and said I was going to be a big help to him. I never asked him what he would pay for my services, I trusted him to make it fair. That probably wasn't a good business decision but I knew it was going to be more than I was making at that point and it would be fun.

I stayed with this part-time job until I graduated.

Other than the mandatory slaughtering events on the weekends, the hours I put in during the week were decided upon by me. Elmer was grateful for the help whenever I was available and we got along great together. Sometimes when Elmer was really busy I would handle the complete butchering of some of the smaller animals all by myself, other than removing the hides and the waste byproducts. Those two items were definitely jobs for more than one guy.

One of the more memorable phases of the butchering business was the ever-important phase of killing the animal. Cows were much easier to kill than pigs. We used a .22 caliber pump action rifle.

The rule of thumb was to draw an "imaginary" line between the animal's eyes and the opposing ears, like a cross, and where these two lines intersected was the killing zone. To make a clean quick kill with a cow, you had to put the bullet inside an imaginary circle (the size of a silver dollar) at this perceived juncture.

To achieve the same effective result with a pig, you had a killing circle about the size of a quarter. The skull of a cow must not be as thick as a pig's. If you missed the exact spot because the animal would possibly move just prior to the shot, the cow would still go down. This gave you another chance to shoot again while he was on the ground.

Conversely, with a pig if you missed that quarter-sized circle the pig wouldn't even flinch. It's like you just tapped him on the shoulder and he turns around and says . . . 'Yes?' It gives a whole new meaning to "hard-headedness."

I have heard stories of farmers making the mistake of just walking in among a herd of pigs and trying to shoot just one and end up shooting several (they all look alike) before one finally goes down.

I will never forget this one incident. Elmer, as a rule, didn't butcher really large cattle because they were just too hard to handle. It was a lot of trouble getting them inside the butcher shop. This particular time the owner of this huge Holstein bull, with a full set of horns, talked Elmer into taking it. He said it was tame so it would be easy to get him inside. Also, the animal would be easy to process: Because of its age, the owner wanted all the meat ground into hamburger. The job sounded like a piece of cake.

Elmer made an arrangement with the owner of the bull. He wanted me to be at the shop next Saturday. Everyone was there at the appointed time. The owner led the animal into the shop just like he said he would. The critter looked twice as big once he was inside as he did on the truck.

Elmer and I had everything ready to go so there would be no wasted time. Elmer shot the bull and he went down like a ton of bricks. Elmer then cut his throat to bleed him out and proceeded to block up the carcass to start the skinning procedure. All of a sudden— the bull gets up and does his best to try to destroy the butcher shop with that magnificent set of horns.

Elmer and I couldn't get to either door to get out, so we climbed up on the steel tables that lined one wall. There was some sturdy shelving above the tables and I climbed up high on one and sat down and watched the show.

Elmer was able to avoid his charges by hopping from one table to the other. The big animal wreaked havoc until his blood supply waned and he finally lay down and died.

The shop had a policy of not taking an animal that large for the very reason we had just witnessed, and Elmer breeched it against his better judgment. He almost lost his shop and could have lost his life and mine in the process. It was not a wise decision on his part.

CHAPTER TWENTY-NINE

New Friends

*Cleanliness becomes more important when
godliness is unlikely.*

— P. J. O'Rourke

Going into high school was a whole new phase of
my life. I had my familiar circle of friends that I
was comfortable with.

Each year for those entering the ninth grade, there
was a brand new crop of freshmen coming in from the
farm community. Some of this year's students I had
seen occasionally on Wednesday and Saturday nights.
Many of the new students knew each other, and most
had strange names like Matulka, Jirovshy, Machacek,
Vanicek, Zetocka, and Polak. Most were bilingual.
They spoke Bohemian and English.

One thing I didn't like about the newcomers was,
when they didn't want you to know what or who they

were talking about they would converse in Bohemian. After a few years of being exposed to the language I managed to pick up some key phrases and words, at least enough to know when I was being denigrated.

The one thing they had in common was they were all farmers, and most had to do their livestock chores before they came to school. You could always tell the pig farmers, especially in the wintertime—*Phew!*

The school was heated with steam heat. The boiler was in the basement and every room had a steam-heated radiator along one wall. If the teachers were smart they would situate the students from the pig farms as far away from the radiators as possible. No matter how hard you tried to clean your shoes after coming out of the pigpens and sties you could *never* get all the pig crap off. Let me tell you, there is no worse smell than fresh pig manure. The steam heat from the radiators would inevitably revive the stench of *any* unseen residue and it would quickly permeate the whole room.

During the winter, a lot of the farm students wore long-john underwear. For you city folks, long-john underwear was a one-piece undergarment that went from your ankles all the way to your neck and wrists. The garment had a buttoned "trap door" flap in the rear, and also your standard vent in the front for excreting bodily wastes. This popular item of clothing was made from different types of, i.e.: wool, cotton, or flannel.

Not to be unkind (I am sure it was out of necessity), but for whatever reason some didn't change these items very often. There was one young fella named Reynold whose winter attire was always the aforementioned woolen undergarment covered by a long sleeved blue denim shirt and standard bib-overalls, with high topped work shoes . . . *every day*. His wardrobe varied in the warmer seasons *only* by the elimination of the long underwear.

In high school it was mandatory to attend one hour of PE, in some form, each school day. The activities were performed inside the auditorium during the winter. It was also mandatory to be attired in school approved gym shorts and T-shirts during this activity.

The hour-long workouts associated with PE varied, but all were designed to make you work up a sweat. Because of this activity, it was strongly suggested that everyone take a quick shower before changing back into their regular clothes prior to going home.

Reynold did as he was instructed. He wore his school-approved shorts and T-shirt *ove*r his aforementioned long-john underwear. After participating in the PE activities, and perspiring profusely, Reynold always waived the suggested shower and promptly put his clothes back on and went home on the bus.

The rumor was that Reynold was *sewn in for the winter*. Anyway, come early spring Reynold would be getting a little gamey. He was a nice friendly kid and was always smiling, but due to his personal hygiene habits the timing and extent of his friendships were . . . seasonal, at best.

He was never, I repeat, n*ever* allowed to sit next (or anywhere close) to the radiators.

CHAPTER THIRTY

Scouting and Munitions

I refuse to join any club that would have me as a member.

— Groucho Marx

Towards the end of my freshman year in high school, a new family (husband, wife and son) moved to town. The father Lowell was going to work at the bank in some management position. They had a young son named Skipper.

After they were settled in Lowell, who had been a Boy Scout, decided that our little community needed a Boy Scout troop and started to take applicants. We ended up with a troop of three members: Lowell's son Skip, my friend Wayne (the academically challenged one), and myself.

Even though we had a tiny troop, Lowell made our activities interesting and enjoyable. We learned all the traits, traditions and crafts in the Scout Handbook. I advanced from Tenderfoot to Second Class in the two years I was in Scouting (pretty impressive . . . huh?).

I was always a sucker for a uniform.

The principles that Scouting promoted were lofty goals for any young boy to emulate. I promised myself if I ever had kids they would all be in Scouting. The Scouting values and guidelines I learned helped me many times throughout my life.

Lowell always had fun projects for us to participate in. He would get projects and crafts from Scout Headquarters and present them to us in our meetings. One such craft was making a rubber gun shooter. This was a pistol shaped out of pinewood, and on the back of the handle you tacked a clothespin. The front of the barrel portion of the gun was a Vee-shaped notch.

The concept was, you would take a fairly good-sized rubber band, tie a knot in the middle and stretch it from the notch on the end of the (perceived) barrel, across the top of the gun and secure it with the clothespin at the handle.

The theory was to load the gun with a rubber band (bullet) and when you were ready to fire you would squeeze the clothespin (which opened it) and release the rubber missile. We three Scouts each made one and we would have rubber gunfights Western-style.

Wayne's dad had a woodworking and machine shop on at his grandfather's farm a short distance from town. Because of Wayne's on-the-job training by his father, he was a master mechanic and craftsman. He could fix most any automotive motor or anything made of wood.

He had no problems—as long as he didn't have to read any instructions.

We decided to take the small rubber gun concept and expand on it. Shooting the original rubber gun was OK, but it wasn't very accurate because the rubber bands were light and any little amount of wind would blow them off course.

Back then, all the automobile tires had to use inner tubes, the part of the tire assembly that held the air. Inner tubes of those days were made out of rubber— "real rubber" that stretched quite well (they had red and black ones; the red was best for our purpose). Our plan was to get some old inner tubes and cut them in strips. What we ended up with was a larger, heavier rubber band. Heavy enough that the wind wouldn't affect its flight.

Because the new rubber bands were heavier, you needed more power to launch them, so conversely you needed a *bigger* gun. Using a prototype of the same version of the original small gun, we made a longer barrel. The theory was sound but the clothespin spring wasn't strong enough to hold the heavier new rubber band so we increased the spring strength by wrapping smaller rubber bands around the handle and clothespin until it would hold the stronger band. What we ended up with was a long, cumbersome weapon with a fat handle and a hair trigger that required both hands to fire, but it worked. That weapon was lethal. The length and tension of the rubber band was adjusted by tying more or fewer knots in it.

The new design shot farther and straighter than we had expected. If it hit human flesh it definitely raised a welt . . . *now we're talkin'!* We made a half dozen of these monsters and started recruiting some of the local youth and organized our own version of "Laser Tag."

The problem we were starting to experience was an inadequate supply of ammunition. These new rubber missiles flew so far that in the heat of battle you would lose track of their location. Therefore the supply had to be replenished regularly.

Since the automobile inner-tubes were made out of rubber, real rubber, the automobile owners could repair them when they developed leaks. They lasted a long time. This was a small town with not a lot of vehicles to wear out inner-tubes. By the time someone decided to throw away an inner-tube it usually had a lot of patches, which limited the amount "un-patched area" of the tube that could be cut into strips used for our purposes. This restricted supply of useable tubes meant we had to spend an inordinate amount of time searching to reclaim our ammunition. This in turn drastically curtailed and limited our battle time . . . *we had another poser.*

Wayne and I went to our local auto repair garage/

gas station and asked our friend Cecil (he was the guy that ran the facility) if he had any ideas on how we could get our hands on more tubes. He said he would check on the availability of discarded automobile tubes the next time he was in Lincoln, while picking up new tires and inner-tubes. He did say he had a fair amount of *truck* inner tubes (red in color), and he gave us a couple dozen of them to take with us.

When we got to Wayne's place we cut some of them into thin strips the same way we did the automobile tubes, and right away we knew we had a problem. The truck tubes were much bigger in diameter; therefore the rubber bands were a lot larger in length. The only way they would work on our newly made pistol shooters was if we would tie about a dozen knots in them. Their size made them inoperable for our purpose (they wouldn't stretch with that many knots).

The truck tubes were just as good as the auto tubes, but they were just too big . . . Hmmmm. When you have big ammunition you need . . . you guessed it . . . a *bigger* gun.

We immediately went to work on the problem. What we came up with was a rifle or "long gun." We used the same principle as the pistol but, with the rifle, the distance from the Vee-notch at the end of the barrel to the clothespin trigger was greater in order to adapt to the larger rubber band.

It worked great and it was definitely more powerful, with the same accuracy. It changed the strategy of our war games considerably. We were getting proficient with the long gun but its design was still in the Civil War era in the sense that all our weaponry only had "single shot" capabilities.

Wayne (displaying his usual genius) came up with a completely new weapon design (Samuel Colt would have been proud): Instead of using a clothespin trigger on the stock, he cut a series of saw tooth notches on the top of the gun with the vertical portion of the notch situated toward the front end of the barrel. The last notch was located near where your rear hand would hold the trigger on a normal rifle. His design incorporated this ingenious addition: In front of the first notch (toward the barrel) he attached a sturdy string that extended all the way to the butt end of the stock. He enlarged the Vee-notch on the end of the barrel so it could hold more rubber bands. The loading process was: Put one looped portion of the knotted rubber band in the Vee-notch and stretch it into the first available notch, making sure the string was situated under the rubber band. You repeated this procedure until you loaded six rubber bands (this was the optimum number after numerous exhaustive field tests) into the six notches.

What we had here, boys and girls, was a prototype replica of the up-to-date *B.A.R.* (Browning automatic rifle), with almost as much killing power. You could set it on single shot (just pull the string hard enough to release one rubber band) or set it on full auto (give the string a yank hard enough to release all six bands).

Wayne proceeded to duplicate another half dozen of these beauties—*Let The Games Begin!*

We had some great fun playing the rubber-gun war games but not without a few causalities. Every once in a while someone would get hit in a sensitive spot with the big rubber bands from the long guns and our parents would discover the welts, which lasted some time. We tried wearing baseball caps with the brim pulled low to try to protect our eyes.

One time while playing our games in an abandoned barn I was sneaking across the barn floor trying to reposition myself to get a shot at the enemy hidden in the loft. As I peered out from one of the stalls and looked up to see if I could find my foe—he let me have a *full auto load* (six shots) right in the face. Luckily my cap protected my eyes but the next morning my face looked like the rear end of a baboon with an *extra bad* case of hemorrhoids.

This new gun was devastating, and because of its increased firepower our parents insisted we at least use some effective protection over our faces. The results of that little episode prompted a détente in our war games until we could convince our parents we could find a way to minimize our casualties.

The local hardware store was owned and operated by a guy named Howard whom we approached for ideas on what type of face protection we could obtain—*cheap*. He showed us some baseball catcher's face masks in one of his catalogs. They weren't the "official" high quality masks a real catcher would use. These were the cheap imitations sold to younger kids who wanted to act like real catchers. They looked like they would be perfect for our purpose.

Howard was a real nice guy who always supported any activity that would help keep the local kids off the streets (in our town's case the correct term would be "street"). Howard asked how many of these masks we would need. We told him six. (That was the full complement of guys who would participate in our battles).

Howard said, "If you kids could come up with $2.00 apiece I would order them and would pay the difference, including the shipping."

We said, "We'll get back to you."

As a side note of immense significance to this story, Howard was a heavyset, solid individual with a unique talent I have never seen, or heard, duplicated in my lifetime. I don't know how or what he ate but he *always* had an inordinate amount of intestinal gas. He seemed to have a never-ending supply and would pass it in the most unusual way. I'm sure he held the world's record for the longest duration of expelling these noxious fumes, but the part that set him above everyone else was, he could change the pitch of the tone he was emitting. In other words, *Howard could fart like a flute.* He had built quite a reputation because of his magnanimous talent. Many folks would ask him to perform his flatulent symphony every time they patronized his store. What an advertising gimmick. *Howard was a marketing genius!*

All of us were excited to get the masks and get on with the games. The problem was, how we were going to come up with $12. We tried to think of some way we could earn the money but I seemed to be the only one who had access to employment.

My mother still monitored my earned income cash flow closely. She wouldn't allow me to go out and blow my money on just anything. Remember she's the one with the "save for a rainy day" philosophy.

I still had my occasional discretionary jobs at my friend John's beer joint. To reiterate, my job was relocating all the recyclable beer bottles from various locations in his bar, placing them in cardboard cases, and stacking them in his locked storage shed, ready for pickup by the brewery company.

We finally came up with a plan to raise the money. I have agonized over the decision of whether to share this plan with you or not. I am not proud of the devious scheme we devised. The only reason I will divulge this is that my friend John is dead. If he should get wind of what I did—*from where I know he is right now* . . . John, I hope you will forgive me.

I knew where the keys were hidden to John's storage shed, the place where the recycled beer bottles were kept. There was an old abandoned barn close to the shed. The town's beer joints always closed at six o'clock on all the nights except Wednesday and Saturday.

We all made an excuse to our parents that there was some phony function we had to attend for a couple hours one evening; I had worked it out that I was going to spend the night with one of my friends.

After it was dark we went to John's shed and moved a bunch of cases of empty beer bottles into the old barn, took the bottles out and put the emptied cases back in the shed and stacked them so it appeared like they were still full of bottles.

The plan was, over the next several days each of us would take the loose bottles back in the beer joint a few at a time and get the refund (we were re-recycling). I would then, as was my regular job, in turn take them back to the shed and refill the empty cases.

I couldn't have felt guiltier if I had knocked over Fort Knox. I just knew everyone in town had seen us pull this caper off. I couldn't look John in the eye when

I redeemed the bottles and I could never enjoy the "rubber gun" war games or the new face masks the same way as I had before this scam. I told my friends that "under no circumstances would I ever do something like that again, so don't ask."

Over the next months I secretly worked extra hours without telling John to try to repay him for his loss I had caused. The irony of the entire scenario was, if I had just openly asked John for the money he undoubtedly would have freely given it to us. That's just the kind of wonderfully generous man he was. My self-esteem level was at an all-time low . . . the term "*pond scum*" readily came to mind.

CHAPTER THIRTY-ONE

Close Shave

*Every time I go and shave, I assume there's
someone else on the planet shaving. So I say,
"I'm gonna go shave, too."*

— Mitch Hedberg

One of my three closest friends, Ray, always had a heavy beard, the entire time I knew him through high school. I think maybe he may have been born with it. His beard was so thick that his five-o'clock shadow showed up about three-thirty, every day.

Bill, another of my friends, decided he wanted to start shaving. I don't know why, all he had for a beard was a little peach fuzz. Bill, Jack (my third close friend) and I were all in the same boat. We really didn't have enough facial hair to require shaving yet, but Bill was making a good case as to why we should start.

We were always told by our parents and other adults

to put off shaving as long as possible because once you started your whiskers would grow faster and you could never quit.

Well we collectively decided that we *had indeed* put it off as long as we possibly could. We were ready to look like Ray. We were going to shave—*now*.

We couldn't go to Jack or Bill's house because their mothers and other siblings would be home. Since both my parents worked my house would be the obvious place to launch our adventure.

We had all watched the various shaving techniques at the local barber shop and had witnessed our own fathers' grooming rituals long enough that we were comfortable in our ability to apply those techniques to our own faces. How hard could it be? Every adult male did it. Everyone we knew used straight razors. The shaving procedure using this implement is as follows: You place a hot wet towel over your face for a short period of time to *soften* the beard, put water into a shaving mug (coffee cup look-alike) which held a round cake of soap in the bottom. After pouring the water out of the mug, take a soft-bristled brush with a handle and work the soap into a lather and spread it on the areas of your beard. Then proceed to take a cutting device sharp enough to easily *sever your head* and gently *scrape* off all of your coarse facial hair, pausing periodically to clean the blade of accumulated soap and hair debris in a basin of hot water.

When you are finished and cleaned up, then proceed to hone (re-sharpen) your razor on what is known as a razor strop (everyone pronounced it razor strap) before putting it away so it will be ready for the next episode. Sounds simple enough—*piece of cake!*

We arrived at my house and as expected found it empty. We anticipated having a couple of hours before my dad got home. Plenty of time to shave, clean up and hide all the evidence and vacate the premises. This was going to be fun.

Just to set the stage where this "carnage" was about to take place: We had a small room next to our kitchen, technically known as the washroom. It was about the size of a modest bathroom typical of most modern homes. Its layout was as follows: On one wall was a "washstand" consisting of a shelf with a porcelain sink at one end. Located in the middle of the sink was another one of those mysterious "drains to nowhere." Next to the sink was additional shelving space with room for an enameled bucket with a notched lid with a dipper in it (it was always filled with clean water for drinking, washing your hands and the daily dishes).

On the wall was a large medicine-style cabinet with a mirrored door which held all of our toilet items and Dad's shaving paraphernalia. With these few trappings, when you entered the room and squinted a little you could get the feeling of walking into a *modern* bathroom. In fact the only things missing to meet the minimum qualification were running water, a faucet, a tub or shower and a toilet. We *almost* had a real bathroom.

We all went into the washroom. I got out the shaving gear and we were ready to start. We didn't want to take time to pump water and start a fire in the stove to heat it up. We opted to go cold turkey.

We also figured we could waive the wet-towel step because our beards (a term loosely applied) were probably soft enough. Bill was the most anxious to do this so he would go first. Dad only had one razor. Jack and I would watch and give critical *technological* advice.

Bill was lathered up and took out the razor while looking at Jack and me kind of sheepishly. I think actually holding and preparing to wield that lethal instrument was a little daunting, but he was committed. After all it was his idea. He started to scrape. The shaving soap was coming off just as we had expected and seen on so many occasions. Unfortunately, so was a thin layer of Bill's chin. We suggested he hold the razor flatter to his face and stretch the skin with his other hand. While trying to master this move he cut his thumb.

We had a goodly amount of blood flowing by now. I took the towel off the towel bar and gave it to Bill to sop up some of the blood before it got everywhere. He was determined to finish the job. He didn't want to only have "half" a beard. He repeated the procedure on the other side of his face. He was consistent, ending up with a matching wound on the opposite side of his chin.

I took the dipper and poured clean water in the basin located in the sink and Bill started to wash up. I had seen Dad use an object (what looked a white crayon) to rub on cuts and nicks when he shaved and it seemed to stop the blood flow. Bill began applying it to his chin and thumb.

Jack was confident, after watching Bill butcher himself, that he could do a better job. After the prepping and soaping he was ready. He held the blade just at the right angle and started scraping. At first glance it looked like he had the hang of it. The soap was coming off smoothly. He would wash the razor and take the next swipe. *Good Jo*b we cheered. *Then it started to happen.* Apparently every time Jack would start his stroke he had applied too much pressure on the razor because he had about a dozen small cuts that were starting to produce a rather copious amount of blood. Bill handed him the towel and the white crayon and Jack went to work cleaning up *his* face. Blood was everywhere. It looked like we were attending a vampire convention.

I decided that this massacre had gone far enough and it was going to take time to clean it up—more time than we had before Dad came home. I wisely told the guys I would have to forego my shaving experience for another day and they would have to help me destroy all the evidence.

Being fearful of my Dad's wrath, they readily agreed. We needed to get this butcher shop cleaned up . . . *fast*! I told them to wet the towel they were using and clean up all the blood and to use the water from the bucket to wash it down the drain to nowhere, then go out to the pump and get a fresh bucket of water to replace that which we used.

In the meantime, I would sharpen Dad's razor on the razor strop so he wouldn't notice it had been used. Little did I know there it is an art to "stroping" a razor properly. I had watched Dad slide the blade back and forth on the strip of leather on numerous occasions but I had never noted—in *which direction* he was sliding the blade. I soon found out that if you went the wrong direction the blade would cut into the leather, which in turn (I found out later) dulled and sometimes ruined the edge.

We took one last look around the crime scene and were satisfied the place was free of any incriminating evidence.

Bill asked what we should do with the towel, which was still heavily stained with blood. We couldn't wash it so I said, "Bring it with us. We'll bury it somewhere.

I don't think Mom will miss it because she has a lot of towels."

Jack and Bill were a mess. Come to find out the crayon-looking stuff turned white when it dried and they both looked like they were ready to go on the warpath. They couldn't have done more damage to themselves than if they had kissed an electric fan.

The next morning when Dad was starting his shaving ritual I heard a lot of grumbling coming from the washroom. I heard him shout, "Pearl, have you been cutting stuff up with my razor again?"

Mom answered, "No, James. I haven't touched it."

After another short grumbling interlude my dad *yelled*, "Donnie come here!" Oh crap, here it comes. I reluctantly went into the washroom and Dad handed me his razor case with the blade inside and said, "Your mother dulled my razor again. I want you to take it over to Uncle Fred's place and have him put an edge back on it." He added, "I don't know why your mother just won't admit she used the razor. Here look at the strop. See where it's all nicked up where she tried to sharpen it, she's just hardheaded."

I answered, "Yeah, it's getting to be a problem—we will have to keep an eye on her." The next evening, Mom pulled me aside and stated, "Give me some straight talk about you bringing your friends over here to try shaving." *How do they do that?* Great! Now Mom had the same perceptive powers that Dad has. I don't have a chance!

Finally I had to come clean. I told her everything and apologized for leaving her holding the "blame" bag. She assured me that Dad would get over it. I asked her, "How did you find out?"

She said, "It was easy. I saw Jack in the store earlier today and his face looked a lot like Dad's when he shaves before he's fully awake. There was still some blood on the washroom floor and lastly, I was missing my favorite face towel."

I asked if she ever considered going to work for Scotland Yard.

CHAPTER THIRTY-TWO

Restaurateur

A cannibal is a person who walks into a restaurant and orders a waiter.
— Morey Amsterdam

Each of my last four years in school, I spent two to three weeks of my summer break in Lincoln at my sister Dorothy's apartment. I really looked forward to that vacation. She would get me a bus pass and I could travel around town as much as I wanted.

I would go the university and wander though all the interesting facilities on campus. They have one of the most complete Natural History museums I have seen, anywhere.

There was a radio station studio nearby. I would go over and watch them record radio programs. I especially enjoyed watching and listening to a gospel singing quartet. I would sit in chairs outside the sound booth.

It was fascinating to see how the radio programs were made especially after all the time I had spent listening to the radio before television.

The singers were friendly guys and I got to know them well. They would always sit and talk with me before and after the recording sessions. I liked the fellas but they talked kind of funny. Just about every sentence uttered would be interjected with the phrase, "Praise the Lord," and at times I would make a statement and they would answer "Amen." Occasionally they asked me if I had been saved. I wasn't sure what that meant but I always answered, "You bet."

They sorta reminded me of when the "Holy Rollers" would come through town and set up their big tent just outside of town. While they were visiting, their members would take many of us kids aside and ask us the craziest questions and read off a long list of things we shouldn't be doing and try to get us to attend their revival meetings. To my knowledge, none of us ever went to an official meeting, but Jack, Bill and I would sometimes sneak a peak under a corner of their tent and watch their antics—those folks did some weird things.

When Dorothy wasn't working, she would take me to the movies with her and her boyfriend Ed. We also went to a place called Capital Beach, a big amusement park with a huge swimming pool. The pool had salt water in it and they had sand around the edge—this was as close I had ever been to a real beach.

One of my close friends, Jerry, moved to Lincoln when I was in the tenth grade so I would often hang around with him and his friends.

He worked part-time at a drive-in restaurant as a carhop when he wasn't in school. We used to hang out there a lot.

He told me if I wanted to work while I was visiting in Lincoln he probably could get me a job for a couple of weeks. I jumped at the chance. I was always interested in learning about another business and of course picking up some extra money.

I met him the next day at the drive-in and he introduced me to his boss, who said he could use some extra help on the weekends when it was really busy. I filled out all the paperwork. He gave me a white shirt with his logo on it and a weird little white hat and told me to come in while Jerry was there and they would train me and get me ready for the weekend. I was excited . . . my first *real* big-city job.

It was a Thursday night when I went in for training and Jerry showed me the ropes. He introduced me to the cooks and the other carhops, most of whom were girls—cute girls. They were dressed like cheerleaders. The manager watched me while I took a couple of orders and put the order form in a clip on a big wheel at the window and turned it so they could see it from the kitchen. When the order was ready they would call my name over the loudspeaker. I was to pick up the order, put it on a tray that hooked onto the car window, take their money, give it to the cashier and return with the change.

The boss said, "The most important part of the order besides taking it and giving it correctly to the cooks is to pick it up *promptly* when your name is called so it can be served hot" . . . *piece of cake*. I was ready for the big time. "Bring on the masses!"

I got to work early on Friday afternoon, dressed in my weenie-looking uniform shirt and that dumb "Dixie cup" hat and started taking orders. When a car would pull into a stall next to the microphone they would push a call button and a light would appear on a big board showing which stall was ready to order. I took two quick orders and went through the kitchen and delivering process without a hitch . . . this was going to be fun, and *I get paid for it!*

The place started getting busy and most all the stalls were full. I had just placed an order when a car full of older guys pulled in (they looked like college students), they hit the call button and I was off like a shot out of a cannon.

I greeted them and asked if I could take their order. I don't know if they had been drinking or not but they were obviously out for a good time. First thing out of their mouths was they wanted a girl carhop, not "Little Lord Fauntleroy." Not knowing what a "Little Lord Fauntleroy" was I wasn't sure if that was a compliment or not. But the way they were laughing and yelling at me I finally got the impression they didn't care for my uniform or gender.

I asked them again if they wanted to order and they started yelling their orders at me all at once. Just when I thought I had it all down they started changing their minds.

I heard my name called to pick up the last order I had placed. I asked these guys if they would mind if I went and picked up my order, adding that I would be right back. They said, "*No way*," they wanted their order taken right now. They weren't going to wait.

I had a dilemma. The manager said I had to pick up the order quickly when it was ready and these guys were telling me if I didn't take their orders now they were going to complain. I finally thought I had their orders straight but each time I would try to leave one of them would make another change.

The kitchen had called my name two more times and sounded mad. The guys at last said they were satisfied that they had ordered what they wanted and told me to *hurry up* with their food.

I ran back to the kitchen to pick up the previous

order that was ready and the cook told me he was going to have to remake the whole order because it was cold. I had to go tell my last customer their order was going to be delayed. They weren't happy about that at all, and said I should send someone else to check on it as obviously I didn't know what I was doing.

When I tried to turn in the large order from the belligerent guys, I had made so many corrections I wasn't sure what was right. This whole mess was quickly getting out of hand. I wasn't about to go back to the jerks in the car and ask them to repeat their order, so I made my best guess what they wanted and turned it in.

My previous re-made order was ready. After I listened to the cook threatening me to not be late picking up orders again, I took the food to the customers and had to listen to a bunch of crap about how they had never had such poor service and not to expect a tip . . . *Tip*! At this point I didn't care if they even paid for the food—I just wanted this nightmare to end.

After some time, the jerks' orders were ready and it took me two trips to take it all to their car, but I just knew it wasn't going to be right . . . and it wasn't. They started to complain about what was wrong, but before they could get into it too far I told them I had to go to the restroom and would be back shortly.

I went into the restroom, took off my weenie shirt

and Dixie-cup hat, folded and stacked both next to the sink and snuck out.

I went to the corner drugstore and called my sister to come get me, saying that my shift was over. I told her to pick me up at the drugstore on the corner, not at the drive-in. When she got there she was all cheery and asked me how my first day at work went.

I answered, "Fine," and we went home.

The next day my friend Jerry called and asked what happened last night and where I had gone. He said, "There was a near-riot by a bunch of guys complaining about their food." He asked again where I had gone.

I said in a raspy horse voice, "*Sick*."

He said, "The manager asked if you were coming in tomorrow."

I whispered in the same pitiful voice, "*No . . . sick bad*," and hung up.

I never went to that drive-in again and never even went back for my check. I figured I probably owed them money. My sister inquired when she would have to take me back to work again. My answer was, "You don't. Business was slow and they don't need me anymore." She shrugged and went on her way. I don't know what inspiring business applications I learned from that traumatic experience. I'm aware of one thing since that happened. I *never* complain about service in a restaurant.

CHAPTER THIRTY-THREE

Cool Cars

I know a lot about cars, man. I can look at any car's headlights and tell you exactly which way it's coming.

— Mitch Hedberg

I got my learner's driving permit when I was fifteen and a junior in high school. I had been practicing driving prior to that time, to and from town with my mom. She was a nervous wreck by the time I got the hang of it (sort of like my bicycle learning experience, but without all the crashes).

Before my dad would allow me to drive on my own, he required me to pass *his* driving tests. In theory I was not supposed to drive by myself without a licensed driver in the car with me until I was sixteen. I guess Dad knew that once I was out of his sight I would probably *waive* that requirement (like every other fifteen-year-old did). Remember, no cops, no tickets. Most farmers' kids drove a lot earlier than that out of necessity. Nobody complained unless they got reckless, and in that case their parents would find out about it and they were toast.

My dad had me go through the basics and then he said we'd take it out on the highway and see how I reacted to *heavy* traffic on a "high speed" thoroughfare. The "high speed" highway he was referring to was a two-lane graveled road maintained by the county that stretched approximately twenty-five miles from our town, where it connected with an honest-to-goodness "concrete" highway into Lincoln. Peak traffic use at any one time, over the twenty-five mile stretch, maybe fifteen to twenty cars, tops.

As I mentioned before, our family car was a 1938 Ford Tudor sedan (V8 engine), and once we were out on the highway he said, "Open'er up."

I did a double take and said, "Are you sure?" The speedometer was bouncing between 55 and 60 mph. I looked at him out of the corner of my eye and his hands (white knuckles) were clutching the dash.

Finally he said, "Shut'er down . . . I didn't think it would go that fast. *That was fun!*"

Once my dad was assured I could handle the car under these extreme conditions, I was given a reasonable amount of freedom of its use, as long as it didn't conflict with his or Mom's needs.

OK. . . I was almost a "townie" and had the use of a good car. What else was there? Only problem, the family car wasn't a *cool* car. Some of my older friends had *cool* cars, lowered in the rear, foxtails on the aerials, fender skirts, and loud pipes (exhausts). Most of what I just mentioned cost money which we didn't have. I did have the raccoon tail that was on my bike. I proudly attached it to the aerial (it was a start).

I checked with my friend Cecil at the garage/gas station and inquired how much it would cost to put one of the "dual tone" Smittie mufflers he had in stock on the car. He gave me a price of the muffler and added that for me, he would put it on for free (what a guy).

I put a plan in action. I approached my dad and told him the car wasn't sounding so good. I said I thought it needed a new muffler.

He went to the car started it up and said, "Sounds good to me" and turned and walked away.

Well, that didn't work, so I quickly went to Plan B. A couple of days passed and I found an old cement block, put it in the trunk and drove to town to the firehouse where my dad was helping with a remodeling project. I parked off to the side and secreted the cement block out of the trunk and propped it under the car's muffler and backed over it. That did it. There was no doubt that the car needed a new muffler after that. The car sounded like an old John Deere tractor.

I brought it to Dad's attention. I lamented that someone had left out an old cement block and I hadn't seen it. He said to take it to town and have Cecil install a muffler. It never ceased to amaze me how clever I was . . . it was almost too easy.

Cecil installed the new muffler and it purred like a kitten (a *Tiger* kitten). I never said anything about this when I got home, just parked the car in the shed and went inside. When Dad came home he asked, "Did you have the new muffler put on?"

"Yup," I answered. That was it!

The next morning, Dad went off to work with Uncle Fred, and Mom went to start the car to go to work. She came hurrying back in the house, wide-eyed and asked, "What's wrong with the car? It sounds like a tractor."

I told her that the old muffler was ruined and this was a new one we had put on yesterday.

She asked, "Your dad put that noisy thing on our car?"

"No, I did," I answered.

"You mean it's always going to sound like that?"

"I'm afraid so," I stated.

Mom lamented, "What will people think of me driving something like that? You will have to take me to work from now on."

That night, Dad wasn't very happy with me after the tongue lashing he received from Mom. He asked, "Why did you have to get such a loud one?"

I said, "It was the only one he had."

"I guess we'll just have to live with it. I can't afford to buy another new one," Dad stated. The car was getting cooler by the day.

As I mentioned before, my friend Wayne was a mechanical genius, especially with cars. His grandfather had an old Ford Model T stored under a haystack in his barn. For some reason a lot of the older farmers stored old cars in this manner. They thought somehow the hay and straw kept the upholstery and body in better condition, who knows?

His grandfather, in his 90s, was sick and about to pass away. He wanted his grandson Wayne to have his old car. The car had one of the classic body styles (it looked sort of like an outhouse on wheels). It was a two-door with a four-cylinder engine that ran on gasoline, kerosene or ethanol.

We figured it must have been made prior to 1915 because it didn't have an electric starter. It had to be started with a hand crank, which had a reputation of inflicting bodily harm by "kicking back" if you didn't have the spark adjustment set just right.

Wayne's father (who taught Wayne everything he knew) knew all about the idiosyncrasies of this particular model. His dad found a place in Lincoln that carried all the parts needed to repair or restore this and other cars of that era. Wayne was excited and he wanted me to help him with the task at hand. I wasn't much of a mechanic but I followed directions well.

We had the engine up and running in no time. I was quickly learning how this thing ran. It didn't have a battery so when you wound the hand crank it generated a low voltage, alternating current via a flywheel magneto, which in turn powered a "trembler" coil that produced extremely high voltage. This in turn passed though a distributor to the four combustion cylinders (boring, I know, but stay with me—this is important).

We found out by accident, much to our chagrin, that if you touched the contact points of that coil after it had been charged it would knock you on your butt!

That got me thinking. Wayne's grandpa had several of these coils in his barn. How could we turn this power into a *weapon?*

What if we hooked that coil up to a car battery, would it work . . . yes it did . . . it *really* worked. I think it even increased the power! Next step, what if we mounted the coil under the hood of a modern-day car and hooked it to the battery. Would the car body be electrified? Nope, it wouldn't.

Wayne's dad knew something about electricity. We asked why it didn't work and he said the car needed a ground to bypass the rubber tires, which were acting as an insulator and couldn't complete the circuit. "How do we fix it?"

He said, "You need a metal ground from the frame to the ground (earth)."

"How are we going to do that? We can't drag an anchor behind us?" we asked.

Wayne went in his dad's shop and found a piece of heavy chain and welded it to the frame of his car. It was just long enough to drag about two or three links on the ground.

He hooked the coil to the battery and then we drew straws to see who was going to test it. I won, or lost, however you want to look at it. *It worked!* . . . That thing was so powerful it would almost stop your heart (these must be what they used on the electric chairs in prison). The problem was, it worked, but it *always* worked. How were we going to get in and out of the car without getting killed?

With a little more thought we decided to try installing an electric light switch between the battery and the coil, and locate it under the dash. We had harnessed the power.

Now came the time to test it out on the masses. It was a blast (literally). I decided I had to have one of these also, so we duplicated the same setup on our family car.

The problem with living in such a small town was: Between the two of us it only took about a week and we had shocked just about everybody we would *dare* shock, and still live. The element of surprise was over. We had only exhausted one segment of the population. So we redirected our assault on the only feasible alternative, *the farmers*, on Wednesday and Saturday nights.

Two unmarried farmer brothers worked a small farm east of town and they always came into the big city on the open nights. These two guys were always dressed like they were permanently auditioning to be extras for the movie "The Grapes of Wrath."

The one brother, named Emile, also had a few personal problems. For one, most of the folks used tobacco in one form or another. Several used snuff (Skoal was the brand of choice). And again, most enjoyed it in their mouth. You know the commercial, "just a pinch between the cheek and gum." Emile, on the other hand, stuffed both nostrils full of the obnoxious concoction . . . *all the time*. Because of this vile habit, he had this real high-pitched nasally voice. Secondly, mentally, Emile was about two balls short of a full rack (a little billiards lingo).

Farmers in general (my dad included) had a funny, quirky habit. When they would stop and talk to each other on the street they would always have to lean on something (a pole, bench, chair, or sign) and if something else (an object a little closer to the ground) was handy they would put one foot (either foot was optional) on it while debating the world's plight.

This was the sanctioned technique of conversing (I think it had something to do with blood flow to the brain or something like that).

Taking this lore into account, Wayne and I would park our cars on the street in an area devoid of any of the aforementioned props. The only thing they could use was one of our cars for conversational stimuli. The theory: They would lean on the hood and put one (designated) foot on the bumper. Our cars proved to be a satisfactory substitute prop in lieu of usual standards and would be an adequate substitute to inspire a meaningful dialogue.

I always felt, "it took a lot of nerve to lean on someone else's automobile and put their "pig-crap encrusted" shoes on the bumper. Because of their calloused display of bad behavior, I decided I wouldn't feel sorry the intended victims. They deserved the *almost* lethal dose of electricity they were about to receive.

Emile, on this particular day, was draped all over our family car, like a polar bear lounging on a melting iceberg. I'm thinking . . . *OK, Emile, hang on to your snuff. Here comes your "talking point" for the day* and I let him have it.

Usually the technique was to flip the switch on and

off quickly so you wouldn't inflict permanent brain damage, but with Emile I turned it on and left it on.

Emile didn't flinch and never skipped a word in his chat. I must be having a malfunction, so I disengaged and re-engaged the switch again and waited for the inevitable reaction . . . nothing. What's wrong? . . . That sustained surge would normally knock down a full-grown steer. The coil must have burned out or something. I got out to open the hood to see what the problem was . . . *my eyeballs lit up!* No human could have sustained that much electricity for that length of time and lived, let alone still carry on a conversation.

I don't know if it was because Emile was slow and he had a detour sign between his nerve endings and his brain and he would start hollering later that evening, or what caused his immunity to electricity, but I had a whole new respect for Emile. He was my new hero. If he ever committed a capital offense they would have to come up with a new form of execution.

So now our family car has a raccoon tail on the aerial, loud street mufflers and a built-in execution chamber. It was getting close to where I wanted it—*It was almost 'cool.'*

Dad, on the other hand, was receiving so much flack from Mom that he finally had to take control and mitigate the damages. He decided to buy me a car, can you believe that, *my own car. If* I promised to put the family car back the way it was, with the exception of the muffler (I guess he was getting used to it)!

One of the local farmers was selling a 1931 Ford Model A. It was great deal, $35.00 cold, hard cash on the barrelhead.

I wouldn't be able to fix this one up like the family car, but heck the trade-off for ownership was worth it. After dad bought the Model A, I took it to my friend Cecil at the garage/gas station and had him check it out and he said it was in fine running order. I drove that car for two years and did my darnedest to destroy it. But it survived and when I graduated I sold it for, guess what? . . . $35.00 cold, hard cash.

Two of my classmates owned cars just like mine. We would race them against each other. The cars were supposed to be capable of going sixty M.P.H., but at forty-five M.P.H. my front wheels would start to shimmy.

In the wintertime after a big snow the road grader would push the snow off the roadway and pile it up on the edges. During the daytime if the sun came out it would melt a portion of the snow left on the roadway and at night it would freeze. When it got good and slick (icy) we would race on that. We would slide around the corners and use the snow banks as bumper guides. It was like the bobsled run in the Olympics.

I remember one time; one of my friends hit a low

snow bank and his car flipped over on its side. We all jumped out and tipped it back up. It was still running and he took off and finished the race. You just couldn't hurt the old cars.

When we really wanted to get the attention of the townsfolk, we would unbolt the exhaust pipe from the manifold headers, drop it down and tie it off with baling wire. It was unbelievable how noisy those small engines were without a muffler. All three of us would then drive down the main street, and when we got to the intersection, we would let off the gas and retard the spark and they all would backfire in unison. It was a beautiful thing. Although not appreciated by the townsfolk.

I remember once, one of the cars must have had some gas leaking out of the carburetor because it caught on fire during one of our backfiring concerts. We all stopped our cars and started throwing dirt on the engine to put it out. Amazingly, after the fire was out the thing started right up and we went on our way.

One of my friends took it a step further. He drilled a hole in the back floorboard and on into the tailpipe. He inserted a piece of copper tubing into both holes and inside the car he mounted a small funnel. While he would drive in formation with us (he was in the rear) someone would be in the back seat pouring used motor oil into the funnel and through the tubing. You've never seen such a smokescreen.

My poor mother while working in the grocery store, always caught the flack for our antics. The people would come in and complain to her about us and *strongly* suggest that we not do the backfire and smoke thing anymore. Mom would then talk to Dad and when he got tired of listening to her, he would get my attention and *strongly* insist that if I didn't stop it he would throw my car keys away. That usually did the trick.

Shortly after I got my car, Mom convinced Dad that they should get rid of the old 1938 Ford family car and get a newer one (I think she had just about had it with the loud exhaust noise).

Dad went to Wahoo and made a deal to trade our car for a five-year-old, 1949 Mercury four-door sedan, maroon in color with mohair upholstery. Great car. It looked like the same car that the Green Hornet used. The one he had his trusty valet and chauffer, Kato, drive for him. The body looked like it was designed by General George Patton. All it needed was a gun turret on top. It was a real heavy car and fun to drive. My mom had to use the usual two pillows under her to see out. She looked funny driving a car that big. Everybody gave her a wide berth when they met her. I was allowed to use the new car in the winter if I had a date because it had a good heater (my model A didn't have a heater), but I couldn't take it out of town under any circumstances.

CHAPTER THIRTY-FOUR

"You're in the Navy Now"

I'm inclined to think that a military
background wouldn't hurt anyone.
— William Faulkner

When I entered my junior year, the school's focus was on our careers after graduation. As I mentioned before, the only way to make a living and still live in this town was to farm and/or work for the railroad.

Burlington Railroad had an assembly plant for their railcars in Lincoln and employed a multitude of local workers. The railroad company would send recruiters to the area high schools hoping to lure high school graduates to their facilities.

For the majority of the students in our school, college wasn't an option because of cost and logistics. Most area colleges recruited from the metropolitan cities because of a larger population base. Recruiting in these more populated venues was cheaper and easier than traveling to the rural remote areas.

The only students I could recall that attended institutions of higher education were a few girls who wanted to be teachers, and they would attend the smaller teachers colleges.

The military also recruited at our school. The branches of services that participated were the Army, Navy and Air Force, and they always had an enlistment gimmick to entice young graduates into their ranks. At this particular time, the Navy had an attractive program called "The High School Seaman Recruit" (I wonder how long it took them to come up with that catchy phrase).

The plan was: The student would join while in the eleventh grade, choose his billet (job) and take the appropriate school courses pertaining to that job description. Upon graduation, if he or she was at least seventeen prior to induction, would enter the service, serve close to four years and be discharged the day before the recruit turned twenty-one years of age.

Our parents' signatures were needed on the enlistment application because most students were underage if they were still in high school.

I brought home the brochures, application, and a list of career opportunities I would be eligible for upon entrance. I told my parents what I had decided I wanted to do upon graduating. The timing couldn't have been better. The Korean *Conflict* (don't let the wimpy portrayal fool you, it was a war . . . a lot of young men and women in the military died) was over. My brother had recently returned home to a hero's welcome.

Although my brother didn't actually see action on the frontlines due to that fortunate random reassignment to Japan for duty instead of Korea, back in those days anyone who answered the call of duty was considered a hero.

Some who did serve in battle were never the same again. And then there were those who came home in a box. In our town, *all* who served were publicly honored every Memorial Day with an honor-guard ceremony at the cemetery.

My brother didn't need any medals to be my hero. What he did and how he did it has always been an inspiration for me. He was my brother and I loved him . . . most of the time!

My parents asked my brother to come to the farm over the weekend so we could discuss my decision to enlist, and he did.

Lloyd recounted the maturity and experience he gained in the Army. He explained the advantages he enjoyed by being eligible for access to the benefits of the GI bill: Such as educational and technical training subsidies and assistance to buy a home with subsidized loan rates. He told our parents that he was already participating in some of the programs and was planning to buy a small home.

Knowing our family's financial situation and my bleak outlook for meaningful employment, he highly recommended that they allow me to join the Navy. My parents respected my brother's opinion and they both agreed they would sign the application.

My brother and I went over the job rates (billets) that were available to me. We chose a brand new rate, which was electronics mate. I wasn't sure what an electronics mate did, but Lloyd thought that electronic technology would be an ideal field for the future.

I notified the recruiter through the school of my intentions and he came to our home to finalize the paperwork. The whole thing was wrapped up in a very short time. He left me a list of school courses that would assist me in preparing for my new job after graduating. This was really exciting. Technically and for all intents and purposes—*I was in the Navy!* The last thing the recruiter told me and my family was that I couldn't change my mind once the papers were signed.

I found out the following week that three of my classmate buddies had done the same thing. They had come in from the farms to attend high school recently and we formed a tight bond in our senior year. Two of them were my Model A cohorts.

It was comforting to know my future was set and I didn't have to worry about what would happen when I graduated. This also meant I could now *really* enjoy my senior year.

CHAPTER THIRTY-FIVE

Senior Year Events

*It is a thousand times better to have common
sense without education than to have
education without common sense.*
— Robert Green Ingersoll

My senior year was finally at hand. My grades were good, and because of that I had a lot more freedom at home. I was allowed to skip my farm chores from time to time when school functions came up, like sporting events. Elmer, my boss at the butcher shop, was a lot more flexible with my work requirements. He and my dad attended as many of my sporting events as they could, they were both my fans. That's about all we talked about while we processed animals into food.

I was almost as tall as my dad, he was five feet ten and I was five feet nine, and I was in the best shape of my life because of football and Charles Atlas. Dad and

I were becoming good buddies. We would kid around with each other. He made jibes like, "You may be too big to still take over my knee but don't get too cocky, I can still kick your butt."

I would reply, "Don't be too sure, old man."

One day we decided we would have a friendly wrestling match. When it started out it was all in good fun *until* I got Dad in a headlock (just like on TV, Gorgeous George would have been proud of me) and wouldn't let go. Dad was doing his best to get out of the hold when he panicked. For some reason he grabbed my hair and pulled pretty hard. This ticked me off and I really clamped down the headlock. I put enough pressure on his head to the point that he had to give up so I would release the hold.

I have never forgotten the look he gave me. His shoulders slumped; he turned and just walked away without saying anything. I felt bad, but he shouldn't have pulled my hair.

I never knew the extent that I had wounded him or what I had taken from him until now that I have myself reached that age and can identify with his plight.

Men consider themselves invulnerable and immortal. Until late in life you think mortality is only for those who are "less fortunate." In making him *give up* I had forced him to accept something a man is the most reluctant to admit, his vulnerability. The destruction of his perceived immortality, that he is a mere mortal, on the ebb of that transience.

What I unwittingly took from him was something he could never regain. It was his *power* and I have regretted that ever since because *he wasn't ready to give it up.* I have since faced my mortality and am dealing with it, but I don't mind telling you . . . I don't take it kindly.

I was fairly popular with my schoolmates; everyone seemed to like me (especially since I was, technically, in the Navy—something about a uniform). I was on the student body council. I had a good part in the school play and helped plan "senior sneak day".

Senior sneak day was: One school day was designated for the senior class to play hooky (with permission of the faculty, of course). Volunteer parents would take the whole class to different planned points of interests for the day.

We could go just about anywhere we voted on, as long as we could obtain permission and/or reservations for tours conducted by the companies or institutions we planned to visit. The only exception was, we had to include two *mandatory* visits to two locations in our itinerary. These two particular facilities visits were traditional and were always arranged by the school principal well in advance.

One of these two facilities was Boys Town in

Omaha. I don't know if you have ever heard of this village but you would have to see it to believe it. They made a movie about the village in 1938 aptly named "Boys Town," starring Spencer Tracy and Mickey Rooney. The movie was good but didn't come close to recognizing the quality and dedication of this great man . . . the founder (*the following was taken from the Boys Town official Web site*):

Father Edward J. Flanagan came to Omaha, Nebraska in 1913, and a drought that year filled the streets with unemployed farm laborers. When he saw the many homeless young boys outside his Workingmen's Hotel for impoverished men, Father began to formulate his philosophy that assisting a boy when he was young might prevent him from turning into a homeless man.

On December 12, 1917, Father Flanagan borrowed $90. from an anonymous friend believed to be Henry Monsky and opened the first Father Flanagan's Boys' Home, a nonsectarian, non-proselytizing home for boys. It was an old run-down Victorian mansion near downtown Omaha. Five boys were the first to benefit from Father's vision, and those first residents barely had time to get settled before a steady stream of additional boys began to arrive. They were sent by the court, referred by sympathetic citizens, and often, simply wandered in on their own. The front door was never locked, and any boy who came was allowed to enter, regardless of race, color or creed. There was *hardly enough money to feed them, but these boys received stronger nourishment than food – love, care, patience and understanding in rich quantities. With this new venture, Father Flanagan began his pioneering effort to rehabilitate children instead of imprisoning them.*

Father Flanagan also knew the boys needed more to become successful adults. He began to focus on their educations. A horse and wagon carried the boys to and from school, music was always a part of the home's life and recreation in the form of supervised sports took place on the back lot. Tending to the boys' needs was no small task, but Father Flanagan's enthusiasm quickly attracted helpers. Neighborhood men and women volunteered their evenings and weekends, and the diocese sent nuns to help with the daily work.

The second mandatory visit was to the Nebraska State Penitentiary for men, in Lincoln. Our school had been participating in this tour for many years, so the penitentiary personnel knew what kind of student enlightenment our school expected from them. We got the "cooks tour." We saw behind the scenes, and felt the austere environment the prisoners lived in. We even got to have lunch in the cafeteria. I think the town fathers wanted us to know what it would be like if we ever decided to stray from the straight and narrow. It was an impressive deterrent that worked (on me anyway), as I made a mental note that was one place I never wanted to visit again.

One of our other two stops on our sneak day was the Roberts Dairy and ice cream factory. The one experience at the facility always stuck in my mind. I could never forget the most important job there—the guy who physically tasted and graded all the cream that came form the local farms—Yuck! Going through the tour had rekindled the pride of remembering that our little farm had contributed to the quality of the ice cream they were selling by sending them the cream from our two milk cows. I'm sure our cows were proud also. After the dairy we toured the University of Nebraska, Lincoln; I found it interesting, even though neither I nor none of my classmates would be able to attend.

Chapter Thirty-Six

Bleacher Bums

It took me seventeen years to get three
thousand hits in baseball. I did it in one
afternoon on the golf course.

— Hank Aaron

After the senior sneak day I had only two major events scheduled before graduation. The senior prom was one and the other was a trip to St. Louis, Missouri, to see the Brooklyn Dodgers play the St. Louis Cardinals.

My friend Jack was going to get the use of his dad's car so he and my other two friends Bill, Ray and I were going to take a three-day trip try and take in two games at Busch Stadium.

As I stated before, I was a rabid Dodger fan. The other three guys were not, but they weren't Cardinal fans either.

The Dodgers were tearing up the National League that year, 1955. They were thirteen games ahead of the second-place Milwaukee Braves and a shoo-in to take the National League pennant.

The Cardinals were out of contention at thirty games behind, but they always played the Dodgers tough and they had the great Stan "The Man" Musial and Red Schoendienst on their team so both games promised to be great, hard-fought contests and we would get to see some of the *all-time* great players.

The Dodgers club's starting players were: Roy Campanella, catcher; Gil Hodges, first base; Junior Gilliam, second base; Peewee Reese, shortstop; Jackie Robinson, third base; Sandy Amoros, left field; Duke Snider, center field; and Carl Furillo, right field—what a lineup. To top it off, the Dodger pitchers of the two games we were going to see were Sandy Koufax and Don Newcombe. It just doesn't get any better than that. I couldn't wait for the trip.

We called ahead and reserved rooms at a cheap hotel not too far from the Stadium; our plan was to leave really early the day of the first game and try to make it before it started that afternoon. We couldn't buy advance tickets so we would have to take our chances on getting tickets because, after all, it was the Dodgers and Jackie Robinson was playing.

We had to miss two days of school but when we

told our teachers and principal where were going they all thought it was a good idea, saying they just wished they could go along.

The night before the trip it was hard for any of us to sleep. It was the first time we were going to attend a major league baseball game and the first time we were taking a trip without an older member of our families with us.

We got an early start because the trip was over 400 miles long. Luckily the car we were driving was newer and would go over sixty miles per hour. I think the speed limit was fifty-five but there weren't a whole lot of cars on the roads during the week.

The trip took a little longer than we expected. We hadn't budgeted time in for eating along the way, and we did a lot of that. We had a good map and drove right to the stadium, parked and made our way to the ticket booth and suffered out first setback—they were sold out. We could buy tickets for the next day's game, which we did. This meant we were going to get to see only one game.

Dejected, we started to make our way back to the parking lot when we were approached by a couple of guys who said they had four tickets on the second row. We couldn't believe our luck. The tickets were a little more expensive than the ones we had purchased for the next day but . . . what the heck, they were on the second row.

It was about thirty minutes before the game was to start so we stopped by a souvenir booth and each bought a team T-shirt. The regular T-shirts were expensive, so we got the much cheaper, "wife beater" style (tank-top), and a cap. Of course my purchase bore the Dodgers logo. My friends said they were tired of me talking about the "Bums" all the time, so they decided to get shirts with the Cardinals logo. We went into the bathroom and changed, then went to try to find our seats.

Once we got inside the stadium we were all in awe; it was huge, the diamond, the grass, the field was beautiful and people—people were everywhere, music was playing and most of the seats were already filled.

We were tracking the section numbers on our tickets with the corresponding numbers printed on the aisles when we discovered we were in dead center field. We got to our assigned section and there was an usher stationed at the top of the section before we went down the rows.

Before he even looked at our tickets he said, "You guys must be in the wrong section."

We assured him we were in the right place and showed him the tickets.

The usher checked the tickets, looked up at us and remarked, "Are you guys sure you to want to sit here?"

We said, "We're sure, we're in the correct section, and we're supposed to be in the second row. Is there something wrong?"

He answered, "No, you folks are in the correct section and you are definitely in the second row all right, but you also are in the colored section."

Not being sophisticated and learned in the ways of the big city, we asked inquisitively, "What's a colored section?" We thought, *maybe the seats were painted different colors and if so, what's the big deal?*

He cleared his throat and stated, "You guys aren't from around here, are you?"

We replied, "No, we just want to see a ball game, we bought the tickets, you said there wasn't a problem, so why don't you show us to our seats—*pal!*" So he did. Our seats were definitely in the second row (just like we expected), we couldn't figure what that guy's problem was. Who knows about city folks; I guess they are just weird by nature.

We got seated and started to go through our programs, still amazed by the enormousness of the stadium. Jack is looking around and suddenly he leans over to me and, in a hushed voice says, "Look around us—but do it casually." How do you look casually?

Not knowing what the problem was, I look around and, confused, I leaned back over to Jack and say, "I didn't notice anything . . . what did you want me to look at?"

He said, "Take a closer look at the other people sitting around us." Suddenly we knew what the usher meant by the "colored section."

Our other friend Ray, overhearing our conversation says, "Just scrunch down in your seats. Maybe they won't notice us." To say that Ray was naïve in his suggestion would be like all of us breathlessly expecting Tiny Tim to win the "Man of the Year" award.

Picture this scenario. Here are four white guys. When I say that I mean *white* guys. Guys from rural Nebraska don't spend a lot of time at the beach. The only places on our bodies having anything resembling a tan . . . let me rephrase that, the only place on our bodies that are "less white" is from the neck up and the biceps down, those damn sissy T-shirts we bought just compounded the problem—it showed more skin. When the sun hit us just right, *we glowed*. I was surprised the umpires didn't make us move because of the glare of four "lily-white" guys imbedded in a dark background. It had to be a distraction and would probably hurt the hitters' eyes.

A rather large gentleman sitting behind us leaned over our shoulder and asked, "What the hell you four crackers doing sitting out here with us?"

I answered meekly, "Nothing . . . just wanna watch the game."

He said, "It's a good thing one of you is a Dodger fan," referring to my shirt and hat.

I told him, "My favorite player of all time is Jackie Robinson, and I love the Dodgers because of him." Come to find out most of the people in our section felt the same way. The four of us would cheer every time Don Newcombe would strike someone out and every time Robinson, Amoros or Gilliam would get a hit.

The Dodgers won and by the time the game was over we were bosom buddies with most of the people sitting around us. We were telling Polack jokes, which everyone seemed to enjoy. All in all we had a great experience, one I have never forgotten.

The next day we discovered all four of us weren't as white as when we came. We were now a lovely shade of pink.

The second game we planned to attend was the last one of the meeting. It wasn't much of a contest. The Dodgers murdered the Cards and Sandy Koufax pitched a shutout.

During the game, I don't remember who hit it, but a foul ball line drive was coming our way much too hard to try to catch with your bare hands. I took my new souvenir Dodgers cap off and held it by the bill like a first baseman's glove and *almost* caught it. Problem was, after the ball passed by, the only thing I had left of the cap was the bill. No matter . . . it was a cheap hat anyway.

The main difference between this game and yesterday's game was, this day we sat in an all-white section, with all-white neighbors. When the game was over we had talked to nobody new, and knew nobody around us, and we couldn't tell any Polack jokes. Go figure.

My friends were anxious to beat the crowd out of the stadium but I had heard someone talking about the possibility of going to stand by the players' buses and try to get some autographs. I told the guys I was going to go and try to get some of the Dodgers 'autographs, and to wait on me. They said they would wait at the car, so off I went program and pen in hand.

I found where the team buses were parked and saw there was a big line in front of the lead bus so I found a spot closer to the dressing room and waited there.

I ended up with signatures of (be still my heart) Jackie Robinson, Gil Hodges, Sandy Amoros and Carl Furillo on the back of my game program. What a treasure!

Just for your information the Dodgers won the World Series that year. They beat the Yankees four games to three.

We decided we were going to stay a second night

in our fleabag motel and leave for home early in the morning.

We discovered something else after the game. In Missouri, you could buy beer at eighteen years of age, albeit it was only 3.2 beer. This beer was supposed to have less alcohol by weight than regular beer. We weren't eighteen but Ray looked like he was thirty, with his heavy beard.

We sent him to the store to see if he could buy the low-alcohol beer without showing his driver's license and it worked. He came back with a case of it. None of us were rocket scientists but even we could figure out the simple solution of getting high on low-alcohol beer was to drink more of it . . . *duh*!

Because of some substantial overindulgence, we didn't leave as early the next day as we had planned and we had to switch drivers often to stay alert.

Come to think of it (as an interesting side note) Nebraska had some of the dumbest drinking laws I have ever encountered. Until just a couple of years prior to 1955, in our town, Valparaiso, only beer (regular alcohol content beer) could be sold in taverns, and you had to be twenty-one years of age to purchase it.

The last two years I was in high school, they started letting the beer joints sell liquor, but you couldn't drink it on the premises. They could only sell it in half-pint quantities and you couldn't take it out of the bar unless it was encased in a plain brown paper bag (like no one knew what you had just bought).

Think about that for a moment. Consider the mindset and mental capacity of the people who enacted that law. What could possibly be the (I use the term loosely) logic behind it?

Like the scenario of 3.2 beers sold in other states: It had less alcohol, so it could be sold to those eighteen years of age or older, resulting in more beer consumed by younger intoxicants.

Likewise, in the case of liquor, for some unknown reason they're selling it in tiny quantities, presumably so you will drink less. Do you think that worked? Wouldn't it be better to consume liquor in an establishment designated for that purpose instead of on the way home while you are driving?

In some of the neighboring towns, you could not sell any alcoholic beverages on Sunday, and in our town they opened the beer joints when the churches let out, but you couldn't take any home with you (other than what you had consumed, of course).

In the big city of Lincoln, they wouldn't allow alcohol beverages to be sold on Sunday.

In fact the liquor stores weren't allowed to even be open. But you could take your own "unopened" bottle of whatever to most any restaurant or private club and they would open it for you and serve mixes and ice.

It gets better. There was a small town between our town and Lincoln named Raymond that was allowed to sell beer on Sunday but for take-out only. That meant that every Sunday people would come from miles around and from all over the county to Raymond to buy beer. You're probably thinking that everyone was going to wait to get home before they drank it, right? Wrong—the ditches on either side of the highway in and out of the town had to be dredged out almost once a month to clean up all the discarded beer bottles.

Wait, it *still* gets better. In the metropolitan city of Lincoln, *the capital of the state*, in the fifties, if you wanted to buy hard liquor any day but Sunday, you had to go to a "drive-up" window at a liquor store to purchase it.

The consistent thread that ran through all these different laws and statutes governing a relatively small geographical area was . . . there was no consistency. It was like the powers that be would wake up each day and say, "Let's try this today because what we did yesterday was really stupid."

CHAPTER THIRTY-SEVEN

A Loss of Adolescence

First love is only a little foolishness and a lot of curiosity.

— George Bernard Shaw

This is the part of my story that I have been dreading—*girls!* I'm reluctant to relate the intimacy of my dating experience. I didn't want this magnificent manuscript to degenerate into a continuous string of sordid, lurid love affairs. However, I feel I must at least give you a peek into my deep secret relationships, lest you wonder that I may have been a little light in the loafers. Nothing could have been further from the truth . . . honest. I will lay a little groundwork and then I will try my best to enlighten you in a tasteful, non-erotic manner. It's going to be tough but here we go.

Human sexuality was never discussed in my family. As I said earlier, I have never seen another member of my immediate family naked.

The only attempt my dad made to enlighten me on sexuality was when we took our milk cow, Bess, to the neighbors to be bred. I guess he figured a picture was worth the few words he was too embarrassed to utter. But somehow, watching two animals mate is just not the same as a meaningful relationship between a man and a woman.

The only attempt my mom ever made to explain the facts of life was the night before I was to leave for the Navy. She was so uncomfortable and hesitant in her effort that I took pity on her and told her that I appreciated her concern, but it was too late. She was so relieved I thought she was going to cry.

I know, you are probably thinking—*what about the BIG (medical) BOOK*. It must have had some explicit depictions and explanations. Why didn't I satisfy my curiosity and gather the sex-ed information there? I tried, but all the pictures of sexual organs and the reproductive process were illustrated without skin, and somehow it just wasn't a stimulating medium (like say, modern-day *Playboy*).

My best source of erotic information was from my male friends in high school. I don't know if you realized this or not, but young teenage males love to talk about their sexual conquests, in detail. They will always relate their escapades to their close friends (in fact, they will tell anyone who will listen).

The downside of this conduit of information is that most, if not all, young male teenagers lie. They relate their intimate events (fantasies) in the way they would have liked them to turn out instead of the real outcome (if they took place at all).

I noticed that most of my male acquaintances carried wallets and in these wallets they carried a condom. You could see the raised outline showing through the leather. They proudly showed me the imprint of their valued treasure and told me, "You have to be prepared and ready whenever the occasion arises and you never know when that might happen."

OK, I came to the conclusion that if I'm going to be "one of the guys" I have to get a wallet. The closest thing I ever had to a wallet was when Mom would tie my lunch money inside a knot in a corner of my handkerchief so I wouldn't lose it.

I started pricing out wallets in the dry goods and drug stores. They were pretty expensive so I asked Mom, "Do you or Dad have an old wallet lying around that I could use?"

She said, " No, and Dad is using his, but your brother Lloyd may have left one in the belongings he left in an old trunk, when he moved out." We looked and sure enough there was one.

Mom asked, "Why do you need a wallet?"

I blushed and said, "Everyone else has one. I think it's time I have one too."

She just shrugged her shoulders, did the head-shaking thing, and left it at that.

Wallets were strange accessories. Some were small and compact and some were huge.

Some men carried big long ones on a chain that looped over their belt, so no one would steal it. Those folks must not trust banks. What could you carry that would fill up something that size?

Anyway, I had the wallet. Now I needed the customary talisman—the condom. There was no way I had enough nerve to go into the drugstore and buy one from the couple that owned the place. They knew my mom, and I used to hang around with their daughter. How was I going pull this one off?

Fortunately in the male teenage world, perception is as important as if not more so, as reality. I went to the hardware store and purchased an "O" ring washer the exact size and shape of a condom and put that in my wallet. The physical impression it made through the leather was identical to the real thing. It would temporarily serve the purpose until I could get "the real thing." The only problem was that if "the occasion" presented itself, unexpectedly, the 'O' ring would be sorely inadequate and quite laughable.

So now I have an old, used "empty," wallet with a

rubber washer in it and, just like that, I am an accepted member of the brotherhood of men. With this amulet in my possession, a mere casual presentation (like checking on my nonexistent money), "like a cop with a badge," signifies I am a recognized honorary associate, in good standing, in the society of masculine prowess . . . Is this a great country, or what?

As I suspected, most of my friends weren't any more sexually experienced than I was. Again, perception was the key. Among my circle of boastful, naïve, male acquaintances, Wayne, my friend from Scouts, was the exception. He would relate some of his sexual escapades to me in confidence, and in great detail. At first I kind of lumped his forays in with the others as the musings of wanna-bes, but Wayne was more believable. We had a code of honor in Scouting that whenever you held up three fingers and swore to something evoking the term, "Scout's Honor," it was most assured that what followed was the truth.

I know he had all the equipment to hold up his end of any co-ed sexual venture. Wayne, to put it delicately, was "well-endowed." Now don't start thinking that I went around checking out other guys' masculine apparatus. It so happened on a couple of Scout campouts that we skinny-dipped in the ole swimming hole, and you can't help but notice when a guy's male appendage is measured—by the pound.

If what Wayne was relaying to me about his sex-capades was in fact true—then he was seeing more action than the bench seat in the women's community outhouse.

My sexual exploits were—nonexistent. My first actual boy/girl encounter was when I was in grammar school and two of the town 'hotties' (girls) lured me to a basement under an abandoned house to participate in the ritual of "I'll show you mine, if you'll show me yours." At that age I wasn't sure what we were going to show each other, but I was game. There were two of them to one of me so whatever we were sharing I was going to get twice as much as they were.

When we got under the house the girls gave the appearance of being a little embarrassed and were giggling, but I had the impression they had played this game before. They wanted me to go first but, since I was the chivalrous gentleman, I insisted they go first. So they did. They counted to three and in unison dropped their drawers and quickly pulled them back up. I don't know if it was our ages or if they just did it too fast, but quite frankly I didn't notice much difference between them and me. I wasn't impressed.

They excitedly said that it was now my turn. By now I was disenchanted, uncomfortable and reluctant to participate any further, so I proceeded to fake a buckle malfunction on my bib-overalls. When it was apparent they were disappointed and became insistent, I just shrugged and gave them my best "sorry, not my fault" expression, and we all left.

Just to let you know, I dated a lot of girls in our town. Well, to be fair, I guess, we should establish the guidelines and agree as to what actually constitutes a "date."

In our little town, the young eligible males had limited resources and entertainment options, so a date usually consisted of sitting next to a girl at the free show, skating next to one at the weekly skating sessions in the town hall, walking a young lady home from school, or, on rare occasions, accompanying one of the female gender to at dance at the VFW hall.

In that context of the art of dating, I did quite well and there were many dates. If, however, you narrow the definition somewhat and include actually touching the girl at the movie; holding hands while skating, if you carried her books as you walk her home, or actually danced with the girl you went to the VFW hall with, then my *actual* number of dating companions would fall off considerably.

If you really get technical you could restrict the terminology of a date to just hugging and kissing, and you excluded the casual yawn and arm-stretching when one arm just happens to fall around the girl's shoulders, or your knees just happen to touch at the movies. Or you exclude the May basket kissing tradition. If you mean you had to plan something, then pick them up, take them somewhere, neck a while and bring them home, then I'm down to three or four girls.

Ok . . . "OK" . . . why it is so hard to tell the truth about this subject. It must be a guy thing, I going to have to work on that. Here is the truth: *Scouts honor*, I only dated one girl in high school, but they were real dates, honest—under anybody's definition.

Her name was Mildred. I called her Millie. I first noticed her when I was a junior, and she was a sophomore. She had just made the junior varsity cheerleading squad. The first time I saw her in her short uniform skirt and tight sweater, something happened to me. I knew then and there that she was the one for me. She also made the varsity volleyball team and they wore really short uniform shorts . . . her legs were gorgeous (I've always been a leg man).

Both Millie and I were shy people so it took quite a while for us to actually talk to each other. Her sister Geraldine was one grade ahead of me and she was real friendly and outgoing, so I got to know her pretty well. I would ask her what things Millie liked and how best to get to know her. Geraldine told me her sister was also shy and would never be the first one to make the first move and talk to me. She suggested the best thing

I could do was just walk up and say, "Hi." . . . I was afraid of that.

One afternoon, I had just gotten out of baseball practice and was on my way to my car when I noticed Millie walking off the school grounds by herself. There was another girlfriend of hers walking the other way and I asked her why Millie was walking—she usually rode the bus to her home on the edge of town. Her friend told me Millie had to stay late and missed the bus.

Here was my chance, it's now or possibly never, I'm rationalizing. *What's the worst thing that could happen? All she could do is say, "no," but that's also what I was most afraid of* . . . oh what the heck, I'm going for it.

I pulled alongside her and meekly introduced myself and asked if I could give her a ride home.

She stopped, slowly turned, stared at me for a while and answered, "I know who you are" (that was a good sign).

"I thought you would never ask," she said, and hopped in my car.

I was on top of the world. The only regret I had then was all the time I had wasted getting to this point. We sat out in front of her house and talked for a long time. I never met anyone up to that point that was so easy to relate to. In a matter of a couple of hours, we knew just about everything we needed to know about each other.

Her sister Geraldine came out to the car and told us that Millie had to come inside and do her chores.

Before Millie left I asked her if she would go with me to the annual carnival, which was coming to town in two weeks. She said she would love to, but she'd have to ask her parents first.

That was good enough for me to know that she, at least, wanted to go with me. I was so excited I didn't even remember the drive home.

Millie's sister Geraldine liked me, so she helped convince their parents that it would be all right for Millie to accompany me to the carnival.

I told my mom and dad of my impending date and they both seemed to be pleased. My dad mumbled something about being relieved; it was about time I had *finally* got a date.

I went to the bank and drew a few bucks out of my savings account (with my mom's permission, of course), got dressed up and drove over and picked up Millie and we were off to the festivities.

We had a great time riding rides, and walking along the carnival's vending booths. At one point she took my hand and I don't remember ever letting go for the rest of the evening. As we strolled, we noticed a lot of other couples (I couldn't believe we were now a couple) carrying big teddy bears and other stuffed animals. Obviously the guys had won them for their girlfriends.

Millie kind of hinted that it would be fun to have one of them in her room.

I, in my best macho voice, said, "Then you shall have one." I told her to pick out a booth that offered the stuffed animal she liked and said, "I'll win it for you."

The booth she chose gave huge teddy bears as prizes. The booth was one that had rows of stuffed dolls on three shelves. You would buy three baseballs and if you could knock two dolls *off* the shelves you won the prize. The dolls were lined up so closely on the shelves that they were touching each other, so I couldn't see how I could miss. This was going to be a piece of cake.

I threw until my arm felt like it was going to fly off. What wasn't apparent when I started this quest was that the dolls had a thick fringe around them, and the actual doll part was very small. If you didn't hit the doll square in the middle and just hit the fringes, the ball would sail through like you never threw it. I could knock the dolls down but you had to knock them *OFF* the shelf to win.

I had almost gone through all the money I'd brought and there were still two nights of the carnival left. In the past, I had always gone every night when I was by myself.

Millie kept pulling on my arm and telling me I

was spending too much money and she really didn't have a space in her bedroom for the thing anyway, but I wouldn't have any of that. I was determined to stay with it until either my money or my arm gave out. It was now personal . . . It was me or the dolls.

Millie said she had to go to the bathroom and she'd be right back. When she left, the guy that ran the booth pulled me aside and said, "Man, you are being a fool. You could have bought two or three of those animals with all the money you have spent trying to win one."

I told him, "I have to win one for her. It's my first date and I really have to impress her."

"OK", the guy said, "here's what I'm going to do. When she gets back, I'm going to give you three free balls. I want you to knock down two dolls on the bottom shelf, then distract her and when I go back to pick up the balls, I'll push them off the shelf and you act surprised. It'll work, trust me."

I distracted her, and he did his thing and nobody was the wiser.

Millie's eyes lit up like a Christmas tree. She couldn't have been more proud than if I had won her a mink coat. She was beaming the rest of the night.

On the way home, I asked her if she would like to go again the next night and she eagerly agreed. I told her I couldn't afford to try to win any more stuffed animals, but we could ride the rides and just walk around.

She said, "I would prefer doing that because watching you work that hard to win the stuffed animal was too stressful."

When I picked her up the next day, she wanted to bring the stuffed teddy bear with her and we lugged that darn thing around all night. She made sure all her friends knew I had won it for her. It was worth all the money I spent to make her happy.

We dated off and on through my junior year. When I was a senior, we decided to go steady until I left for the Navy. It wasn't that big a deal since neither of us had actually dated anyone else anyway. Graduation time was quickly approaching. We became more serious about each other and the word love had cropped up on several occasions. We never actually had sex but at times there was some heavy petting.

There were two major detractors standing in the way of consummating our relationship. The main one was her religion. She was Catholic, and her priest and her parents were constantly bombarding her with propaganda about not having sex before marriage . . . who came up with that nonsense? No matter what argument I would come up with to counter that logic just wasn't enough.

She would say, "Don, I would love to, but I just can't. It wouldn't be right. If you love me you won't insist on it."

What is a guy to do? I really cared for her, but . . . a guy has needs. The second problem was a personal one on my part (this is a delicate issue, so bear with me). Millie was developing, physically, in every way. She was getting lumpy in all the right places and she was driving me crazy.

I on the other hand, was maturing *much* slower. I was 5 feet 9, 135 pounds and in great shape (because of football and Charles Atlas), but to say that I was anatomically challenged would be "kind."

Luckily, we had stall showers in the dressing rooms at the school gym. I didn't have to 'flaunt' my meager manhood before the masses. I know you are thinking— *it's no big deal*— but it was to me.

To modestly put things into perspective, my friend Wayne (to use the animal vernacular) would be compared to a Shetland pony stallion. I, on the other hand would be more in the *stud* field mouse category.

When football season started, all the players had to submit to an in-depth physical examination, to make sure we were healthy enough to play. I imagine that was because of the violent nature of the sport, and probably to lessen the liability of the school.

We had to strip down, and one phase of the exam required us to stand in front of this doctor who was sitting on a high stool. The next thing I knew the guy had a hold of my testicles and told me to turn my head and cough. This really caught me off guard. At first I thought he might have been one of those Homo sapiens my friend Jerry, who had moved to Lincoln, told me about. He looked at me and asked, "How old are you?"

I cleared my throat and in my deepest voice replied, "Fifteen and a half." I guess he wasn't impressed with my manhood any more that I was.

I've always looked younger than I actually am. Even today I'm seventy-two and a half but everyone tells me I don't look a day over seventy. It's a curse. People don't take you seriously if you don't look your age.

Just so you know, my inadequacy problem wasn't a permanent malady. I did eventually mature physically, reaching six feet in height and 175 pounds, *everything* became normal, but it didn't happen until several months later, on the Island of Guam. It must have been the South Seas climate. I can remember welcoming my new normal male member into my anatomy and thinking: *It's about time you reported for duty!*

I recall my first exposure to mass masculine adulthood at the huge pool at the Naval Training Center. There were about 100 naked men standing around this huge body of water. As I was taking it all in I had a sinking feeling that I had brought a knife to a gun fight.

I took Millie to the senior prom. The whole affair

was built up to be something really special. The dance was to be at the VFW hall.

One of the local dance bands was going to be playing the music. Since the majority of the students were of European/Polish descent, most of the dances were polkas. I didn't know how to dance, so my sister Lucille tried her best to teach me before the prom. She and my brother-in-law Audry were probably the most-accomplished dance team in town. After a couple of weeks of intense instructions, Lucille finally gave up on my dance lessons. She decided she just couldn't make a silk purse out of a sow's ear, as they say. Lucille told me I had about as much rhythm as the sow whose ear we were trying to transform into a silk purse.

Not many of the male students in the senior class were any more proficient at dancing than I was. The prom turned out like any other typical dance. The guys sat on the sidelines and discussed *guy things* and watched the girls dance with each other.

Graduation came off without a hitch, even though the school had to deal with the largest senior class ever to graduate from Valparaiso High School (twenty-two students; twelve girls and ten boys).

The time was fast approaching when I was to leave for the Navy. I turned seventeen on April 19th, 1955 and graduated shortly thereafter. The Navy didn't tell me exactly when I had to report to the Naval Training

Center, in Great Lakes, Illinois. I figured I would have most of the summer to have some fun before I left for boot camp.

I recently saw a war movie, but I don't remember the title. The first part of the film was about a young couple, in love, trying to cope with the traumatic reality of their imminent separation. The young lad had been drafted, in time of war, and there was the possibility that he may not come back to her. They previously promised each other they would postpone their sexual intimacy until their anticipated marriage.

The war changed the dynamics of their well-laid-out plans. They mutually decided to accelerate their lovemaking union. They weighed the odds that this may be their only opportunity and they didn't want to completely miss the divine experience.

This concept stimulated my glands. I was wondering if I could convince Millie of the urgency of our *similar* circumstances. I know I wasn't going off to war, but the possibility of impending danger still loomed over us. I could be on one those big boats and it could spring a leak and sink. I wasn't that strong of a swimmer yet, so it was well within the realm of chance that these few remaining days could be our last.

As the time of my departure quickly approached, Millie was becoming pretty upset about us being apart for an extended period of time. I had planned to give her my class ring to wear while I was gone, assuring her that I definitely intended on coming back to her.

It wasn't like I was going to take advantage of her. Our union would have to be consensual. I was definitely going to suggest we talk about it in the next few days. But first I would have to get prepared just in case I could pull it off.

I was going to have to get a *real* condom. The "O" ring just wasn't going to cut it.

I couldn't buy one in our town for reasons I have already mentioned. I couldn't ask any of my friends to buy it for me since I was supposed to have had one all this time. It was another poser.

I was scheduled to spend the following weekend with my sister and brother in Lincoln, for a going-away party. I remembered there were two drugstores within walking distance of their apartment. This would be my best chance to buy the condom.

Upon my arrival, I told my siblings I was going to take a walk. I went to the closest store, which was a Rexall Drugs. Inside I noticed the clerk was a woman. They weren't too busy but I didn't want to buy something like that from a woman if I didn't have to.

I walked a few blocks to the other store; it was a Walgreens. It also had a woman clerk but they were really busy—too many people.

There is just no way you can pretend you're buying a

condom for any other reason than to have sex. Nobody is going to believe you're buying ammunition for a water balloon battle.

I opted to go back to the Rexall store, thinking, *if I had to buy from a women clerk, at least I would do it with fewer people around as witnesses.*

I hung around inside the store looking at comic books until the clerk wasn't busy. Then I went up to her, leaned over the counter, and said in a really low voice, "I need a condom."

She looked at me quizzically and answered, "The gum is over by the cash register."

I said, in little louder voice, "No, no, I don't want any gum. I want to buy a condom."

She nods her head and said, in a *loud, distinct* voice, with perfect diction, "Oh . . . you want to buy some condoms! OK—follow me. They are kept down at the end of the counter."

Oh great, why did she have yell it out? Now everybody in the store knows what I'm planning. I knew my face was turning red because I could feel the heat. I couldn't have appeared guiltier if I had come in the store to rob the place! I was really tempted to just bolt for the door, but I quickly reasoned the damage has already been done. Everyone now knows that I'm a sex fiend getting ready to prey on some unsuspecting damsel. I might as well stick it out.

I followed her to the location of the counter she indicated. I just knew the eyes of the other people in the store were following every move I made. She pulled out a rather large box and started naming off brand names, which meant nothing to me, so I said, "Whatever's the cheapest."

She then informed me there were different sizes (will this never end), "small, medium and large." I'm thinking, *There must also be an industrial size for guys like Wayne, but you probably had to special order those.*

I cleared my throat and in my deepest voice said, "M*edium!*" I was praying that was the last decision I had to make so I could get out of there, but that was too much to hope for.

Her next test question was, "Do you want a package of six or twelve?"

I said, "I want one."

She says, "Are you sure? . . . they are cheaper if you buy them in a box of six or twelve."

"No, I don't want a box; I just want one—*PLEASE.*"

I didn't see any sense in buying more than one. What would I do with the leftovers? The Navy had sent me a list of things I could bring with me to boot camp, and condoms weren't on it. Besides, sex had to be similar to hunting . . . if you are a good shot you only need one bullet.

Finally she gave me my purchase; I paid her and quickly left. I never looked around at the other people as I left, but I imagined I could hear them applauding.

As I was walking back to my sister's place I was kicking myself, thinking, *Why did I order a medium size, I just had to let my male ego take over and now I'll probably have to use a garter to keep the darn thing on.* This escapade is becoming a whole lot more complicated than I thought it would be—it better be worth it!

The following week I received a letter from the Navy with an itinerary, and a train ticket. I was leaving in six days. So much for a fun summer.

I picked up Millie in my parents' Mercury and broke the news to her about my early departure date. I gave her my class ring, ran the concept of the leaky boat past her, floated the idea of possible accelerated intimacy, and waited for her response.

I guess I threw a little too much at her at one time because she broke down in tears and said, she knew the day would come when I had to leave and she had promised herself she would be brave. Now that the time to leave was actually here, she realized just how much she would miss me.

I was leaving on a Monday, so I promised her we would have the weekend together just the two of us. We held each other for a long time, and then I took her home.

I informed my parents that I wanted the weekend to myself so any going-away festivities they had planned needed to be completed by then, and they were OK with that.

I was looking forward to the weekend with mixed emotions. I wanted to experience the lovemaking but it was a big step for both of us. When I picked up Millie, she was trying her best to be upbeat and cheerful. We drove to Wahoo and had supper at my sister Lucille's in-laws' restaurant, The Wigwam Cafe. Lucille told them I was coming with a date and they treated us to our meal as a going-away gift. It was impressive to Millie that we could order anything on the menu, "on the house," like we were celebrities.

The city of Wahoo had just recently opened a small theater, so we took in a movie. Afterward we drove home. It was getting dark; I went to our usual parking spot near the cemetery.

Millie was very nervous and pensive. I asked if she had thought about what we had discussed earlier in the week.

She answered, "Yes. I want to do whatever makes you happy."

I kissed her tenderly. I didn't want to rush this. She kissed me back more urgently and things heated up from there. We were both breathless. We moved to the back seat. I could tell Millie was losing her inhibitions; there was more aggressive kissing, some clumsy groping, and urgent removal of clothing. It looked like this was really going to happen . . . my heart was pounding.

We were down to our skivvies. Millie began to quietly cry. I could tell she was unbearably conflicted about what to do. It was like her priest was peering through one side window of our car and her parents were ogling us through the other, but she cared enough for me to put all that guilt aside to give me what she thought I needed. She was a brave girl, and our hormones were taking on a mind of their own.

I, on the other hand, was just as conflicted. My body was saying, "Go for it," but my heart was hesitant. I truly cared for her and I didn't want to hurt her, and there was this other thing I worried about all the previous night, that damn condom. I read the instructions on the package, as vague as they were, and all it said was, "Apply prior to sex," like it was some kind of salve (it must have taken them weeks to come up with that pearl of wisdom). My concern was how long before sex was the *approved* time frame? What if I chose the wrong time, what if the darn thing fell off and I lost it? . . . I only had one!

Finally I decided to take charge of our emotions. I pulled her up by her shoulders into a sitting position and looked directly in her eyes and said, "Millie, we shouldn't do this at this time in our lives."

She said breathlessly, "But I want to. I really want to make you happy."

I told her, "Honey, I want to too. Believe me, I *really* want to—but it's just not right for us at this time. If we truly care deeply for each other we will have a lot of opportunities when we are both better prepared and not under so much stress."

But she opined, "What if you don't come back, like you said. Look what we will have missed."

"Millie, I promise I will come back to you, hey . . . you're my girl, who else would I come back to?" I added, "Besides, I'm sure the Navy isn't really going to put me on a leaky boat, so don't worry."

She grabbed and hugged me tightly and said, "I'm so relieved, I love you so much," and the tears really came then. I assured her that I loved her too, and then I was crying.

We put out clothes back on and I drove her home. I parked in front of her house and we made two vows: one, we would write to each other at least twice a week; two, we would stay celibate until we were back together (we were successful in keeping at least one of our vows).

She gave me a nice picture she had taken by a professional photographer (she was beautiful.) I asked if she wanted to see me off on the train the next day. She declined. She felt she just couldn't handle it, so we said goodbye and I went home.

I don't know if we were truly in love, but the way we felt that night, our emotions certainly fit *our concept* of love. On the way home I felt really good. I couldn't believe I had talked myself out of something I had thought so important. I was within a couple of heartbeats of having sex . . . *I Almost Made It!*

But I did the right thing, I was still *horny* but happy . . . it was a good day. I didn't see Millie again for two and half years but we wrote each other every week like we had promised.

The next day some of my family and I were waiting for the train to leave from Lincoln Station. I was the most apprehensive about leaving mom and dad. They were in their late sixties, and I didn't know when I would see them again, or what shape they would be in when I did. Also present was my sister Lucille and her family, my other sister Dorothy and her fiancé Ed, and my brother Lloyd. Now I knew better how Lloyd felt when he had left on the same train, except he was going to war. I wasn't. Big difference.

There I was at the "all important" crossroads of my life, less than two months into my seventeenth year of age, armed only with a few essentials, a picture of my girlfriend, immature physically and mentally, hopelessly naive in life experiences, a virgin, and . . . alone.

I had no idea what I had gotten myself into and no

inkling of the life-changing events I would experience in the next four years.

The train ride was uneventful; I kept pretty much to myself. Our itinerary was to take the train to Chicago and then a bus to the Great Lakes Naval Training Center.

My first earth-shaking incident took place at the Chicago train station. While I was waiting for the bus to take us to the Training Center, I had to use the restroom. When I entered the huge mausoleum-like lavatory with stalls, *it happened*. I had just . . . well . . . that's the beginning of— *another story!*

Shortly after graduation, fully matured, ready for the world.

Post Script

Since obviously you are the one reading my book, I have a favor to ask of you. I'd just as soon you not let that *virgin* thing get around. I still have a reputation to protect.